Roman Obermaisser
Hermann Kopetz

GENESYS

Roman Obermaisser
Hermann Kopetz

GENESYS

An ARTEMIS Cross-Domain Reference Architecture for Embedded Systems

Südwestdeutscher Verlag für Hochschulschriften

Impressum/Imprint (nur für Deutschland/ only for Germany)
Bibliografische Information der Deutschen Nationalbibliothek: Die Deutsche Nationalbibliothek verzeichnet diese Publikation in der Deutschen Nationalbibliografie; detaillierte bibliografische Daten sind im Internet über http://dnb.d-nb.de abrufbar.
Alle in diesem Buch genannten Marken und Produktnamen unterliegen warenzeichen-, marken- oder patentrechtlichem Schutz bzw. sind Warenzeichen oder eingetragene Warenzeichen der jeweiligen Inhaber. Die Wiedergabe von Marken, Produktnamen, Gebrauchsnamen, Handelsnamen, Warenbezeichnungen u.s.w. in diesem Werk berechtigt auch ohne besondere Kennzeichnung nicht zu der Annahme, dass solche Namen im Sinne der Warenzeichen- und Markenschutzgesetzgebung als frei zu betrachten wären und daher von jedermann benutzt werden dürften.

Verlag: Südwestdeutscher Verlag für Hochschulschriften Aktiengesellschaft & Co. KG
Dudweiler Landstr. 99, 66123 Saarbrücken, Deutschland
Telefon +49 681 37 20 271-1, Telefax +49 681 37 20 271-0, Email: info@svh-verlag.de

Herstellung in Deutschland:
Schaltungsdienst Lange o.H.G., Berlin
Books on Demand GmbH, Norderstedt
Reha GmbH, Saarbrücken
Amazon Distribution GmbH, Leipzig
ISBN: 978-3-8381-1040-0

Imprint (only for USA, GB)
Bibliographic information published by the Deutsche Nationalbibliothek: The Deutsche Nationalbibliothek lists this publication in the Deutsche Nationalbibliografie; detailed bibliographic data are available in the Internet at http://dnb.d-nb.de.
Any brand names and product names mentioned in this book are subject to trademark, brand or patent protection and are trademarks or registered trademarks of their respective holders. The use of brand names, product names, common names, trade names, product descriptions etc. even without a particular marking in this works is in no way to be construed to mean that such names may be regarded as unrestricted in respect of trademark and brand protection legislation and could thus be used by anyone.

Publisher:
Südwestdeutscher Verlag für Hochschulschriften Aktiengesellschaft & Co. KG
Dudweiler Landstr. 99, 66123 Saarbrücken, Germany
Phone +49 681 37 20 271-1, Fax +49 681 37 20 271-0, Email: info@svh-verlag.de

Copyright © 2009 by the author and Südwestdeutscher Verlag für Hochschulschriften Aktiengesellschaft & Co. KG and licensors
All rights reserved. Saarbrücken 2009

Printed in the U.S.A.
Printed in the U.K. by (see last page)
ISBN: 978-3-8381-1040-0

Contents

Contents		1
1	**Introduction**	**5**
2	**System Architecture**	**7**
	2.1 Systems, Services and Behavior	7
	2.2 Users of the Architectural Model	9
	2.3 Components and Application Services	9
	2.4 Platform and Platform Services	10
	2.5 Component Model	12
3	**Requirements**	**13**
	3.1 General Requirements	14
	3.1.1 Limited Cognitive Capacity	14
	3.1.2 Composability	15
	3.1.3 Linking Interface Specification	16
	3.1.4 Heterogeneity and Technology Obsolescence	17
	3.1.5 Real-Time Requirements	18
	3.2 Networking and Resource Management	19
	3.2.1 Messaging	19
	3.2.2 Streaming Support	20
	3.2.3 Mobile Networking and Connectivity to the Internet	21
	3.2.4 Dynamic Resource Allocation	22
	3.2.5 Power/Energy Efficiency	23
	3.3 Security and Robustness	24
	3.3.1 Security Strategies and Services	24
	3.3.2 Diagnosis	25
	3.3.3 State Awareness	27
	3.3.4 Testing	27
	3.3.5 System Certification	28
	3.3.6 Fault-Tolerance and Error Containment	29
	3.4 System Design and Evolution	31
	3.4.1 System Modeling	31
	3.4.2 Reuse of Existing Systems and Standards	33
	3.4.3 Product Life-Cycle and Technology Changes	34
	3.4.4 Design for Validation	35
4	**Cross Domain Architectural Style**	**37**

4.1		Complexity Management	37
	4.1.1	Abstraction	38
	4.1.2	Partitioning	38
	4.1.3	Segmentation	38
4.2		Component Orientation	39
	4.2.1	Component Interfaces	40
	4.2.2	Types of Components	41
	4.2.3	Composability of Components	43
4.3		Structuring of Systems	44
	4.3.1	Integration Levels	44
	4.3.2	System Views	46
	4.3.3	Architectural Services	48
4.4		Networking	50
	4.4.1	Availability of a Common Time Base	50
	4.4.2	Communication Modes	51
	4.4.3	Heterogeneous Networks	51
	4.4.4	Internet Connectivity	52
4.5		Resource Management	52
	4.5.1	Universality	53
	4.5.2	Holistic View of Different Resources	53
	4.5.3	Power and Energy Awareness	53
	4.5.4	Continuity of Service	54
4.6		Robustness and Security	54
	4.6.1	Fault Containment and Error Containment	54
	4.6.2	Integrated Security	55
	4.6.3	State Awareness and Robustness	56
	4.6.4	Diagnosis	57
4.7		System Design and Evolution	58
	4.7.1	Model-based Design	58
	4.7.2	Name Space Design	58
	4.7.3	Modular Certification	58
	4.7.4	Legacy Integration and Technology Obsolescence	59
	4.7.5	Evolvability	59

5 Reference Architecture Template — **61**

5.1		Core Services	62
	5.1.1	Basic Configuration Services	62
	5.1.2	Basic Execution Control Services	64
	5.1.3	Basic Time Services	65
	5.1.4	Basic Communication Services	67
5.2		Optional Services	68
	5.2.1	Diagnostic Services	69
	5.2.2	External Memory Management Service	71
	5.2.3	Security Services	72
	5.2.4	Resource Management Services	74
	5.2.5	Gateway Services	76
	5.2.6	Mobility Services	78
	5.2.7	Generic Middleware Services	80
5.3		Domain Specific Services	82
	5.3.1	Data Management Services	82

	5.3.2	Combined Quality-of-Service and Resource Awareness	82
	5.3.3	Multimedia and Graphics	83
	5.3.4	Trust and Privacy	87
	5.3.5	Open Systems and Ambient Intelligence	88

6 Development Methodology — 91
6.1 Principles — 91
- 6.1.1 Embedded Systems Engineering Process — 92
- 6.1.2 Model Driven Development — 92
- 6.1.3 Model Representation — 93
- 6.1.4 Modeling Semantics — 93
- 6.1.5 Formal Methods — 93
- 6.1.6 Quality and Non-Functional Properties — 93
- 6.1.7 Integrated Development Environment — 94

6.2 Process Model — 94
- 6.2.1 Legacy Integration Process — 96

6.3 System Requirements Specification — 97
6.4 Architecture Design — 100
- 6.4.1 Modeling Languages — 100
- 6.4.2 Views, Models and Transformations — 101
- 6.4.3 Application Architecture Design — 102
- 6.4.4 Platform Architecture Design — 108
- 6.4.5 System Allocation/Configuration/Refinement — 111

6.5 Quality Evaluation — 114
- 6.5.1 Performance Evaluation — 114
- 6.5.2 Power/Energy Evaluation — 115
- 6.5.3 Reliability and Availability Evaluation — 116
- 6.5.4 Safety Analysis — 117
- 6.5.5 Evolvability Evaluation — 119

6.6 Integrated Tool Environment — 119
6.7 Conclusion — 122

7 Prototype Implementation — 127
7.1 Introduction — 127
- 7.1.1 Implemented Architectural Services — 128
- 7.1.2 Outline — 129

7.2 Prototype Hardware — 130
- 7.2.1 Mainboard — 130
- 7.2.2 FPGA Board — 130
- 7.2.3 Basic I/O Board — 132
- 7.2.4 Multimedia I/O Board — 132
- 7.2.5 Physical Constraints — 132
- 7.2.6 Partitioning of the Prototype — 132
- 7.2.7 Micro Components — 133

7.3 Demonstration Application — 138
- 7.3.1 Overview — 138
- 7.3.2 Control Distributed Application Subsystem — 139
- 7.3.3 Multimedia Distributed Application Subsystem — 143

7.4 Results of the Demonstration Application — 145
7.5 Validation of implemented Architectural Services — 145

		7.5.1	Composability	145
		7.5.2	Communication in the Deterministic Network-on-Chip	147
		7.5.3	Common Time	147
		7.5.4	Reconfiguration	147
		7.5.5	Off-chip Gateway	148

8 Migration Path and Relationship to Domain-Specific Architectures   **149**

	8.1	Network on Terminal Architecture (NoTA)		149
		8.1.1	System Structuring	149
		8.1.2	Device Interconnect Protocol	150
		8.1.3	Commonalities and Contrasts of NoTA and GENESYS	151
		8.1.4	Instantiation of NoTA as Middleware on top of GENESYS	154
		8.1.5	Résumé	155
	8.2	Integrated Modular Avionics (IMA)		156
		8.2.1	Avionics System Structure	156
		8.2.2	Avionics Software Execution Environment	158
		8.2.3	Realization of IMA on top of a GENESYS Chip	160
	8.3	Automotive Open System Architecture (AUTOSAR)		164
		8.3.1	AUTOSAR ECU Software Architecture	165
		8.3.2	Compatibility of AUTOSAR Virtual Function Bus (VFB) and GENESYS	167
		8.3.3	Instantiation of AUTOSAR on top of GENESYS	170
		8.3.4	Résumé	173

Glossary   **175**

List of Project Partners   **187**

Bibliography   **189**

Preface

It is the objective of this book to give an overview of the cross-domain architecture for embedded systems that has been developed in the context of the European FP 7 research project GENESYS (GENeric Embedded SYStem FP7-213322) from January 2008 to June 2009. GENESYS is a candidate for the ARTEMIS European Reference Architecture for embedded systems. ARTEMIS is a European joint technology initiative (JTI) that bundles the efforts of European players from industry, academia and governments in the domain of embedded systems in order to develop a cross-domain approach to Embedded System Design. Such a cross-domain approach is needed to support the coming *Internet of Things*, to take full advantage of the economies of scale of the semiconductor industry and to improve the productivity of the human resources.

In a two year effort, before the start of the GENESYS project, an expert group from ARTEMIS has captured the detailed requirements and constraints for such a European cross-domain embedded system architecture [8]. GENESYS has taken these requirements and constraints as a starting point. In particular, the following three challenges have driven the development of GENESYS

- **Complexity Management:** The management of the ever-increasing cognitive complexity of embedded systems is a major concern in all application domains. GENESYS attacks this problem by lifting the design process to a higher level of abstraction – to the level of self-contained hardware/software components that communicate exclusively by the exchange of messages. Components can be reused on the basis of their interface specification without having to know the internals of the component implementation. The GENESYS framework supports the straightforward composition of components and supports the classic simplification strategies of abstraction, partitioning and segmentation.

- **Robustness:** An embedded system must deliver an acceptable level of service, even in the presence of software and hardware faults, and operator mistakes. GENESYS supports robustness by establishing a framework for fault containment and error containment, the selective restart of components that have failed after a transient fault, and the masking of transient and permanent errors by the replication of components. Security is addressed at all levels of the architecture.

- **Energy Efficiency:** Energy efficiency is of utmost concern in the mass market of mobile devices. GENESYS provides for energy efficiency by a technology-agnostic model-driven design style that supports the migration of a stable component form of software on a CPU to an ASIC (and thus improving the energy efficiency by orders of magnitude) and by an integrated resource management that makes it possible to individually reduce the power-requirements of components or to turn off components completely that are not needed during a particular interval (power gating). The time-triggered communication paradigm establishes a "green wave" for the transmission of messages without any energy intensive intermediate buffering or arbitration.

GENESYS is a platform architecture that provides a minimal set of core services at the waist and a plurality of optional service that are predominantly implemented as self-contained system components. Choosing a suitable set of these system components that implement optional services, augmented by application specific components, can generate domain-specific instantiations of the architectures.

Acknowledgments

This work has been supported by the European research project GENESYS under project Number FP7/213322. The book is a joint effort of all partners of the GENESYS consortium listed in the Annex. It is based on the project deliverables and many discussions among the project members. The available material has been substantially reorganized and edited in order to support the consistency and readability of the book. Many thanks go to all members of the consortium for their valuable contributions, in particular to Bernhard Huber (TU Vienna) for writing most of Chapter three and Chapter eight, to Michael Goedecke (Infineon), Heikki Waris (Nokia), Ch. Ykman-Couvreur (IMEC) and Valentin Gherman (CEA) for their significant contributions to Chapter five, Eila Ovaska (VTT) and Sergio Campos (European Software Institute) for writing Chapter six and Christian Paukovits (TU Vienna) for contributing to Chapter seven.

Special thanks go to our project officer form the EU, Alkis Konstantellos for the many helpful interactions and the outstanding project management, and to the four reviewers Bran Selic, Miroslaw Malek, Yuriy Sheynin, Janos Sztipanovits, for their constructive criticism and substantial support during the course of the GENESYS project.

R. Obermaisser
H. Kopetz
Editors

One

Introduction

EMBEDDED SYSTEMS enable the real-time computer control of physical devices and systems, ranging from mobile phones, to television sets, to automotive engines and to industrial robots (to take a few examples) in order to achieve an unprecedented level of performance and utility. Embedded systems are also called Cyber-Physical Systems (CPS) to denote the emphasis and the close synergetic interactions of a real-time information processing subsystem (the Cyber System) with a physical device or subsystem that is to be controlled (the Physical System).

The demands on the functional capabilities and the dependability of, and consequently the opportunities for embedded systems grow rapidly as society moves further into the information age. Societal mega-trends demand radical innovations in the following areas:

- Personal communication and information: The phenomenal success of the mobile phone industry over the past twenty years shows that there is a deep human desire for an ubiquitous connection to his peer group and society at large.

- Efficient use of natural resources: We are in the middle of a shift from a resource-intensive economy to a sustainable economy. Embedded systems are a key enabling technology to enable this shift.

- Safety and Security: The increasing dependence of many parts of our society on the correct operation of embedded systems puts increased emphasis on the dependability, safety and security of these systems. The wish for all kinds of information is constrained by the desire to protect the personal privacy sphere.

- Assistance in an Aging Society: The welcome demographic trend to an extended human life-span puts more strain on the medical domain to ameliorate the later stages of life. Embedded systems help to assist medical doctors and increase the productivity in the health-care sector by providing tele-medical services.

The fulfillment of these challenging demands is facilitated by the enormous progress of the semiconductor and communication technology. The 2007 International Technology Roadmap on Semiconductors (ITRS) states [30, page 83]:

The historical ability to reduce the leading-edge product manufacturing cost per function by an average 29% each year has represented one of the unique features of the semiconductor industry and is a direct consequence of the market pressure to continue to deliver twice the functionality on-chip every 1.5-2 years in an environment of constant or reducing prices. Even though the rate of increase of on-chip functionality could slow in the future, the amount of functions/chip is still growing exponentially, though at a slower rate. According to [30, page 84], the marginal production cost of one million bits of DRAM (packaged) is about 1 cent in 2007 - going to decrease to about .06 cent in 2015. This means that today about 10 billion bits can be produced for the cost of one engineering hour. Parallel with this production-cost decrease goes a dramatic increase in the fixed cost of chip manufacturing, such as cost of equipment, design, mask cost, test-cost etc. implying that an ever larger number of chips of a given design must be produced to recover the fixed cost. Furthermore, the time-honored trend that the failure rate per transistor decreases as fast or faster than the increase in the number of transistors per chip will not continue in the near future due to the growing susceptibility of the ever smaller microdevices to internal and external disturbances (e.g., ambient cosmic radiation). As a consequence the failure rate per chip is increasing (although the failure rate of each transistor still decreases). System-level techniques to provide to the end-user robust services despite the occurrence of transient device failures are therefore needed. Giving this future environment of growing demands and greater than ever technological capabilities, the opportunities for the embedded system sector are enormous, provided that the technological and societal requirements and constraints are properly addressed. These requirements and constraints have been captured in detail in the ARTEMIS Strategic Research Agenda [8].

It has been the objective of the GENESYS project to develop a cross-domain framework that addresses these requirements and constraints. By promoting a strict component-based design style and identifying components that can be deployed in different application domains, the design and production costs of new applications can be significantly reduced by reusing components and taking advantage of the enormous economies of scale of the semiconductor industry.

The book is structured into seven Chapters. After a short introduction in Chapter one, Chapter two introduces the notion of a system architecture and the relationships between the platform and the architectural services. Chapter three summarizes the extensive set of requirements that have been captured in the industrial and consumer electronics domain and form the yardstick for measuring the adequacy of the architecture. Chapter four presents the architectural style of GENESYS, expressed as a set of architectural principles that guide the detailed design of the architecture. Chapter five introduces first the core services that are part of the waist of the platform and then the open set of optional services. These optional services can be implemented in the form of self-contained system components that interact with the generic middleware of the application components by the exchange of messages. Chapter six outlines the model-based development methodology of GENESYS. Chapter seven describes an FPGA-based prototype implementation of the core architecture. Finally, the relationships between GENESYS and some domain specific architectures, such as NOTA, IMA and AUTOSAR are discussed in Chapter eight. In the Annex one finds a detailed glossary of terms.

Two

System Architecture

THIS CHAPTER introduces the notion of a system architecture for distributed embedded real-time systems. The overall architecture consists of two types of constituting systems: a set of components and an underlying platform (cf. Figure 2.1). Components are built on top of a platform, which offers core platform services as the basis for the implementation and integration of components. The core platform services enable emergence of global application services of the overall system out of local application services of the constituting components. The core platform services provide elementary capabilities for the interaction of components, such as message-based communication between components or a global time base. The core services are the instrument via which a component creates behavior that is externally visible at the component interface. In addition, the specification of a component's interface builds upon the concepts and operations of the core platform services. The component interface specification constrains the use of these operations and assigns contextual information (e.g., semantics in relation to the component environment) and significant properties (e.g., reliability requirements, energy constraints). Hence, the core platform services are a key aspect in the interaction between integrator and component developer.

2.1 Systems, Services and Behavior

We use the definition of a system introduced in [20]: an entity that is capable of interacting with its environment and is sensitive to the progression of time. The environment is in principle another system. The environment takes advantage of the existence of a system by producing input for the system and acting on the output of the system.

A system combines physical and logical aspects. As a consequence, behavior can be associated with a system taking into account both the value and time domain. This definition excludes, for example, a software module without associated hardware.

In general, systems are hierarchic and can on their behalf be recursively decomposed into sets of interacting constituting systems. The constituting elements of a system are denoted as components.

The temporal awareness of systems requires a model of time. We assume

8 CHAPTER 2. SYSTEM ARCHITECTURE

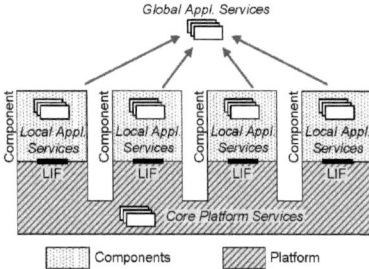

Figure 2.1: Architecture Model

a model based on Newtonian time, where the continuum of real-time can be modeled by a directed timeline consisting of an infinite set of instants [76].

In a distributed computer system, the progression of time is measured by a set of physical clocks. A physical clock partitions the time line into a sequence of nearly equally spaced intervals, called the micro granules of the clock, which are bounded by special periodic events, the ticks of the clock.

Since any two physical clocks will employ slightly different oscillators, the time-references generated by two clocks will drift apart. Clock synchronization is concerned with bringing the time of clocks in a distributed system into close relation with respect to each other. A measure for the quality of clock synchronization is the precision, which is defined as the maximum offset between any two clocks during an interval of interest.

However, due to the synchronization and digitalization error it is impossible to establish the temporal order of occurrences based on their timestamp, if timestamps differ by only a single tick. A solution to this problem is the introduction of a sparse time base [34], where time is partitioned into an infinite sequence of alternating durations of activity and silence.

A service is what a system delivers to its environment according to the specification. Through its service, a system can support the environment, i.e., other systems that use the service.

The specification for a system defines the service. Given a concrete paradigm of interaction between systems, the notion of a service can be refined. For example, in context of message-based interaction, the service of a system can be defined as the sequence of intended messages that is produced by a system in response to the progression of time, input and state [20, page 28]. An overview of formalisms for the definition of services in different interaction paradigms can be found in [13] (e.g., Statecharts, Specification and Description Language (SDL)).

In the presence of faults (e.g., design fault in the implementation or physical faults during the execution), a system can violate its specification. In this case, the system exhibits a failure [10] instead of its specified service.

We used the term externally visible behavior (or behavior for short) as a

2.2. USERS OF THE ARCHITECTURAL MODEL

generalization of the notions of service and failure:

$$behavior = service \cup failure$$

The correct behavior (as defined by the specification) is the system's service. The faulty behavior (violation of the specification) is a failure. In the absence of a specification, we can only reason about the behavior of systems.

2.2 Users of the Architectural Model

When developing a system that follows this architectural model, we can differentiate two roles: component developers and the integrator. The component is the unit of delegation and the unit of integration. Using the platform, the integrator is responsible for binding together the components to an overall system with global application services. The platform offers the means to integrate the components based on the specification of the components' local application services.

The component developers are concerned with the design and implementation of individual components. A component developer can delegate subtasks for the realization of a component to suppliers/subcontractors. Nevertheless, the component developer delivers an entire component with a local application service to the integrator. The integrator need not be aware of the inner structure of the component and the involvement of suppliers/subcontractors.

2.3 Components and Application Services

A component is a self-contained building block of the computer system. The borderline between a component and the platform is called the component's Linking Interface (LIF) [41]. At the LIF, the component provides its local application services to the other components.

A local application service is the intended behavior of a component at the LIF. The component exchanges information with other components at the LIF and the specification of the local application service must cover all aspects that are relevant for the integration of the component with other components:

1. Values: The syntax of the information exchanged at the LIF needs to be defined. In addition, relationships between inputs and outputs are specified.

2. Timing: In a real-time system, the specification of the LIF encompasses temporal constraints, e.g., for consuming inputs or producing outputs.

3. Relationship to the (natural) environment of the computer system: For each component that interacts with the environment of the computer system, the LIF specification must capture the (semantic) relationship between the information exchange at the LIF and the interaction with the environment. While abstracting from the details of the component's local interfaces (e.g., I/O interfaces or fieldbuses), the semantics of the LIF interaction in relation to the component environment need to be described. Due to the inability to fully formalize the relationship to the environment [42], natural language or ontologies are examples of suitable

specification methods. Information that originates from a local sensor and refers to entities in the natural environment is provided at the LIF to other components with a given delay. Likewise, information consumed at the LIF can cause an effect on the natural environment via an actuator. In addition to the value domain, this relationship must be specified in the temporal domain. For example, the lag between sensory information at the LIF and the state of the environment is of concern (cf. temporal accuracy [35]).

In addition, many other aspects can be relevant for the specification of the LIF, e.g., reliability, energy, security.

2.4 Platform and Platform Services

The platform is the foundation for development and integration of components. The platform offers platform services. A platform is of essential importance for two reasons:

Baseline for development of components: Component developers need a starting point for realizing components. The platform offers a foundation on top of which application-specific functionality can be established. This foundation consists of generic services, which are useful for many specific components. Although some of these services could also be realized within the components, their availability in the platform simplifies the component development. As an example, consider a sensor component that periodically samples the lateral acceleration in a car and produces a message on the LIF with this measurement. The local application service of this component would be 'acceleration measurement'. An example of a platform service that can be used to construct this application service would be a time service. Such a time service can provide the periodic sampling points (e.g., with respect to a global time base).

Using platform services, recurring problems are solved once-and-for-all in the platform without the need to redevelop them in every component. Principally, the development of components becomes easier if more functionality is offered by the platform. However, overloading the platform with a plethora of functionality is likely to lead to a high overhead. The reason for the overhead is that part of the functionality will be too specific to be applicable except for a few very specialized components. Furthermore, the complexity of the platform will increase. Thus, the likelihood of design faults in the platform will increase. Such a design fault in the platform is of particular severity. While a design fault of a component would affect only this specific component, potentially all components can be affected by a design fault in the platform. All components build upon the platform and depend on its correctness. The issue of the complexity of the platform and the susceptibility to design faults is of particular importance for safety-critical applications that need to be certified.

Framework for integration of components: Besides serving as the baseline for the establishment of local application services of components, the platform services are an instrument for emergence. The platform services enable the emergence from local application services of the components

2.4. PLATFORM AND PLATFORM SERVICES

to global application services of the system.

Therefore, the platform offers mechanisms to compose the overall system out of the independently developed components. These mechanisms include communication services enabling the exchange of information between components. In addition, other services can serve as a useful basis for integration, e.g., fault isolation services [44] that prevent component failures from propagating between components or clock synchronization services [45] to establish a common notion of time.

Following up on the previous example, the introduced component can be integrated with other in-vehicle components, thereby composing the speed measurement service with local application services of other components. The result is the emergence of a global application service (e.g., passive safety in the example with the lateral acceleration measurement) out of local application services (e.g., brakes, steering, and suspension in addition to the mentioned acceleration measurement service).

A core platform service is an elementary building block of the platform. Inversely, the set of core platform services defines the platform. Each core platform service has three roles. A core platform service introduces a platform capability, provides an instrument for behavior generation and represents a concept for the specification of application services.

Each core platform service is a capability of the platform that is offered to the components. An example of a core platform service is message multicasting that enables components to interact by the exchange of messages. In its simplest form, this service would consume messages from one port and transport these messages to a set of destination ports with defined properties (e.g., latency, reliability). This core platform service would enable a component to deposit messages at a port in order to be delivered via multicast communication to ports belonging to other components.

Secondly, the core services are the instrument by which a component generates behavior at the LIF. The use of the core services results in activities that can be externally perceived at the LIF from outside the component. The core services offer elementary operations, a sequence of which forms behavior at run-time. For example, in case of the platform service message multicasting, the instrument would be the ability to send messages.

The instrument for behavior generation is a part of the capability. The capability is, however, more than empowering the component to generate behavior. The capability is also concerned with the reaction to the component behavior in the platform. In particular, the capability links behavior at different components (e.g., output of one component becomes input of another component).

In addition, the core services provide the underlying concepts for the specification of component services. This statement about behavior relates to behavior on a meta-level. Given a set of core services, different service specification languages are possible that use these concepts. The core services of the GENESYS architecture will be described in Chapter 5.

2.5 Component Model

From the point of view of the LIF, a component provides application services expressed w.r.t. the core platform services. The integration of a system out of components is helped significantly through the existence of the core platform services. The core platform services introduce a uniform instrument across all components for generating component behavior.

However, component developers can favor different sets of platform services to express application behavior. Firstly, legacy applications have been developed for different platforms with different sets of platform services. In order to avoid a complete redevelopment of these legacy applications, a mapping of the legacy platform services to the uniform core platform services is desirable.

In addition, different domains can have unique requirements regarding the capabilities of the platform. For example, a safety-related control subsystem can build upon platform services for active redundancy. A multimedia system, on the other hand, might have to cope with a large number of different configurations and usage scenarios. Hence, a multimedia system needs dynamic reconfiguration capabilities that go beyond the reconfiguration support of the core platform services.

We introduce a layered component model in order to resolve this discrepancy between uniform core services and the need for application-specific platform services.

In order to provide application services, the component can employ an intermediate form of the application services: application services expressed w.r.t. optional platform services.

On top of the core services, the optional platform services establish higher-level capabilities for certain domains (e.g., control systems, multimedia). Besides, the optional services within a component establish an instrument for behavior generation just as the core services do.

In contrast to the core platform services, the optional platform services provide additional constructs that are not always needed or useful in all types of components. The optional services reflect the heterogeneity of a system by no longer enforcing uniformity of platform services throughout the system. A particular optional platform service can prove to be useful in one component, whereas the deployment of this service in another component might impede the component development. Consider for example an optional service for dynamic reconfiguration, which would make difficult the certification of a safety-related component.

The instrument for behavior generation of the optional platform services must have a defined mapping to the underlying instrument for behavior generation of the core platform services. Hence, the optional platform services transform the application services towards the core platform services.

Three

Requirements

THE FIRST PHASE of the GENESYS project has resulted in an impressive collection of requirements for future embedded systems that have to be taken into account for devising the GENESYS architecture, in particular the GENESYS architectural style. These requirements originate from different application domains, thereby reflecting important challenges for a broad range of embedded systems.

The first report - GENESYS deliverable D1.1 - presents the results of the requirements analysis from the point of view of industrial applications. This report incorporates requirements from the automotive application domain, the avionics application domain, as well as, requirements originating from industrial control systems. Deliverable D2.1 gives an analysis of requirements from the consumer applications point of view. Thereby, the document primarily focuses on product property related and product creation related requirements of embedded systems for mobile devices and ambient intelligence.

Besides those two application-oriented reports, the four technology-oriented requirement analyses have resulted in four corresponding documents. Deliverable D3.1 describes the requirements for a methodology framework that accompanies the GENESYS architecture for the development of systems according to the GENESYS architectural style. The report D4.1 gives an analysis of the requirements form the point of view of networking, security, and resource management, whereas the scope of deliverable D5.1 is robustness and diagnosis. Finally, deliverable D6.1 examines requirements for the GENESYS architecture from the point of view of composability.

It is the purpose of this chapter, to merge and condense this impressive collection of requirements in order to ease the later evaluation of the architecture. Therefore, the present collection of requirements originating from different partners has been subdivided into different categories. The first category incorporates those requirements that are cross-cutting the technological challenges addressed in GENESYS and include, amongst others, requirements for handling the cognitive complexity of future systems, for supporting composability of components and systems, and requirements with respect to the specification of services based on interface specifications. The second category deals with requirements with respect to networking (e.g. messaging, support for data streaming, or mobile networking) as well as with respect to resource management (e.g. dynamic allocation of resources or the improvement of power/energy efficiency). Robustness and security are the focus of the next category of requirements in this chapter. This category includes requirements for the GENESYS architecture from the point of view of system certification, diagnosis and testing, fault-tolerance, and security (e.g. security services and strategies). The fourth category is devoted to system design and evolution. This category addresses issues such as system modeling, reuse of existing systems and standards, and system validation.

3.1 General Requirements

This chapter covers requirements for the GENESYS architecture that are crosscutting the technological challenges addressed by GENESYS. The first section is concerned with requirements for the architecture that evolve from the need to overcome the limited cognitive capacity of users of the architecture. On the one hand, those are system engineers who develop systems according to the GENESYS architecture. On the other hand, those are end users who should profit from the achievements enabled by GENESYS (e.g., by providing highly optimized optional services such as security services to applications in different domains). To reach this goal, the GENESYS consortium has decided from the very beginning of the project to support a component-based design principle. Requirements that are strongly related to the specification and interconnection of components are subsumed in the sections "Composability" and "Linking Interface Specification". To enable the use (and mixture) of a wide variety of component technologies, which is a prerequisite for reuse of components and the integration of legacy subsystems, the subsequent group of requirements is concerned with the support of heterogeneity within the GENESYS architecture. This general requirement section is finished with requirements with respect to real-time guarantees, which is of importance for most applications in the world of embedded systems.

3.1.1 Limited Cognitive Capacity

In present embedded systems, the complexity and wide-ranging functionality makes it almost impossible to reason about the behavior of the system without decomposing the system into subsystems and without being able to analyze the behavior of those subsystems in isolation. Therefore, an architecture for future embedded systems has to provide a framework which supports to build artifacts (hardware components or software modules) for decomposing the overall system and permits to model subsystems at different levels of abstraction and to analyze their relevant properties.

In order to further benefit from the complexity reduction achieved by the system decomposition during system integration, the GENESYS architecture shall support the aggregation of components to constitute compound components in a way that ensures that all functional and non-functional properties of components must not be invalidated after integration. Furthermore, in order to ensure that the cognitive complexity required for reasoning about the system's behavior grows linearly with the number of subsystems, the architecture has to ensure that if n subsystems are already integrated into a system and the amount of available resources permits the integration of an nth+1 subsystem,

3.1. GENERAL REQUIREMENTS

then the nth+1 subsystem must not disturb the correct operation of the n already integrated subsystems.

All issues related to the composition of a set of subsystems can then be investigated by referring only to the specification of their linking interfaces (LIFs) [41]. Due to this advance of the level of abstraction, the cognitive complexity of the whole system is significantly reduced. To keep the LIF simple and understandable, the architecture shall ensure that only those properties of a component (e.g., provided and expected services) that are required for the intended emerging service should be visible at the LIF.

The success of the GENESYS architecture is not only determined by tackling the complexity of embedded systems during system design. Also, the complexity for the end user of the architecture, i.e. its usability, is an important success factor. Therefore, the architecture shall comprise a well-defined programming model that eases application development. Furthermore, the architecture should enable the implementation of user-friendly user interfaces, whose design considers learnability (the quick and intuitive use of the interface), memorability (easy to remember how to use), efficiency (easy and productive usage), error tolerance, relevancy, and satisfaction. In addition, multimodal interfaces (e.g., audio, visual, touching, moving/tiling, gesture recognition) by optional platform services should be enabled by the architecture.

3.1.2 Composability

Besides its benefits w.r.t to managing cognitive complexity, the decomposition of systems and the support for modularity and composability of the architecture is essential for fast and cost-effective product creation in multi-vendor environments, since it enables the independent design, development, and verification of subsystems. Therefore, the architecture shall support composability in a way that larger systems can be composed out of smaller subsystems. A system, i.e., a composition of subsystems, is considered composable with respect to a certain property, if this property, given that it has been established at the subsystem level, is not invalidated by the integration. Examples for such properties are timeliness or certification [8]. That means, the architecture shall ensure that a validated service of a subsystem, both in the value and in the time domain, is not refuted by integrating the subsystem into a larger system. Therefore, for correctly operating subsystems the architecture shall ensure that there is no unintended interference between different integrated subsystems, since those interferences would add an additional accidental complexity to the inherent complexity of an application. In addition, in case a fault affects the correctness of a subsystem, the architecture shall provide error containment between subsystems (see Section 3.3.5).

A prerequisite for the integration of (independently developed) subsystems is the existence of separate name spaces for those subsystems without the need for a central naming authority that coordinates the naming process for the entire system. Therefore, the architecture shall support a unique, but uniform identification of subsystems and enable the provision of dedicated namespaces for subsystems, even if multiple subsystems share the same physical communication infrastructure.

Furthermore, reasoning about system behavior and properties should be possible relying solely on the component specifications, regardless of the order of subsystem integration, which facilitates the assembly process. That is, the properties of the system can be inferred solely by the analysis of properties of the components carried out independently for each component. This avoids exponential (combinatorial explosion of the) analysis complexity.

3.1.3 Linking Interface Specification

Because of the increasing complexity of embedded applications, the level of design abstraction has to be elevated in order to cope with the cognitive load for understanding today's and future systems. Such an abstraction can be achieved by composing a system out of subsystems based solely on their interface specifications; hence, abstracting over the inner structure of the subsystems. With a full specification of a subsystem's linking interface all issues related to the composition of a set of subsystems can then be investigated by referring only to the specification of their LIFs. Therefore, at the lowest integration level of the architecture, the GENESYS architecture shall restrict interactions between subsystems, to occur exclusively by the exchange of messages (defined data structures for inter-process communication) via the LIFs of the subsystems. These messages have to be fully specified in the value and the time domain in a LIF specification.

A LIF specification in the GENESYS architecture shall comprise an operational specification and a meta-level specification. The operational interface specification captures the syntactical and temporal properties of the linking interface, which are a prerequisite to ensure interoperability. In this context, interoperability is only concerned with the integrity of the mechanisms for the exchange of information chunks among components without evaluating the compatibility of the meaning of these information chunks at the sender and the receiver. The gap between the syntactic description of the information chunks determined with the operational specification and the user's mental model of the service provided at the interface is bridged by the meta-level LIF specification. The meta-level part of a LIF specification in the GENESYS architecture shall describe the meaning of the information that is exchanged over the interface. The concepts used in the specification must fit well with the conceptual world of the user of a given subsystem (i.e. it must be expressed in terms and notations that are common knowledge to the user). The meta-level specification may contain formal descriptions, but can also incorporate natural language, pictures, and diagrams that are commonly used in the user's domain.

Besides helping in the reduction of the complexity, an exact LIF specification is a prerequisite for independent development and reuse of subsystems and for enabling evolvability. A key enabler for reuse of subsystems (e.g., legacy components or components developed by a third party supplier) is the protection of intellectual property. Therefore, the architecture shall provide mechanisms to prevent the disclosure of intellection property at different abstraction levels (e.g., the contents of an FPGA or of on-chip flash memory).

In many application domains, it is not possible (or even desired) to design a system and decide once and for all which subsystems are integrated to comprise the overall system. In such systems the constituting components (sensor/actuator nodes, mobile devices) might even not be known at design time. In addition to this, the topology and hierarchy where subsystems are integrated might not be known a priori. Therefore, the architecture shall also support the

3.1. GENERAL REQUIREMENTS

definition of the LIF for reconfigurable systems covering temporal aspects as well as non functional aspects such as safety.

3.1.4 Heterogeneity and Technology Obsolescence

For many application domains enabling a fast time-to-market is a key requirement of an architecture that co-decide over success or failure of a product. Using pre-validated component libraries (e.g., hardware components or software modules for often needed functions like security services, memory services, etc.) may help to speed up the development time of future applications. Thus, the GENESYS architecture shall support commercial component-of-the-shelf system development and permit the integration and reuse of heterogeneous components. Examples for such heterogeneous components are components that are realized in different technologies (e.g., an algorithm provided as software component running within a general purpose CPU or as a dedicated customized hardware IP core) or implementations of components within the same technology requiring different configurations (e.g., hardware IP cores running with different operating frequency in order to optimize the power consumption). The architecture shall support this integration of components based on the interface specifications solely, i.e., without having to understand the internals of the components. This would allow third party suppliers to deliver, e.g., pre-compiled software modules in order to protect their intellectual property (e.g., the source code).

This reuse of such intellectual property (IP) modules across different applications can increase the number of reusable components and has to be supported by the architecture (e.g., an IP core that realizes security functions should be suitable for e-commerce applications as well as for the automotive sector). This will also address the issue of non-recurring semi-conductor engineering costs as barrier for implementing new functions as customized hardware IP blocks. The non-recurring costs (design, masks, test pattern, etc.) of a submicron SoC are continuously growing (tens of millions of dollars). Low-volume applications can hardly afford the design of a custom SoC. Thus, the architecture shall enable the cross-domain reusability of once validated components in order to enable low production and low parts costs.

As a consequence, when integrating components from different domains (or different product generations), system developers will face a multi-vendor environment, i.e. components and entire subsystems that have to be integrated are developed by different vendors. Therefore, the architecture shall have the capability to support multiple standards (e.g., protocols, interfaces) that allow the integration of IP blocks from multiple vendors without demanding a redesign of core elements of the architecture. For this purpose, standards should be encapsulated in subsystems that can be modified and exchanged without violating the established architectural style. Particular attention has to be paid to handle heterogeneous data representations at the interfaces of components developed by different vendors. In order to avoid inconsistent data representations, the architecture shall support dedicated components (e.g., gateways) that resolve potential property mismatches of two independently developed subsystems.

Besides improving component reuse a component-based design methodology facilitating heterogeneous components is also beneficial for the performance of systems: Achieving performance enhancements only by increasing the clock frequency of chips will lead to a dead end. Therefore, new strategies to enhance the system performance are requested. A feasible approach for embedded systems in terms of cost and power consumption could be scalable heterogeneous multi-core processing. That is, the architecture shall ensure that the scalability of a system must not rely on an increase of the performance of a single processing element, but enable the system designer to choose that implementation alternative out of a set of heterogeneous components that fits best his performance/power goals. This will result in a different approach to system-level design. Instead of mapping a selected function to a predefined architecture, the future goal of system-level design is to map a maximally parallel function to a maximally parallel implementation. Methodologically, this defines a new design domain that emphasizes distributed implementation over centralized implementation; this reprises the need for communications-centric design.

Further performance improvements within components could be achieved by supporting multithreading with steady runtime behavior, which means to block one thread during the time of a code memory fetch by executing the instructions of a second thread. In this way, the execution pipelines of the processor can be almost fully utilized.

3.1.5 Real-Time Requirements

Timeliness is vital property for the majority of embedded applications addressed by the GENESYS architecture. Examples range from multimedia applications that are required to deliver synchronized audio and video streams, which require to specify and guarantee a certain amount of bandwidth for data exchange between sender and receiver(s), to control applications where the temporally correct (i.e. with low and bounded jitter) acquisition of information, its processing, and finally the triggering of an appropriate action is required for providing a control service with high quality.

Therefore, the architecture has to provide means to enable to reason about the temporal properties of an application and to provide guarantees (and enable to monitor these guarantees) for the timely execution of an application service. In order to analyze application-specific temporal constraints, the architecture shall enable the development of software for which the calculation of tight bounds on the WCET is possible with feasible effort. The key to calculate tight bounds on the WCET with feasible effort is deterministic behavior in each layer of the system that is to be analyzed (e.g., constant instruction timing of processors, predictable memory hierarchies instead of implicitly loaded caches, compilers that generate single-path code ...). Nondeterministic behavior in any layer (hardware, operating system, middleware, compiler, and application code) can preclude the feasible calculation of tight WCET bounds, and can result in highly pessimistic and overestimated WCET bounds. Furthermore, the architecture shall ensure that the start-up time of a component is a priori known and bounded, since the start-up time of a component is, on the one hand, an important issue for implementing fault-tolerance, e.g., by restarting the component after a transient fault, and on the other hand, in many applications an important factor to guarantee user satisfaction (e.g., for consumer electronics devices like digital cameras).

In addition, the architecture shall enable the synchronization of computation and communication of distributed services and to check the temporal validity of real-time data that originates from distributed subsystems. A prerequisite for this is the existence of a common time base: The architecture shall provide a consistent global time service for a defined set of nodes, which establishes a common time base with bounded precision, bounded accuracy, (an application-dependent) sufficiently fine granularity, and (an application-dependent) sufficiently wide horizon.

3.2 Networking and Resource Management

The following requirements for the GENESYS architecture address challenges for future embedded systems that are mainly concerned with networking and resource management. First, different communication modes that have to be supported by the architecture are stated. These requirements mainly originate from the different fields of applications that are targeted by the GENESYS architecture. The subsequent requirements analysis focuses on particular aspects of networking: the efficient support of data streaming, wireless networking, and Internet connectivity. Thereafter, requirements for dynamic resource management are stated, which is an important architectural feature that enables efficient use of shared resources, advanced fault-tolerance strategies, and offers the basis for establishing power and energy efficiency. Requirements concerning power and energy efficiency are completing this part of the requirements analysis.

3.2.1 Messaging

As a cross-domain endeavor, the GENESYS architecture has to unify requirements originating from highly diverse fields of applications. A central and essential part of each architecture is its communication infrastructure. The communication infrastructure provided by the GENESYS architecture has to provide architectural services for enabling the interaction of components belonging to different application domains. These services have to be tailored to the individual fields of application in order to gain usability across domains.

Basically, one can distinguish best-effort and guaranteed communication services. Whereas best-effort communication services offer to each user a share of the overall communication resources depending on the current load without guaranteeing a quality of service level, guarantees with respect to communication bandwidth, maximum transmission latency, and maximum latency jitter are given for guaranteed communication services.

Best-effort communication can be implemented by using event-triggered message transfer. Thus, in order to enable the implementation of best-effort communication services, the GENESYS architecture shall support event-triggered message transfer. Event-triggered message transfer enables a communication system to be designed with respect to the expected average communication load; thus, allowing timing failures to occur during worst-case scenarios.

In addition, the GENESYS architecture shall support guaranteed event-triggered message transfer, i.e. despite the use of the event-triggered communication paradigm guarantees for maximum latency, bandwidth, and latency jitter shall be possible. Otherwise, quality-of-service guarantees as required for many multimedia applications cannot be provided. Therefore, the architecture shall support predictable communication within the system interconnect so that the temporal and/or reliability constraints of applications and services can be met.

For hard real-time systems the temporal guarantees for message delivery provided by the communication system have to hold under all considered fault and load scenarios. In control loops, for instance, where the sensing elements and the actuators are realized on different nodes, the delay and the jitter of the communication service are important parameters for the quality of control. To support such applications, the GENESYS architecture shall provide a real-time message transfer service, which supports a deterministic and timely transport of messages. In addition to bounded transmission latency and bounded transmission jitter, also bounded error detection latency for transmission errors shall be supported by the architecture. This communication service is required for the temporal coordination of distributed actions and depends on a (distributed fault-tolerant) common time-base.

Besides the communication paradigm, the concrete implementation of the communication infrastructure can take significant impact on non functional properties such as cost-effectiveness, resource utilization, and dependability of the system: The GENESYS architecture shall support the sharing of the same physical communication infrastructure among multiple subsystems. Such an integrated system enables the reduction of the required hardware components, communication busses, cables and connectors, which can lead to an increase of the dependability of the overall systems, since there are fewer components that can fail, as well as to improved utilization of the resources since the flexibility of resource allocation is improved. This has also a direct beneficial impact on the cost-efficiency of the system.

3.2.2 Streaming Support

A particular type of information exchange is data streaming. Data streams are content that is consumed while it is being delivered, i.e. it can be processed - listened, viewed, analyzed - before it is fully received. An example where data streaming is the first choice delivery method is streaming media. The major benefit of data streaming is its cost-efficient implementation, in particular with respect to storage requirements: Since the content of data streams can be processed online during its reception, the receiver(s) of the content are not required to reserve memory buffers for the entire data stream, but only for a single data fragment of the stream (or a few fragments depending, e.g., on the quality of the network connection). Especially for streaming media where the size of the entire data stream can easily reach thousands of mega bytes, these storage savings are essential.

Since many multimedia systems are inherently streaming based services (e.g., television or radio), the GENESYS architecture shall support data streaming. Of particular importance for streaming media is that interruptions of service delivery are not tolerated by the user. Present streaming systems typically use pre-buffering of several data frames in order to provide a stream delivery without connection break-offs. In order to avoid such a pre-buffering (or at least minimize the number of required buffers) by still providing a given quality-of-service level, the architecture shall provide tight guarantees for la-

3.2. NETWORKING AND RESOURCE MANAGEMENT

tency and bandwidth of data streams.

Related thereto is the requirement for timely and time-dependent combination of data-streams from different subsystems. This issue, denoted as real-time data fusion, is a generic problem that occurs in many applications (e.g., lip synchronization in multi-media systems, sensor fusion in control systems like the fusion of video and radar data in an obstacle recognition system).

3.2.3 Mobile Networking and Connectivity to the Internet

Ubiquitous computing is a keyword that subsumes a multitude of presently appearing embedded applications in our everyday life. Intrinsic to this group of applications and for the provision of their service is the requirement for mobile networking in order to form (steadily) connected groups of mobile devices or connect stand-alone mobile devices to other existing systems such as the Internet. Mobile networking requires a wireless communication infrastructure, which has, compared to wire-bound communication systems, significant differences with respect to dependability and predictability. Wireless communication links are typically more vulnerable to interferences with other devices/systems than a wire-bound communication system, which can exhibit protection mechanisms (e.g., shielding) and fault-tolerance strategies (e.g., replicated wires) at lower cost. Furthermore, applications using wireless communication infrastructures are typically designed as open-world systems where an (unknown) number of uncoordinated clients compete for the resources of a server.

To address these challenges, the GENESYS architecture should enable the establishment of dependable mobile ad-hoc networks. A mobile ad-hoc network is a self-configuring network of mobile nodes that are connected by wireless communication links. Since the nodes are mobile, the network topology can change rapidly and unpredictably over time. As a consequence, the network should not be centrally organized, and the configuration of the network (e.g., finding a suitable topology) should be done by the nodes themselves. Due to the minimal centrally performed configuration effort and the ability for quick deployment, ad hoc networks are suitable to establish survivable dynamic communication for applications like military networks or emergency operations.

However, especially wireless communication links impose great demands with respect to security on the design of the architecture. Therefore, the GENESYS architecture shall particularly consider the aspect of security for wireless networks (e.g., integrity of network address).

In addition to mobile connectivity, the connectivity to the Internet (or other existing (legacy) networks) is an absolute requirement for many upcoming applications, in particular in the consumer electronics domain. For such applications, ontology-based standardized descriptions of the service semantics should be provided in order to enable the user to select one service out of the multitude of services provided in an open-world system such as the Internet. In addition, the GENESYS architecture should enable the interconnection with many services based on existing Internet standards and to provide network connectivity over different technologies through a single, easy to use and stable API.

This requirement entails several sub-challenges, in particular with respect to service discovery, content access and networking protocols, which are outside the scope of GENESYS. However, it is an absolute requirement that during the design of the GENESYS architectural style those issues are considered in order to ensure that the architecture is not at conflict with enabling Internet support.

3.2.4 Dynamic Resource Allocation

The ability of a system to dynamically adapt the allocation of its resources to its hosted application subsystems and to dynamically modify the configuration of application subsystems is a mandatory requirement for the GENESYS architecture, which enables many emergent properties of the system, which would not be achievable without dynamic resource management: Firstly, dynamic resource management permits to optimize the utilization of hardware resources within the system with respect to changing communication and computational demands of its hosted applications (e.g., applications exhibiting scalable Quality of Service (QoS) with respect to audio/image quality). Hence, the GENESYS architecture shall support the dynamic allocation of the overall communication bandwidth to subsystems in order to enable the efficient implementation of applications with non-uniform communication load patterns (e.g., multimedia applications).

Secondly, dynamic resource management provides the foundation for fault-tolerance and maintenance strategies like graceful service degradation (i.e. the controlled degradation of a system's service in case of resource shortage) or service migration (e.g., hot replacement of components) in the presence of hardware faults. Furthermore, it provides the instruments for achieving system evolvability (e.g., updating, adding, or removing software in order to adapt to user-specific behavior.

Finally, most aspects of power and energy management require the dynamic modification of the system's configuration, including software as well as hardware. Power consumption is a key issue for mobile devices in order to achieve longer operation times with cheaper and lighter batteries. Even for devices that have permanent access to an energy supply, the topic becomes more and more important, because the consumed power manifests itself in heat which can be very difficult to dissipate (e.g., the need for large and noisy ventilators in modern personal computers). Therefore, the architecture shall support dynamically scalable performance of hardware resources (e.g., processing elements, communication infrastructure) with respect to the actual level of available power respectively energy of battery powered devices. Exemplary strategies to achieve this scalability and to control power consumption and heat dissipation of the overall system are to use dynamic voltage and frequency scaling techniques to adjust the clock frequency for parts of the system's hardware or to dynamically switch off/on currently unused components.

The envisioned wide applicability of the GENESYS architecture imposes further requirements on the resource management mechanisms provided by the architecture. First of all, the architecture shall ensure that the above mentioned mechanisms for managing the allocation of computational and communication resources shall not rely on cooperative behavior of subsystems. In contrast, the architecture has to be enabled to enforce resource reallocation. Otherwise, the system would not be able to tolerate a malicious fault of one or more subsystems. Furthermore, the architecture shall enable the development of systems that cover a wide range of performance targets, i.e. to find and enforce the optimal trade-off between the quality levels supported by the application,

3.2. NETWORKING AND RESOURCE MANAGEMENT

the user requirements, and the available platform resources.

In addition, for enabling the implementation of safety-related or safety-critical application services, the architecture shall ensure the coexistence of static and dynamic resource allocation mechanisms, i.e. the provision of guarantees for computational resources (e.g., lower bounds on the availability of processing time) and communication resources (e.g., lower bounds on the availability of bandwidth and upper bounds on latency and jitter of message transmission), even if resources are shared among subsystems. That is, despite the possibility to dynamically modify the allocation of resources among subsystems, it must be ensured by the architecture that a given share of the overall resources is provably available to a particular subsystem. This way, it is possible for applications to meet real-time constraints, also when applications with different kinds of (or even no) real-time requirements requiring the same shared resources are active simultaneously. Even more restrictive requirements have to be full-filled for applications of safety-critical application domains. For instance for system certification in the avionic domain, it has to be ensured that resource allocations are performed deterministic and static, i.e. that time, space and I/O allocations have to be determined at compilation, assembly, or link time, and have to remain identical at each and every initialization of a program or process, and are not dynamically altered during runtime.

3.2.5 Power/Energy Efficiency

Power and energy efficiency are key quality attributes of many products, especially for battery operated handheld/mobile devices. In order to tackle these challenges, low power design and power-awareness are identified as one of the grand challenges for future embedded systems. Low power design primarily addresses the minimization of the power consumption from single gates to complex system-on-chips (SoCs), as well as, the optimization of the communication among the individual gates/cores. Current design tools give power/energy information on a too low level back to system designer. Ideally, one would like to see direct energy efficiency feedback at all phases of the design flow. Therefore, pre-implementation performance and power/energy evaluation should be supported by the GENESYS methodology and tools in order to ensure that all technical solutions on the chip-level are implemented in a way that minimizes chip-area and power consumption. In addition, low-power design is important for reducing the stand-by power consumption of electronic devices. Since the maximum stand-by time that can be achieved without changing the battery is an important aspect of many portable devices and body applications, the GENESYS architecture shall also enable the minimization of stand-by power.

Power-awareness describes systems, which modify their behavior based on current power/energy availability during runtime. Hence, power-aware design deals with the development of techniques and algorithms that influence the system's behavior in order to meet power and energy goals under given performance constraints or vice versa. Therefore, the GENESYS architecture shall support system-level power management, which includes the adaptation and adjustment of components to application and use case specific performance needs so that applications run with lowest possible resource and energy usage. Furthermore, system level power management deals with the partitioning and separation of optional application features into individual components, which enable turning off unused components or the reduction of the component's performance with techniques such as dynamic voltage and frequency scaling (DVFS) or dynamic power management (DPM).

Since energy consumption at run-time also largely depends on user behavior (e.g., display brightness of mobile devices), it is essential to give also the user feedback of energy consumption and means to influence it. Therefore, the architecture shall enable collecting, storing and providing energy, thermal and power information about device energy and power capabilities, such as energy supply information (e.g., the remaining energy), current power usage, estimated usage time, and peak power. It should enable presenting this information to users (consumers and developers) with a proper user interface. However, the architecture should also provide default settings for component configurations in order to support that the end user does not necessarily need to do anything related to energy efficiency in order to use the device or applications (e.g., default clock frequency of an IP core or default application mode such as full-quality video display).

3.3 Security and Robustness

The results of the requirements analysis for the GENESYS architecture with respect to robustness and security are presented in the following subsections. For enabling the recovery from an erroneous state caused by a transient fault, a clear notion of state is important for the GENESYS architecture. Requirements regarding state awareness are formulated in the following. Afterwards, diagnosis and testing are in the focus of the requirements analysis. The important issue of system certifiability is the topic of the next section, which is followed by requirements with respect to strategies and services for security. This chapter is closed by elaborating on the importance of fault-tolerance and error-containment for the GENESYS architecture and the resulting requirements for architectural services.

3.3.1 Security Strategies and Services

System security and data privacy are becoming key issues when increasing the connectivity of systems beyond their traditional system boundaries (e.g., connecting parts of the in-vehicle electronic system of a car via gateways to the Internet in order to enable in-system updates). In addition, private user security is becoming more and more important as consumer devices are used increasingly for identification, authorization, payment as well as for storage of sensitive personal information. Hence, the GENESYS architecture shall provide mechanisms and services to ensure the primary concepts of security: integrity, availability, and confidentiality as well as secondary concepts which are composed out of primary concepts like authentication and authorization.

To ensure integrity, the architecture shall provide mechanisms to prevent undetected modification of hardware or software by unauthorized persons or systems (on architectural level as well as on application level). In many applications integrity is explicitly required for a dedicated set of application data such as the mileage counter of a car or transaction data of online banking applications. In addition, with respect to sensor values and control commands integrity can even become a safety-relevant system property in safety-critical

3.3. SECURITY AND ROBUSTNESS

applications. Therefore, to enable integrity protection, the architecture shall include mechanisms against message injections, message replay, message modification and message delay on the network.

In the context of security, assurance of availability is usually conceived as the provision of mechanisms to ensure that unauthorized persons or systems cannot deny service access to authorized users. The violation of availability may cause economic damage by a significant reduction of the user-value of a given system. Additionally, safety-relevant consequences can also be caused by the violation of availability as operators may lose the ability to monitor and to control a safety-critical process.

Confidentiality is concerned with the protection of private information such as personal data in office applications or performance data and product recipes in automation systems, as well as, information that is specific to the security mechanisms themselves (e.g., user names, passwords). Confidentiality is also important for enabling the support of Digital Rights Management (DRM) as required for many applications in the consumer electronics domain. Therefore, the architecture shall provide mechanisms to prevent the disclosure of information to unauthorized persons or systems.

In order to discriminate between legitimate and illegitimate use of system services as required for the assurance of confidentiality, integrity, and availability, the architecture has to provide mechanisms to determine the identity of a system or a user. Hence, it shall support the authentication of users and systems and the authorization of already authenticated users and systems with respect to a given service.

Closely related to the above mentioned security principles that shall be supported by the GENESYS architecture is non-repudiability, i.e., to *"provide an irrefutable proof to a third party of who initiated a certain action in the system, even if the actor is not cooperating"* [15]. Since non-repudiability is becoming extremely important to commerce, the architecture shall provide mechanisms to support this property of electronic contracts.

In addition, in some cases (e.g., to deal with system liability) component suppliers want to assure that their hardware can be used only with their own software. For such scenarios, the GENESYS architecture shall provide mechanisms to prevent the out-of-specification use of single components.

3.3.2 Diagnosis

The GENESYS architecture addresses the importance of system diagnosis and health state monitoring for improving the robustness of a system by regarding diagnostic mechanisms as integral parts of the system, which are considered from the very beginning of system design. Therefore, the GENESYS architecture shall provide diagnosis services, which provide consistent information about the health state of a defined set of subsystems with known and bounded latency at different integration levels (i.e. at chip level, at device level, and at system level). The timely information about the health state of subsystems enables the system (or the end user) to trigger corrective actions such as an autonomous reconfiguration of the system or the discovery of an alternative service provider.

The diagnostic services provided by the GENESYS architecture shall support systematic diagnostic methods (e.g., to detect the power down of a component or problems in the power supply) and application-specific diagnostic methods (e.g., detecting anomalies in the program execution sequence due to programming errors). Systematic diagnostic methods, on the one hand, are used to detect system anomalies that are application-independent, i.e. those methods can be generally applied without requiring application-specific knowledge. On the other hand, application-specific methods can be used to detect anomalies, which cannot be detected by the exclusive use of systematic diagnostic methods (e.g., results with wrong values that are temporally and syntactically correct) at the cost of needing additional parametrization with application-specific knowledge. The basic requirement for all diagnostic methods is that they must not interfere with the operation of the subsystems that are to be diagnosed, i.e. the avoidance of the probe effect. If the diagnostic service would interfere with the subsystems that are to be diagnosed, it would be able to induce errors into these subsystems. Thus, the diagnostic service would always have to be certified according to the same criticality level as the given subsystem.

A further requirement for the diagnostic services is to classify faults on the basis of their persistence (e.g., transient or permanent faults) in order to trigger the appropriate corrective action. The restart and subsequent reintegration of components is an adequate measure to deal with components that are affected by transient faults. For handling permanent faults, the GENESYS architecture shall provide a maintenance-oriented diagnostic service. For system maintenance, it is an important aspect to correctly identify those subsystems that have to be replaced or repaired. In systems that consist of a large number of subsystems, the identification of faulty subsystems is a very challenging task and can consume a lot of working effort if it is done purely manually. In order to minimize the number of components that are replaced by mistake (i.e. they are replaced although they are still working), the architecture shall support the diagnostic service by tracing back the source of a fault. That is, the architecture shall establish the notion of fault-containment regions that encapsulate the effects of faults. Furthermore, it is important that the diagnostic service shall support the establishment of a holistic view on the system in order to detect correlated failures and anomalies. As soon as integrated systems are developed by different suppliers, the issues of traceability and liability are of utmost importance. Therefore, the architecture shall provide mechanisms that provably identify subsystem that have violated their specification in order to support liability.

Furthermore, different vendors will design their subsystems according to different models of computation. In order to increase the acceptance of the GENESYS architecture on the part of the vendors, the architecture should comprise a design methodology framework, which supports the usage of different models of computation.

In addition, for subsystems and components where life-time prediction is not possible, an improvement of availability and dependability can be achieved by supporting predictive maintenance. Therefore, the GENESYS architecture shall support the identification of components that are likely to fail in the near future (e.g., the early detection of faults in Flash and EEPROM memory technologies by monitoring the charge loss in such devices).

3.3. SECURITY AND ROBUSTNESS

3.3.3 State Awareness

The reliability of today's electronics devices is significantly impacted by the increasing vulnerability with respect to soft errors. Soft errors induced by extraterrestrial radiation (cosmic rays) or by materials (due to alpha particles) are no longer confined to SRAM bit cell upsets - beyond the 90 nanometer feature size of electronic devices, as it is state-off-the-art today, logic circuits and latches become also increasingly vulnerable. Therefore, it is a requirement of utmost importance of the GENESYS architecture to provide mechanisms at the architectural level to handle the resulting increasing transient failure rate of electronics devices, in particular of giga-scale SoCs.

Recovery from a transient failure can be performed by restarting a component. In order to fasten the recovery/restart time, regular reintegration points of a component shall be defined, at which the component can resume its operation after the occurrence of a transient failure. To this end, the architecture has to provide mechanisms to regularly distribute the component's state at these reintegration points and to restore it in the component after restart. During system design, this requires the definition and externalization of those parts of the component's state that are relevant for the component reintegration.

In addition to the handling of transient failures, the GENESYS architecture shall support robustness mechanisms such as fault-tolerance, error containment and graceful degradation of applications. A prerequisite for many robustness mechanisms is the detection of an erroneous component state with sufficient error detection coverage. A requirement for a feasible realization of such detection mechanisms is that as little as possible knowledge on the internals of a component is required and that components need not be modified in order to deploy detection mechanisms: On the one hand, modifications could induce new faults and, for particular application domains, it would cause enormous costs, since a recertification of the component would be entailed. On the other hand, this requirement helps to protect the IP of suppliers, because they need not reveal component internals. State-awareness at the design of components and externalization of state helps in discriminating correct from erroneous component behavior solely on the interface state of a component.

An error-containment technique that is widely applied in the automotive and avionics domain is active redundancy by the replication of components (e.g., using a triple-modular redundancy (TMR) configuration). A systematic voting strategy over the results of replicated components is bit-by-bit comparison of the produced outputs of the components, which has the advantage of not requiring any application specific knowledge about the values to be compared. For such systems, the GENESYS architecture has to ensure replica determinism of replicated components. Replica determinism states that a set of replica determinate components, which are required to have the same encapsulated state, produce the same sequence of output messages at points in time that are at most an interval of d time units apart (as seen by an omniscient external observer).

3.3.4 Testing

Testing is an integral part of the development cycle of a system that involves a notable amount of the overall costs for system development. In order to reduce these costs and to improve the testability of the system, the GENESYS architecture shall provide a standardized test interface for component testing. A standardized test interface will significantly reduce the efforts concerning the adaptation of test equipment and test methodology as well as the costs for training of test engineers by eliminating the existing multitude of different test methods and technologies. Furthermore, a standardized test interface would help to achieve test reuse and test composability. For instance in high volume markets like the consumer electronics industry, the costs for end-of-line tests in manufacturing are a determining success factor. To confine these costs, the architecture has to support fast and simple end-of-line tests by workers of normal qualifications. In addition, the architecture shall limit the impact of product changes (e.g., elimination of bugs or updates) on the required modifications of the production line, which would also require the reusability of existing test procedures. To improve the reproducibility of test procedures and to speed-up test sequences, the GENESYS architecture shall enable a dedicated test mode of components in which it is possible to set the state of a single subsystem. This way, testing effort is reduced since the number of test sequences that is required to achieve the given component state is minimized.

The design and development methodology of the GENESYS architecture shall support design-for-testability, i.e. requirements for testing shall already be considered during system design, since this is also expected to substantially decrease the efforts for design testing, system-integration testing, manufacturing testing, and assembly testing. Furthermore, it should enable automatic test generation in order to support feasible test development.

In addition to improving design and reuse of tests during design time, the GENESYS architecture should enable the implementation of mechanisms for component testing at run-time. In particular at the chip-level, the architecture should support efficient built-in self-test techniques for System-on-a-Chips (SoCs). Since a complete system self-test during system start-up is often too time consuming, the architecture should enable the development of intelligent self-test functionality, which are reconfigurable and exhibit a different test procedure (e.g., starting from a different history state) depending on the results of the last test run.

3.3.5 System Certification

In particular in the application domains of avionics, automotive, and industrial control systems, system certification plays a cardinal role in the system development cycle. Since the GENESYS architecture aims to be deployed for many different applications operating in different contexts, the architecture shall enable the certification of core architectural services independently from concrete applications using the architecture's services. Hence, the core architectural services of a particular implementation of the architecture shall be certified only once, so that the already certified platform can be reused for many applications. In addition, the design and development methodology devised for the GENESYS architecture shall support the principle of design-for-verifiability, which means that requirements for verification are already considered during the design of the system (e.g., algorithms that cannot be verified should not be used in safety-critical systems). Without adherence to this principle, it would be unlikely that system verification and certification will be tractable. Further-

3.3. SECURITY AND ROBUSTNESS

more, in order to optimally support component-based design and thus enable the independent development of individual components, the architecture shall support the modular certification of subsystems. This is also a necessity for cost-effective reuse of components.

Further challenges with respect to system certification that have to be taken into account by the GENESYS architecture originate from the introduction of integrated systems: The progress the semiconductor industry has made in the past decades has encompassed a tremendous increase of processing power and has enabled the construction of complex embedded applications and has increased the number of deployed component in present applications. Many application domains such as the avionics and automotive domain attempt to reduce the overall number of components by the introduction of integrated system architectures, which share the overall resources among different types of embedded applications (e.g., safety-related ABS functions and multimedia applications). Whereas these approaches promise cost savings as well as improvements with respect to dependability, they create challenging demands for system certification for GENESYS: The GENESYS architecture has to support certification of subsystems with different criticality levels, i.e. each subsystem is certified according to its criticality level and the architecture provides mechanisms to ensure that subsystems with higher criticality are not impaired by subsystems with lower criticality. Otherwise, every subsystem would have to be certified according to the criticality level of the most critical subsystem within the system. For this purpose, the architecture should also consider safety composition rules as, for instance, defined by the IEC-61508 standard, which is the common base certification standard for multiple industrial domains.

3.3.6 Fault-Tolerance and Error Containment

Electronic systems need to operate in the presence of faults, either originating from the external environment (e.g., cosmic radiation or misbehaving users) or from the system internals (e.g., design faults or wear-out of hardware components). Hence, the tolerance of faults is a key factor determining the success of a system. In particular for present chip manufacturing technology enabling the construction of complex chips comprising billions of transistors, systems built according to the GENESYS architecture must not rely on the requirement of 100% correctness for devices and interconnects. By relaxing the requirement of 100% correctness for devices and interconnects, the costs of manufacturing, verification, and test may be dramatically reduced. Such a paradigm shift is likely to be forced in any case by technology scaling, which leads to more transient and permanent failures of signals, logic values, devices, and interconnects.

For safety-critical systems, the construction of a fault-tolerant system requires a specification containing the assumptions regarding the type and frequency of faults that the resulting system is supposed to handle. Therefore, the architecture shall be based on such a fault hypothesis. However, if the faults that occur in the real world are not covered by the fault hypothesis, then even a perfectly designed fault tolerant computer system can fail. Therefore, in particular for systems for which a thorough analysis of the expected fault scenario is not feasible or too costly, the architecture shall also provide robustness mechanisms that help a system to survive in case only incomplete or imprecise specifications of the fault-hypothesis are available

A further requirement for building fault-tolerant systems is error containment, since without error containment a single fault has the ability to corrupt the whole system. Therefore, the architecture has to provide an error containment service that allows the establishment of Error Containment Regions (ECR) with known error containment coverage. An error containment region is a well-defined subsystem where the consequences of an error within the subsystem will not propagate outside the subsystem without being detected. The probability for preventing the propagation of the consequences of an error is called the error-containment coverage.

However, different applications have different demands with respect to reliability and therefore require an appropriate degree of fault-tolerance. This has to be taken into account by the GENESYS architecture. For instance, increased communication service reliability will normally imply increased communication cost. Therefore, during the design of an application one should have the capability to select the appropriate level of communication reliability.

Furthermore, the architecture should provide an application programming interface (API) to the application that is independent of whether the underlying platform is fault-tolerant or not. By providing a generic fault-tolerant layer that separates application software from the mechanisms regarding fault-tolerance, the complexity of the application software can be reduced and it is sufficient to implement and validate the fault-tolerance mechanisms only once.

Particular requirements for the fault-tolerance mechanisms that should be provided by the GENESYS architecture that have been identified for various application domains are:

- the tolerance of software errors, since is not feasible in many cases to provide application code that is absolutely free from software errors

- the support for delay/disruption-tolerant networking, since unpredictable delays and disruption may be unavoidable in some cases (e.g., when using wireless communication)

- the handling of transient faults affecting Flip-Flops and memory cells, since low-level recovery (e.g., on-chip recovery) increases the availability of single components and thus increases the dependability of the overall system

- the support for error masking by the use of replicas and voting mechanisms (e.g., self-checking pair, triple modular redundancy)

Several application domains addressed by GENESYS (e.g., automotive domain or industrial process control) have dependability requirements for their systems that exceed the dependability that can be achieved with single components at present implementation technologies. For such systems fault-tolerance strategies such as active redundancy of components in a TMR configuration have to be supported by the architecture. To this end, the architecture shall ensure that all subsystems of a system see a sequence of events (e.g., message reception) in the same order. This is necessary because the temporal order of incoming events can have an influence on the internal state of a subsystem, a consistent view on the temporal order of events is generally necessary to achieve replica determinism.

A further strategy to improve the reliability of systems using redundant subsystems is to support fault tolerance mechanisms that adapt to reliability changes of subsystems during the system's life time. For instance, if the ability to recover from errors is exhausted for a particular replicated subsystem because too many permanent errors have accumulated (e.g., one replica of a TMR system has failed permanently), appropriate actions have to be taken to restore the initial reliability (e.g., the migration of the replicated system functionality to a different IP core in a multi-core system). This is a requirement for enabling the sustained operation of components, which is demanded for applications that require a non-stop operation throughout their entire lifetime.

In addition, since on-call maintenance can be very cost intensive due to maintenance contracts and service outages, the GENESYS architecture shall enable the shift of on-call maintenance to periodic maintenance. A shift to periodic maintenance can be achieved by fault-tolerance techniques that retain, in case of an internal error, the correct system functionality until the next scheduled service date.

3.4 System Design and Evolution

The last part of the requirements analysis is devoted to aspects of system design and system evolution. Firstly, requirements for the GENESYS methodology framework concerning the support for system modeling are stated. This is followed with requirements regarding the reuse of existing systems by supporting the integration of legacy systems. Thirdly, requirements of the GENESYS architecture and the methodology framework for the management of the product life-cycle and to cope with changing technologies are presented. The chapter is concluded with an analysis of the requirements w.r.t. system validation.

3.4.1 System Modeling

The GENESYS architectural style will be accompanied with a development framework that supports the development of cross-domain application services by adapting and extending the most promising generic model- and quality-driven architecture development approach by measurable quality characteristics specific for embedded systems. This methodology framework should support the modeling of the system from different views such as computational-independent, platform-independent and platform-specific (as proposed by the Model-Driven Architecture (MDA)). The methodology framework should support a meet-in-the-middle methodology for system development including design and evaluation of systems, which combines top-down (e.g., driven from user or domain requirements) and bottom-up (e.g., technology driven) development strategies, since in many application domains the features and thus the design of a product is not only driven by the users' requirements, but also by the availability of innovative and affordable subcomponents (e.g., mobile phones with cameras or MP3 players).

In addition, the development framework should assist the system designer from the very beginning of system design and development by providing techniques and tools for gathering and analyzing requirements as well as for modeling structural aspects (e.g., the number of components and their interconnection), behavioral aspects (e.g., modeling the expected system behavior), and timing aspects (e.g., maximum latencies of message transmissions) of embedded systems. Furthermore, the development framework shall provide modeling views on the system that include aspects with regard to system deployment and shall enable dependability evaluation according to the needs of the considered integration levels and application domains.

Based on dependability and performance requirements of application subsystems, the methodology framework should, enabled by the core services of the GENESYS architecture, support the transparent allocation of functional blocks to distinct hardware elements (e.g., to map software components on distinct processing elements). For this purpose, a modeling methodology shall be used that permits to abstract away technical details concerning the physical platform during the modeling phase of the application. Such independent abstraction levels of different system details are provided by the Platform Independent Model (PIM) and Platform Specific Model (PSM) in the MDA. The finally required mapping of platform-independent artifacts (i.e. functional and behavioral descriptions of the application software) to the hardware platform shall be supported semi-automatically by the methodology framework.

The usage of the MDA approach promises a better reusability of (platform independent) models of components and thus promises to reduce the time-to-market in case of similar designs or product line designs. To decrease the time-to-market is a significant requirement in many fast-growing semiconductor markets, where the greatest demand is for low-cost, relatively low-performance, and fast time-to-market designs. Products in these markets are typically SoCs with heavy reuse. Addressing this demand requires to describe the characteristics of reusable cores at levels of abstraction that permit efficient design optimization and reuse.

Besides reuse of existing designs, increasing the degree of automation in system development to a semi-automatic interactive development environment (i.e. the automation of repetitive tasks but let the developer to control all important design decisions) is a further enabler for decreasing the time-to-market. One aspect that should be supported by the methodology framework is automatic source code synthesis for architectural services, application services and configuration files, since it will significantly improve the productivity of the development process and the quality of the source code. In order to improve the reuse of existing (legacy) components, reverse engineering from existing implementation level information (e.g., source code or hardware description) to high level models should be enabled.

In addition to the above stated transformations of platform-independent to platform-dependent viewpoints and the support for automatic source code synthesis, the current industrial practice also shows that several different modeling languages are used throughout the development cycle. Therefore, techniques for automatic model transformation are required and should be enabled by the methodology framework. The modeling techniques and tools provided by the GENESYS methodology framework should be able to trace the changes committed to modeling artifacts by the different transformations in order to maintain consistency among the different versions or views of the same model.

Despite the support for model transformations, the methodology framework shall use widely accepted and standardized languages for expressing domain-specific kinds of models in order to avoid unnecessary overhead for distributed and partially independent system development and to support team work as it

3.4. SYSTEM DESIGN AND EVOLUTION

is often necessary to cope with complex systems. Since UML and its profiles are such standardized modeling languages, they should be supported (at least as one alternative) by the GENESYS methodology framework.

The methodology framework should support a service-oriented development of subsystem and systems. Therefore, of particular importance for the methodology framework of the GENESYS architecture is the support for precisely modeling service semantics and service behavior: Reuse of components premises the ability to discover the services provided by existing components and to judge on their usability based on the specification of their service semantics. For this purpose, the methodology framework should provide support for modeling the semantics of services. As different parties will participate or influence the development of components and services, information about components and their provided services should be based on ontologies to counteract misconceptions.

In addition, in order to be able to evaluate the correctness of the system behavior, precise behavioral models (e.g., expressed with temporal logics or abstract state machines) that permit the detection of deviations between specified and actually observed system behavior are needed. For existing components and their provided services the specification of service semantics and of behavioral aspects of services (as well as of requirements) is often only available as textual representation written in natural language. In order to bridge the gap between these informal descriptions and the formal models, the methodology framework should define a transition from natural language representations to models that can be incorporated into the framework.

3.4.2 Reuse of Existing Systems and Standards

In many situations it will neither be possible nor regarded as desirable to design a system completely from scratch. Rather it is the intention of the GENESYS architecture to enable the reuse of existing components and systems and integrate them into larger systems built according to the GENESYS architectural style; thus, allowing a gradual migration of an old system to the new architecture. This support for integration of legacy subsystems into the integrated system is a significant requirement, which promises an improved acceptance of a new architecture. For instance, semiconductor companies have made large investments in libraries of hardware and software IP modules. Rebuilding such libraries to fit a different design/architectural style is not an option. Also, an increasing amount of software is purchased from third parties. A new design/architectural style can be adopted only if it allows the existing hardware and software IP to be reused at little or no additional cost.

In addition, the GENESYS architecture is required to take into account well-established standards (e.g., Ethernet, CAN, USB, protocols for web services, application programming interfaces, etc.), which reduces the effort for many engineers and users required to use the services provided by the architecture and to feature the interoperability with existing systems and designs. For instance in the consumer electronics market, important aspects are the customer's choice of operating system and the (standard) APIs used to access media processing and communications functions.

A key enabler for reuse of existing systems is to provide execution environments with precise and standardized interfaces for (software) components (e.g., application programmer interfaces (APIs)), which enable the reuse of components from third party developers. As important as the reuse of legacy components in systems based on the GENESYS architecture is the ability to integrate new subsystems based on the GENESYS architecture into an old system environment. This will enable a gradual update of old systems with subsystems built according to the GENESYS architecture; and thus initiate a shift towards the GENESYS architecture. Therefore, a strategy for this inverse legacy integration has to be developed.

3.4.3 Product Life-Cycle and Technology Changes

Due to the rapid development and introduction of new technologies in the field of embedded systems, it is essential to be able to upgrade products and product families with minimal effort and to support the development of products that are adapted according to specific needs of a group of customers and thus have to be delivered in different variants (e.g., the electronic infrastructure of a car is composed out of multiple subsystems where each subsystem is available in multiple variants). The goal of product families is to cover a wide variety of different consumer needs with a single architecture. Therefore, the architecture must be scalable and include extension points for product differentiation. This product extension and configuration shall be possible with minimal effort (e.g., without the need for re-compilation of software components), and can be supported by verified typical platform configurations (automated compatibility checking) requiring minimal platform testing.

In addition, the GENESYS architecture shall be technology agnostic in the sense that it does not assume any particular technology to be used and that it allows different technologies to be combined in the solution, i.e. the architecture shall not cause technology lock-in but enable the coexistence of heterogeneous technologies. This flexibility shall also allow mapping of application functionality to software or hardware (fixed or reconfigurable) depending on non-functional requirements and constraints. Thus, the architecture shall support the replacement of single subsystems of a design with subsystems that are realized in another (newer) technology with minimal effort. Therewith, the architecture shall enable covering a wide performance range with the same product (or product family) and shall provide the ability to perform integration at optimal cost level.

This technology independence during the design phase of a system requires a model-driven design in a way that the system functionality can be defined as a platform-independent model, using an appropriate specification language and that this model can be translated in a subsequent step to one or more technology-specific models for the actual implementation. Thus, the application design does not have to be changed when the actual system has to be ported to a new technology generation.

Given the extreme time-to-market requirements in many application domains, products are likely to be changed after their introduction to the market. Therefore, to be successful the GENESYS architecture shall minimize the life cycle costs of systems (i.e. the costs for design, development, production, maintenance, and adaptation to new technology). For this purpose, these different phases of a product's life cycle shall not be considered in isolation by the GENESYS architecture. Otherwise, innovative solutions to identified

3.4. SYSTEM DESIGN AND EVOLUTION

problems may be missed if every part of the life-cycle is viewed independently of every other part. Furthermore, the methodology framework should support innovative life cycle management, i.e. to provide technologies to support all phases of a product's life cycle that are feasible to manage component upgrades even in the presence of components with different life-times, which should not impose any constraint with regard to the used life cycle model followed by organizations implementing the methodology.

In the past, most embedded systems have operated in isolation or in closed groups of components having a statically defined functionality and having to serve static demands from the system's environment. Today, in particular in the domain of consumer applications, embedded systems in home, in office or on the move operate as a part of a larger system; thus, the actual system is formed dynamically and its constituting subsystems are required to dynamically adapt to changing demands and available resources. Therefore, the architecture shall enable dynamic run-time introduction, activation/deactivation and removal of services as well as dynamic binding of applications to services. Furthermore, it shall provide decentralized mechanisms for service announcement, registration and discovery.

A further trend for embedded systems is to increase value of products by enabling customizations of the product based on user preferences, either directly executed by the user (e.g., extension of the functionality of mobile phones by JAVA applications) or carried out by the manufacturer during the production (e.g., different features realized by electronic inventions in the automotive industry). For this purpose, the GENESYS architecture shall support the in-the-field update of hardware and software components. A cost-effective technique, which shall be supported by the architecture, is to upgrade a system over existing external networks such as the Internet. Due to the ongoing integration and cross-linking of applications, it is very likely that a high percentage of components will be connected to some kind of external network in the near future.

3.4.4 Design for Validation

The ever increasing complexity of embedded applications in various application domains requires from an architecture for such applications to pay careful attention to verifiability and testability of the resulting systems. Otherwise, verification and testing will become bottlenecks in product creation. In addition, the certification of embedded systems according to different types of safety standards (e.g., DO-178B) is a requirement for many application domains that should be facilitated by the architecture.

Therefore, as a first important step, the architecture as well as the accompanied methodology framework should support the simulation of application models and of implemented components on all integration levels. Simulation is one of the most important engineering methods for the early validation of system designs and the recognition of possible design problems (e.g., to detect emission and immunity weakness with respect to electro-magnetic radiation of any hardware part of an embedded system in an early design phase in order to prevent costly redesigns. As a consequence, the fast generation of (virtual) prototypes that can be used for this basic validation should be supported, since rapid prototyping is widely used as a methodology to produce working versions of the system under design in order to be able to demonstrate/validate the most important functionalities/properties of the system before the actual development is done. In order to support the independent development of subsystems, which is mandatory in many system development cycles where subsystems from different suppliers have to be integrated, the testing and simulation of subsystems before system integration shall be supported. The system properties that have been tested in isolation shall not be violated by the integration. For instance, the architecture shall support testing of a subsystem before integrating it into its intended environment (e.g., other subsystems, sensors or actuators that are connected to the subsystem) by simulating the environment. This simulation-in-the-loop shall be supported for hardware components (hardware-in-the-loop - HIL) and software modules (software-in-the-loop - SIL).

Furthermore, the GENESYS methodology framework should support the application of formal methods for system verification, which can be applied to existing design methods. For this purpose, two groups of formal methods should be distinguished: formal specification and formal verification. Formal specification can be used to derive an unambiguous specification of a subsystem, an interface, or parts of those, which is also mandatory for enabling the tool-assisted conformance checking of software/hardware modules and for supporting the correctness-by-construction principle, i.e. to transform a specification step by step into a correct design by applying provably correct design methods. Formal verification yields an objective correctness proof for properties that an architecture claims to fulfill. Usually a formal verification process requires a preceding formal specification process. Therefore, the GENESYS methodology framework should support the usage of formal languages for system modeling.

For the purpose of formal verification of applications, the methodology framework should support the application of model-checking and theorem proofing techniques. Since formal verification techniques are often only applicable to very small systems due to their exponential runtime complexity, divide and conquer strategies should be supported for formal verification, i.e. a property can be verified by the sum of individual verification runs. In addition, runtime verification techniques applied to the actual (physical) system and not only to a model should be supported by the methodology framework.

In order to reduce the efforts induced by applying formal verification methods, the reuse of verification patterns and verification environments shall be supported for the verification of subsystems at different abstraction levels (e.g., on-chip IP blocks, devices, etc.). This requires a common and application-independent procedure for the verification of a subsystem and will support the methodology framework in enabling the automation of the validation and verification process as far as possible.

Four

Cross Domain Architectural Style

THIS CHAPTER describes the GENESYS cross-domain architectural style, which is characterized by architectural principles and structuring rules for dependable distributed embedded systems. A principle is an accepted statement about some fundamental insight in a domain of discourse. Principles form the basis for the formulation of operational rules. In GENESYS these principles are operationalized in the reference architecture template of the architectural service specification, which is covered in the following chapters.

The cross-domain architectural style is the result of extensive discussions among the members of the GENESYS consortium, which included experts from the diverse application domains, ranging from safety-critical embedded systems to dynamic multimedia systems, such as mobile phones.

4.1 Complexity Management

In many embedded systems, constraints such as timeliness, power/energy efficiency, dependability requirements, or time-to-market and cost constraints lead to a significant increase of the complexity of the evolving artifact-particularly in the context of the ever increasing functionality, size and connectivity of embedded systems. This increasing cognitive complexity of embedded systems is thus the topic of major concern in all considered application domains. This topic has to be addressed at the architecture level by establishing a framework that takes into consideration the idiosyncrasies and the limited cognitive capabilities of the human mind and leads to an artifact that provides the specified services under given constraints and where relevant properties of this artefact can be modeled at different levels of abstraction by models of adequate simplicity [36].

The report on "Software for Dependable Systems: Sufficient Evidence?" from the National Academies of July 2007 contains as one of its central recommendations that "... *one key to achieving dependability at reasonable cost is a serious and sustained commitment to simplicity, including simplicity of critical functions and simplicity in system interactions. This commitment is often the mark of true expertise* [32]." This section discusses well-established simplification strategies that have been followed in the design of the GENESYS architecture.

4.1.1 Abstraction

Due to the limited cognitive capabilities of the human mind, it is only possible to understand the world around us if we disregard details that are irrelevant for the given purpose and build models of adequate simplicity. Abstraction results in a deliberate simplification of a scenario by focusing only on those properties that are relevant for the given purpose and by omitting the irrelevant details. The purpose determines the viewpoint of an abstraction. It is a major challenge in any scientific endeavor to create appropriate abstractions that capture the essence of the problem at hand and thus lead to an abrupt simplification. A proper abstraction results in an abrupt simplification of a scenario. For example, in Celestial mechanics an abstraction is introduced where the whole diversity of the world is reduced to a mass point in order that the interactions with other mass points (heavenly bodies) can be studied.

In GENESYS we introduce the notion of a computational component that is a software/hardware unit that performs a specified computation within a given interval of real-time, as a basic abstraction. The notion of a component is recursive in the sense, that a set of interacting components can be accumulated and viewed, from another viewpoint, as a single component, thus leading to a structured representation of a large system.

4.1.2 Partitioning

Partitioning (also known as separation of concerns) refers to the spatial division of a problem scenario into nearly independent parts that can be studied in isolation. Partitioning is at the core of reductionism, the preferred simplification strategy in the natural sciences over the past three hundred years. Partitioning is not always possible. It has its limits when emergent properties are at stake. Emergent properties, which cannot be associated with any one of the partitioned subsystems, but come into existence by the interactions of the subsystems, are lost when the subsystems are isolated. Consider for example a car, which provides a transportation service that is more than the sum of the car's parts. As will be seen in the following Sections, partitioning is widely used in GENESYS to set apart issues that can be separated and studied in isolation. For example, in GENESYS we clearly separate communication from computation in order that these two subsystems can be developed in isolation.

4.1.3 Segmentation

Segmentation is the introduction of structure into the behavior of components in order to support temporal reasoning about behavioral properties. Segmentation involves the temporal decomposition of behavior into smaller parts that can be processed sequentially, step by step. At each step, only the limited context of this step has to be analyzed in order to understand what is happening. Segmentation is simplified if a suitable global model of time is available and the behavior is deterministic. It is hindered if concurrent processes with uncontrolled interdependencies generate the visible behavior. In GENESYS we try to avoid uncontrolled concurrency wherever possible and ensure that the basic mechanisms are deterministic.

4.2 Component Orientation

As mentioned above, the GENESYS architecture follows a strict component orientation from the hardware/software point of view. A component is a self-contained hardware/software subsystem that can be independently developed and used as a building block in the design of a larger system. A component is a replaceable part of a system that encapsulates design and implementation and exposes a set of interfaces. Each component represents a part of a design that may be instantiated one or more times and combined with other components to form a system or a higher level component. Each component serves as a stable intermediate form that exhibits aggregated properties, when integrated with other components to an ensuing system. As expressed in [73], *'complex systems will evolve from simple systems much more rapidly if there are stable intermediate forms than if there are not.'* A component can have a complex internal structure that is neither visible, nor of concern, to the user of the component at the architecture level. Thereby, a component offers an appropriate unit of abstraction for the design.

An important principle of GENESYS is the consequent separation of (computational) components from the communication infrastructure. The communication infrastructure provides the means to integrate the components to the overall system. The communication infrastructure of GENESYS is based on the paradigm of message passing. The basic interaction mechanism among components is the exchange of a unidirectional multicast message. A message is sent at a sending instant and will arrive at the receiver at some later instant. Every message has a specific identifiable sender and one or more receivers. Multicasting is required in many real-time applications, e.g., for fault-tolerance by active redundancy. In particular, multicasting supports the non-intrusive observation of component interactions by an independent fault containment region.

The message-paradigm combines the temporal (control) and the value aspect of an interaction into a single concept. The temporal properties of a message include information concerning the send instants, the temporal order, the inter-arrival time (e.g., periodic, sporadic, aperiodic recurrence), and the latency of the message transport. Messages can thus be used to synchronize a sender and a receiver. The message concept supports inherent data atomicity (i.e., atomic delivery of the complete message contents). A single well-designed message passing service provides a simple interface of a component to its environment. It facilitates encapsulation, reconfiguration and recovery. It is possible to implement other inter-process-communication services, e.g., transactional common memory, on top of a basic message passing service

The strict separation of communication from computation makes it possible to design and analyze these two parts in isolation. As long as the behavior at the interface to the communication infrastructure remains unchanged, components are unaffected by modifications of their internal implementation. Given that the temporal properties of a communication infrastructure are not changed, the communication infrastructure can be modified without any effect on the behavior of the components. Furthermore, components can be reused independently of the communication infrastructure. Likewise, a generic communication infrastructure can be used with different computational components.

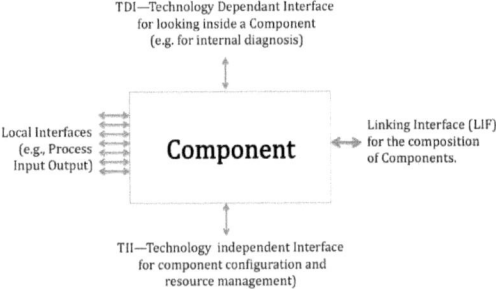

Figure 4.1: Component Interfaces

4.2.1 Component Interfaces

Figure 4.1 depicts the interfaces of a component. In GENESYS four types of message-based component interfaces are distinguished.

The Linking Interface (LIF)

The services of a component are offered at its LIF, which is message based. The LIF is thus the interface for the integration of components at a given integration level. The LIF of a component abstracts over the internal structure and the local interfaces of the component. The LIF is technology agnostic in the sense that the LIF does not expose implementation details of a component or its local interfaces. The specification of the LIF is self-contained and covers not only the functionality of the component, but also the semantics of its local interfaces. A technology agnostic LIF ensures that different implementations of computational components (e.g., general purpose CPU, FPGA, ASIC) and different Input/Output subsystems can be integrated without any modification to the other components that interact with this component across its LIF.

In GENESYS we distinguish between the operational and the meta-level specification of a LIF [41]. The operational specification covers the syntactic and temporal properties of the messages that are exchanged across this LIF. In addition to the structure of all input and output messages, the operational LIF specification should also contain a periodic ground state message that contains information for the restart of a component at the next restart instant. The operational specification must be precise and formal and ensures the interoperability of components.

The meta-level specification of a LIF assigns meaning to the syntactic structures established by the operational specification. It is based on an interface model of the user environment. Since it is impossible to formalize all aspects of a real-world user environment the meta-level specification will contain natural language elements, which lack the precision of a formal system. Central concepts of the application domains and applications can be specified using domain specific ontologies. For example, it is not possible to give a formal specification of the meaning of the temperature of an automotive engine.

4.2. COMPONENT ORIENTATION   41

The Local Interfaces

The local interfaces establish a connection between a component and its local environment, e.g., the sensors and actuators in a process control system or the concrete man-machine interface. From the point of view of the LIF, only the meaning and the timing of the information exchanged across a local interface are of relevance. While the detailed structure and mechanisms of the local interface is intentionally left unspecified. A modification of this local mechanisms, e.g., the exchange of a CAN Bus by a FlexRay Bus, will not have any effect of the LIF specification, and consequently on the users of the LIF specification, as long as the semantics and timing of the relevant data items are the same. A component that does not contain any local interface is called a closed component, otherwise it is an open component. The semantics of closed components can, in principle, be formally specified.

The Technology Independent Interface (TII)

The technology independent interface is used to configure a component, e.g., assign the proper names to a component and its input output ports, to reset, start and restart a component and to monitor and control the resource requirements (e.g., power) of a component during run time, if so required. Furthermore, the TII is used to configure and reconfigure a component, i.e. to assign a specific job to the programmable component hardware.

The messages that arrive at the TII communicate with the hardware (e.g., reset) with the operating system (e.g., start a task) and with the middleware of the component, but not with the application software. The TII is thus orthogonal to the LIF. This strict separation of the application specific message interfaces, the LIF, from the system control interface of a component, the TII, simplifies the application software and reduces the overall complexity of a component.

The Technology Dependent Interface (TDI)

The TDI provides the means to look inside a component and to observe internal variables of a component. The TDI is intended for the person who has a deep understanding of the component internals. The TDI is of no relevance for the user of the LIF services of the component or the system engineer that configures a component. The precise specification of the TDI depends on the technology of the component implementation, and will be different if the same functionality of a component is realized by software running on a CPU, by an FPGA or by an ASIC.

4.2.2 Types of Components

It is an architectural principle of GENESYS to distinguish between different component types, as outlined in this Section.

Hard versus Soft Components

From the point of view of the implementation technology, GENESYS distinguishes between hard components and soft components. The functionality of

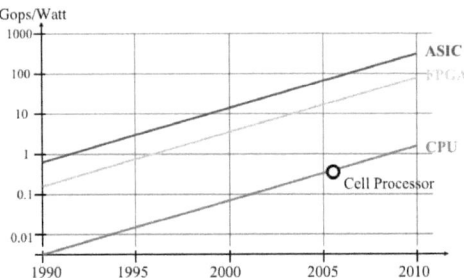

Figure 4.2: Energy implications of different implementation technologies [49]

a hard component is predetermined by the given hardware structure, e.g., an application specific ASIC, and thus cannot be modified. In a soft component, the functionality is determined by software on an FPGA or a CPU. We call the software that is loaded into a soft component a job. The assignment of a job to an appropriate hardware unit that can execute the job creates a new component. The functionality of soft components can thus be modified during the lifetime of the component. A component can also be a mixture of a soft and hard component, i.e., supporting partial modification of the functionality. Soft components allow systems to evolve and adapt to a changing context. However, functionality implemented in a hard component can have superior non-functional properties (e.g., energy efficiency, silicon area). GENESYS provides mechanisms to protect the system from malicious users that try to use soft components for malicious purposes.

Figure 4.2 shows the energy improvement that can be achieved by moving a given functionality from a soft component to a hard component.

System Component versus Application Components

From the point of view of service provision, GENESYS distinguishes between system components and application components. A system component is a component that provides some architectural service. System components are self-contained components that conform to the architectural style of GENESYS and can be considered to form a part of the GENESYS architecture. System components can be widely reused by many different applications.

An application component is a component that implements the specified application functionality. Application components use the services of the available system components to reduce the effort required implement the application functionality. An application designer is only concerned with the development of application components.

We consider it as one of the significant contributions of the GENESYS architecture to eliminate the need for a complex monolithic central operating system to control all resources of the platform. In GENESYS many of the global operating system functions are provided by a set of self- contained system components. In an MPSoC(multi-processor system-on-chip) system com-

4.2. COMPONENT ORIENTATION

ponents map ideally into the IP-cores of such a chip. If they become stable, they can be implemented as hard components, thus significantly reducing energy requirement and silicon area as shown in Figure 4.2. Additionally, each component may have a small local (possibly heterogeneous) operating system that manages the local resources of the component and that is not visible at the architectural level.

4.2.3 Composability of Components

Composability refers to the property of an architecture that is concerned with the easy construction of a system out of independently developed components. It should not be confused with compositionality, which means that the whole can be understood by understanding the parts and how they are compound.

An architecture that supports composability lifts the design process to a higher level of abstraction. In such an architecture new services can be built by reusing existing components, possibly adding only a few new components. Such a component-based design process will reduce the design and validation effort and shortens the time-to-market of new products. In the ARTEMIS strategic research agenda, composability leads the list of properties that the future cross-domain architecture for embedded systems must satisfy.

GENESYS adheres to the following four principles of composability.

Independent Development of Components

An architecture must enable the precise specification of the linking interface (LIF) of a component in the domains of value and time. This is a necessary prerequisite for the independent development of components on one side and the reuse of existing components that is based solely on the LIF specification on the other side. While the precise specification of the value domain of interacting messages is state-of-the-art in embedded system design, the temporal properties of these messages are often ill-defined since in many of the existing architectures timeliness is not an architectural issue. GENESYS provides a global time-base to all components and a deterministic communication infrastructure, such that temporal properties can be precisely specified at the architectural level.

Stability of Prior Services

The stability of prior services principle states that the services of a component that have been validated in isolation (i.e., prior to the integration of the component into a larger system) remain intact after the integration.

An example for the violation of this principle is a message push-interface of a component that must deliver a time critical service to its environment, such as an engine controller in an automotive engine. If, while a time-critical computation is active, the CPU is interrupted by a message arrival, then the deadline of this time-critical computation may be missed. If instead of a message push interface a message pull interface had been implemented, the component can poll the incoming message after the time-critical computation has been finished.

Non-Interfering Interactions

If there exist two disjoint subgroups of cooperating components that share a common communication infrastructure, then the communication activities within one subgroup may not interfere with the communication activities within the other subgroup. If this principle is not satisfied, then the integration within one component-subgroup will depend on the proper behavior of the other (functionally unrelated) component-subgroups. These global interferences compromise the composability of the architecture.

Preservation of the Component Abstraction in the Case of Failures

It is said that Nobel Laureate Hannes Alfven once remarked that in a technology paradise no acts of God can be permitted and everything happens according to the blueprints. The real world is no technology paradise-components can fail and blueprints (software) can contain errors. A composable architecture must ensure that the introduced abstraction of a component remains intact, even if a component is faulty. It must be possible to diagnose and replace a faulty component without any knowledge about the component internals. This requires a certain amount of redundancy for error detection within the architecture.

For example, in order to detect a faulty component that acts like a babbling idiot, the communication system must contain information about the permitted behavior of a correct component and must get rid of a component that does not act as permitted.

4.3 Structuring of Systems

In this Section we first present the three Integration Levels that have been introduced in GENESYS. We then discuss different viewpoints for viewing a GENESYS system. In the last Section we discuss the structure of the GENESYS services.

4.3.1 Integration Levels

The GENESYS architecture introduces three different integration levels: the chip-level, the device-level, and the system-level (see Figure 4.3). At the system level open and closed systems are distinguished. At each level, the architecture provides core services and optional services. The reason for the introduction of these integration levels is that the service characteristics of the three levels are substantially different, e.g., the bandwidth in a network-on-chip (NoC) is orders of magnitude cheaper than the bandwidth at the system level (e.g., WLAN). Furthermore, temporal guarantees can only be given in a closed system.

It should be noted that not all three levels must be present in every instantiation of the GENESYS architecture. For example, in a single chip system the connection to the open world, e.g. the Internet, could already be at the chip integration level removing the need to consider the device level.

System Level (Level 3)

A system consists of devices, each of which is a spatially and logically self-contained apparatus (e.g., ECU in a car, mobile phone, DVD player, smart

4.3. STRUCTURING OF SYSTEMS

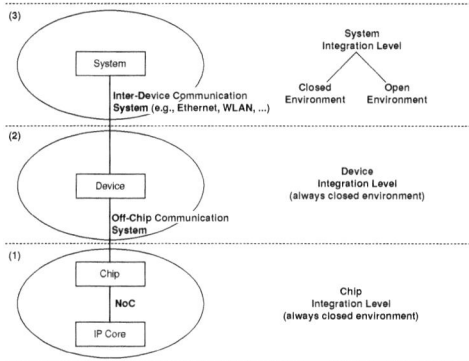

Figure 4.3: Integration Levels of GENESYS

transducer with a standardized network interface, etc.). A device can have local interfaces and linking interfaces (LIFs). The LIFs serve for the connection with other devices. The set of all LIFs of a device is called the interface set of the device. A LIF is of relevance for the architecture and must be compliant to the GENESYS architectural style. The interconnection of devices can occur in an open environment or closed environment. In an open environment the composition of devices always occurs dynamically during the system operation without a priori knowledge concerning the participating devices. A closed system is a system where all devices are known a priori. In a closed environment, the composition of devices can be static or dynamic.

The precise form of a local interface is not relevant for the system integration, since the semantic properties of this interface are captured in the semantic LIF specification.

The interfaces of the devices are thus:

Linking Interfaces: Devices interact with each other exclusively via inter-device LIFs (e.g., wireless connection between a mobile phone and a music player, wirebound connection between ECUs in a car).

Local Interfaces: The local interfaces at the system level are either proprietary interfaces to transducers or interfaces connecting to the cyberspace (e.g., interface to an Internet gateway, mobile base station). From the point of view of the inter-device LIF, the local interfaces of a device are hidden within the device.

Device Level (Level 2)

If a device has an internal structure that is relevant from the point of view of the architecture, then the device can be decomposed into a set of chips that interact via inter-chip LIFs. The interfaces of the chips are:

Linking interfaces: Chips within a device interact with each other exclusively via inter-chip LIFs. The inter-chip LIFs are established using off-chip communication systems such as PCI or SPI.

Local interfaces: Local interfaces are interfaces of a chip that are not considered for the integration of chips, i.e., from the point of view of the inter-chip LIF, a chip's local interfaces are hidden within the chip. However, the local interfaces of a chip can be mapped to inter-device LIFs or to local interfaces of the device. We call a chip that has at least one local interface that is mapped to an inter-device LIF at the next-higher level (i.e., system level) a gateway component from the device level to the system level.

Chip Level (Level 1)

If a chip is an MPSoC that has an internal structure with relevance from the point of view of the architecture, then the chip can be decomposed into a set of IP cores. The IP cores communicate with each other using inter-IP core LIFs via networks-on-a-chip. The interfaces of the IP cores are:

Linking interfaces: At the chip level, IP cores interact exclusively via inter-IP core LIFs (i.e., interfaces to the NoC).

Local interfaces: Local interfaces are interfaces of an IP core that are not considered for the integration of IP cores, i.e., from the point of view of the inter-IP core LIF, the local interfaces are hidden within the IP core. The local interfaces of an IP core can be mapped to inter-chip LIFs or to local interfaces of the chip. We call an IP core that has at least one local interface that is mapped to an inter-chip LIF at the next-higher level (i.e., device level) a gateway component from the chip level to the device level.

4.3.2 System Views

A concrete embedded system can be viewed from many different perspectives (e.g., functionality, timing, power consumption, dependability, physical form, etc.). It can be difficult for any single individual to fully comprehend all views. Behind every view, there is a purpose that establishes an abstract viewpoint. The viewpoint determines which information is relevant for this particular viewpoint and which information can be omitted. Each viewpoint can lead to a hierarchical set of models, where each model exposes more details that are relevant for the chosen viewpoint. In the following we glimpse at the run-time view, the design-time view, the dependability view, and the power/energy view, realizing that many more views are relevant.

Run-Time View

From a run-time point of view, a GENESYS system consists of a structured set of components that interact by the exchange of messages. Each component performs a specified computational function and forms a self-contained fault-containment unit (FCU) that can be restarted in case of failure. The behavior

4.3. STRUCTURING OF SYSTEMS

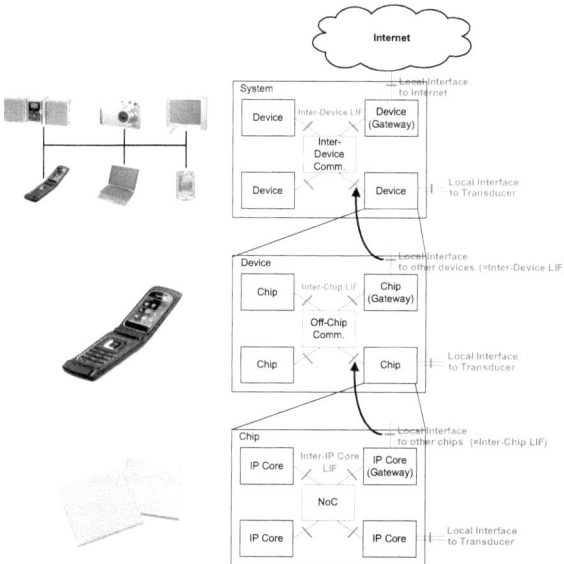

Figure 4.4: Example for Proposed Integration Levels

of each component can be observed from the outside without a probe effect. The recursive notion of a component supports the generation of layered run-time models of a GENESYS system. From the point of view of the architecture, a component is regarded as an atomic unit that need not be analyzed internally in order to integrate the component into a larger system or to find a faulty component. Nevertheless, a component can be internally structured.

Design-Time View

GENESYS supports a model-based design strategy, where a clear distinction is made between a platform-independent model (PIM) and a platform specific model (PSM), as advocated by the model-driven architecture (MDA) of the OMG [61]. In the more abstract PIM the functionality of a component is captured in the notion of a job that is expressed in an executable language, e.g., in System C, augmented by temporal assertions. This PIM-job can be transformed into a form that can be executed on the chosen target hardware, resulting in a PSM-job that, combined with the chosen target hardware, forms the component as seen in the run-time view. If a target hardware is a hard component, i.e., an ASIC (application specific integrated circuit), then the PIM job determines the design of the ASIC and is not identifiable at the PSM level any more. If the target hardware is a computer with a CPU, then the allocation of PSM-job to the hardware as controlled by the TII of the component, can be changed in case the hardware becomes faulty. Such a relocation of a PSM job should not effect the visible behavior of the system.

Dependability View

For the purpose of dependability modeling, another viewpoint is relevant. This viewpoint focuses among others on the allocation of the jobs to the hardware, the independence of the fault-containment units, the error-detection coverage, the error detection latency and the time it takes to restart a component after a transient fault. If the allocation of the PSM job to a soft component is changed, the dependability model has to be modified accordingly.

Power and Energy View

Another point of view of a system, the importance of which is dramatically increasing, is the power and energy view. The power view is important to control the thermal stress in highly integrated system-on-chips, which can lead to significant degradation of the chip's dependability. The energy consumption determines the battery lifetime of a mobile electronic device, which is an important property for market success. This view of the GENESYS architecture supports power and energy modeling and control in all phases of the lifecycle.

4.3.3 Architectural Services

The capabilities of the platform are offered to the components, which realize an application functions, by a set of platform services. These platform services are hierarchically structured as shown in Figure 4.5. At the bottom of this service hierarchy are the core services that define the platform. The core services must be present in any instantiation of the GENESYS architecture. Above these core services are the optional domain-independent services that provide enhanced capabilities to the users of the platform in order that functionalities that are needed in many, but not all application domains, are provided in a ready-to-use form. It is up to the user to decide, which one of these optional services are to be included in a concrete instantiation of the architecture. The implementation of these optional services uses the core services. At the next level of the hierarchy are the domain-specific central services, followed by the domain-specific optional services, as shown in Figure 4.5.

Core Services

The core services are mandatory in every instantiation of the architecture, since they form the foundation for all higher-level services. The core services can be grouped into four categories, the basic configuration services, the component execution services, the basic communication services and the basic time services. The basic configuration services are needed to introduce the components to the platform and to connect the ports of the components, thus establishing communication channels among the components. The component execution services are used to control (e.g., start and stop) the execution of components. The basic communication services enable the components to send unidirectional multicast messages on the established communication channels. Finally,

4.3. STRUCTURING OF SYSTEMS

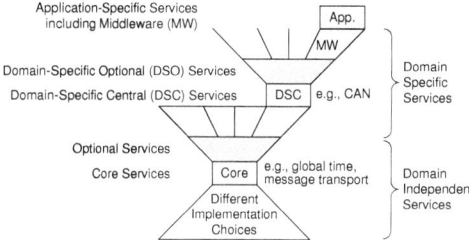

Figure 4.5: Service Hierarchy in GENESYS

the basic time services make the components time-aware and establish a common notion of time.

Optional Services

These services build upon the core services and are generic in the sense that they can be used in multiple application domains. These services are optional in the sense that they are not required in every instantiation of the architecture. If needed, developers can pick them out of the GENESYS reference architecture template, which includes a set of existing, validated component libraries for the different levels of integration. The set of domain-independent optional services is open, i.e., new optional services can be added if the need arises.

At present, the domain-independent optional services are grouped into the following categories: resource management services, advanced communication services, advanced timing services, external memory management services, dependability services, and Internet connection services. These services are explained in more detail in the following Section on the Reference Architecture Template.

Domain-Specific Services

The *domain-specific central services* are those services that are considered essential for the considered application domain and must therefore be present in any instantiation of the architecture for the considered domain. The domain-specific central services build on the core services and a well-defined subset of the optional services, augmented by services that are essential for the considered domain.

For example, in the process-control domain, a stable storage service would be a domain-specific central service or in the automotive domain a CAN communication service would one of the domain specific central services, since CAN is used widely in the automotive domain

Domain-specific Optional Services supplement the service set that is provided to users of a given domain. Again, this service set is open and can be expanded as the need of an extension arises.

4.4 Networking

With respect to networking, the architectural style provides a simple Uniform Network Interface (UNI) with architectural services (e.g., common time base, communication) to the components. Higher-level (application specific) protocols are implemented on top of the UNI using optional services (e.g., encrypted channels at chip-level, CAN at system-level).

4.4.1 Availability of a Common Time Base

A general principle of the GENESYS cross-domain architectural style is the provision of a common time base to all components. A common time base allows the temporal coordination of distributed activities (e.g., synchronized messages), as well as to interrelate timestamps assigned at different components.

In GENESYS, two representation of time are used, the linear representation and the cyclic representation. In the linear representation time is represented according to the TAI notation that is available from any GPS receiver. In the cyclic representation time is represented in the form of cycles and phases. After a phase of 360 degrees the current cycle is completed and the next cycle starts. In the cyclic representation of time any instant, i.e., a point in time, is characterized by its cycle and phase in relation to the global time. For example, if the chosen cycle is the second, then an instant is defined by the cycle (second) and the phase (fraction of a second). The cyclic representation of time is preferred for the description of cyclic processes.

In an ensemble of clocks, each with its own oscillation mechanism and starting with the same initial value, the clocks will diverge over time due to differences in the physical oscillation mechanisms, the differences in the rates of the clocks. In order to keep the clocks in approximate synchrony, we must resynchronize the clocks periodically. In an ensemble of good synchronized clocks (a clock which has failed is a bad clock) we call the maximum duration between the respective ticks of any two good clocks - as measured by the reference clock - the precision of the ensemble. The precision of the common time base depends on the integration level. For example, the precision on a chip will be significantly better than the precision in an open system of loosely coupled devices. In addition, the common time can be synchronized with an external time source (e.g., GPS). Clock synchronization is an architectural service of GENESYS. In safety-critical systems the common time base must be fault-tolerant, since the correct provision of safety-related services can depend on the availability of the common time base. Therefore, the GENESYS architecture has the option to support the use of fault-tolerant clock synchronization algorithms that have been developed for different types of fault assumptions.

The synchronization of the platform-global time with an external time-base, i.e., GPS time, is supported by GENESYS. This external time synchronization will be based on existing standards, such as IEEE 1588 [28] and the NTP Protocol [54].

4.4.2 Communication Modes

As mentioned before, the only communication mechanism in GENESYS is the transport of a unidirectional multicast message. The GENESYS architectural style recognizes that different application subsystems can have different requirements concerning the message semantics. For this reason, the following three communication modes are distinguished:

1. Time-triggered messages: Time-triggered messages provide a predictable time-guaranteed communication service. The instants for the transmissions of time-triggered messages, its cycle and phase, are specified by an a priori planned conflict-free communication schedule, which prevents any collisions between messages by design. This communication schedule is known by the communication system in order to be able to detect faulty components. For time-triggered messages, the communication infrastructure is deterministic and guarantees temporal properties such as latency, latency jitter, bandwidth, and message order. There are no queues associated with time-triggered messages. On sending, a time-triggered message is copied from the send buffer at the sender, but not consumed, while on receiving it will update the contents of the receive buffer, overwriting its current contents. Time-triggered messages are well-suited for cyclic applications, e.g., control applications.

2. Event-triggered messages: Event-triggered messages arrive sporadically and must be queued at the sender and at the receiver. They are characterized by bandwidth, sender queue length, receiver queue length, and minimum inter-arrival time and provide a flexible communication service. The transmission of event-triggered messages can be triggered by any significant event, i.e., not necessarily by time events. Event-triggered communication supports an exactly once semantics. Due to the temporal unpredictability of the events that trigger event-triggered messages, this communication mode offers weaker temporal guarantees, e.g., best-effort communication or probabilistic statements about the bandwidth or latency.

3. Synchronized data streams: Data streams enable the transmission and on-the-fly processing of streaming data. Data streams from multiple sources can be synchronized. Many applications require the temporal alignment of data streams (e.g., synchronization of video and audio sources like lip sync) or multiple video streams (e.g., as input for pattern recognition). Through the synchronization of different data streams, the need for buffering can be minimized, which has positive implications for energy efficiency and the silicon area requirements.

4.4.3 Heterogeneous Networks

The GENESYS architecture supports communication (i.e., time-triggered and event-triggered message exchange and data streaming) across heterogeneous networks with quality-of-service properties (e.g., bandwidth, latency, energy). Heterogeneous networks can exist on the same integration level, e.g., different network technologies at the system level (e.g., WLAN and Ethernet) or heterogeneous networks result from the communication across multiple integration levels (e.g., from a network-on-a-chip at the chip-level to a network at the device-level).

In addition to wire-bound communication, efficient support for wireless communication is required in order to support mobile applications at the system-level. Therefore, the design of the core service at level 3 has to support efficient wireless communication among devices. In particular, issues of stability, source burstiness, delay constraints, multi-hop communications, scaling, and mobility need to be considered.

4.4.4 Internet Connectivity

There is an ongoing trend to connect embedded systems to the Internet. This trend is seen as the beginning of a new era of ubiquitous computing and communication and is named as the "Internet of Things" [31].

To support the seamless connection of GENESYS-based systems to the Internet, the GENESYS architecture supports the Internet naming conventions and Internet protocols using optional services. Gateways to the Internet are provided at the system level. These gateways are responsible for the mapping of the embedded system name space to the name space of the Internet. In addition, the gateways provide security solutions to handle outsider attacks from the Internet.

To be compatible with the Internet, the communication infrastructure of the GENESYS architecture follows the fate sharing principle [12] at all levels. The fate-sharing principle stresses that the hard protocol state is stored at the endpoints of a communication channel and only soft state is allowed in the network.

4.5 Resource Management

Resource management refers to the ability of an embedded system to dynamically adapt to the context. Applications can have multiple application quality levels, which are selected dynamically based on the user preferences and platform resource availability. The importance of dynamic resource management is growing due to the thermal stress that must be controlled in highly integrated system-on-chips.

Since a single resource allocation strategy cannot be expected to fit for all applications and domains, different resource allocation strategies must be supportable. Different resource allocation strategies exhibit different advantages and disadvantages.

Another point of consideration is the interrelationship between local resource management and global resource management. In addition to global resource management, components can have local resource management (including energy and power management). The interface definition of the components includes explicit support for getting resource information and controlling the resource state.

4.5. RESOURCE MANAGEMENT

4.5.1 Universality

Resource management has to be supported for safety-critical applications, non safety-critical applications, and mixed criticality systems with both safety-critical and non safety-critical subsystems. The GENESYS architecture supports hard resource guarantees or enhanced service modes in safety-related subsystems, while sharing of chips and devices among safety-critical and non-critical services. This strategy maximizes the potential for commercial off-the-shelf (COTS) solutions.

4.5.2 Holistic View of Different Resources

The GENESYS architecture enables integrated resource management, which follows a holistic view on different resources. Embedded systems depend on different resources (e.g., power, energy, communication bandwidth, memory) that need to be managed holistically. In many cases, trade-offs between different resources exist that need to be considered. For example, high computing performance typically conflicts with low power operation. When assigning platform resources to the application, it is thus a challenge to optimize for a low power solution, while satisfying the temporal performance constraints.

4.5.3 Power and Energy Awareness

Power/energy awareness is a key requirement in many applications. It is one of the most important drivers in battery-operated devices. In addition, power awareness can be necessary to avoid damage induced by overheating. Finally, ecological aspects motivate power and energy awareness in embedded systems. The GENESYS architecture focuses on power/energy awareness both in design and in operation.

GENESYS enables tools that provide direct energy efficiency feedback at all phases of the design flow, in all abstraction levels and in all design domains. Application development environments (ADEs) should give energy efficiency feedback for application programmers. For hardware design tools and software compilers, energy efficiency is a first class optimization target. Furthermore, the GENESYS architecture supports different component implementation technologies (e.g., software on CPU, FPGA, ASIC), because different implementation technologies can differ with respect to power/energy efficiency by multiple orders of magnitude.

In operation, the GENESYS architecture enables the collection, storing and provision of information about the energy, thermal and power conditions and capabilities (e.g., energy supply state, current power usage and estimated usage time, peak power). In order to control complexity, the energy and power information is abstracted for the application, e.g., by providing to the application software only a number of abstract operating points. The implementation of the architecture, on the other hand, has to deal with the details of the power and energy management, e.g., DVFS with clock frequencies, voltages and the allowed combinations.

Another point for consideration with respect to power/energy efficiency in operation is power-gating. As a prerequisite for the power-gating of components, the ground state has to be stored elsewhere. Thus, the component state can be restored after the wake-up of a component.

4.5.4 Continuity of Service

It is necessary to provide a way to seamlessly switch between different quality levels and operational modes. Firstly, predictability of the service availability after reconfiguration is required. In particular, the effects of reconfiguration to critical services should be known beforehand and reconfiguration activities should not disrupt the behavior of subsystems that are not subject to the reconfiguration activities.

Secondly, resource requirements should be satisfied when reconfiguration is in progress. The architecture enables that resource requirements are satisfied during reconfiguration activities and prevents disruptions of service.

4.6 Robustness and Security

Robustness services are an important scientific challenge for dealing with both physical faults and design faults. With respect to physical faults, increasing transient failure rates will occur due to semiconductor process variations, shrinking geometries, and lower power voltages. Design faults are associated with more and more complex designs, which result from the increasing functionality expected from embedded systems. For example, a current premium car implements about 270 functions a user interacts with, amounting to about 100 megabytes of binary code. In this context, robustness ensures the capability of a system to deliver an acceptable level of service despite the occurrence of transient and permanent hardware faults, design faults, imprecise specifications, and accidental operational faults. A system must be resilient with respect to unanticipated behavior from the environment of the system or of sub-systems. In case such unanticipated behavior occurs, the system should still exhibit some sensible behavior, and not be completely unpredictable.

An aspect of particular importance is the robustness with respect to intentional faults. The current trend shows that the connectivity and extensibility of embedded devices is constantly increasing. In the near future, devices belonging to different application domains will interact with each other in order to provide emergent services and added value to the user (e.g., a mobile phone may act as a key for the car). The increased connectivity and extensibility implies that security is a new dimension in the design of safety-critical systems. Future devices must tolerate perturbations such as accidental faults (e.g., transient or permanent hardware faults caused by radiation, quantum-mechanical effects, electromagnetic interference or aging) as well as malicious attacks aiming at violating desired security properties.

4.6.1 Fault Containment and Error Containment

The GENESYS architecture supports the partitioning of a large system into independent fault-containment regions (FCR). A fault-containment region operates correctly regardless of any arbitrary logical or physical fault outside the region [44]. Conversely a fault in a fault-containment region cannot directly cause hardware/software outside the region to fail. A fault in any one of these shared resources impacts all subsystems of the fault-containment region. Therefore, the subsystems of a fault-containment region cannot be considered to be independent of each other. The structuring rules of the GENESYS cross-domain architectural style guide designers in such a way that components represent fault containment regions. Since a component communicates with its environment solely by the exchange of messages, a fault can propagate to its environment only by an erroneous message.

Components are physical entities (i.e., IP cores, chips, or devices) and are aligned with the logical entities (i.e., the jobs). This alignment between physical and logical entities is the key mechanism for the establishment of clear fault containment regions. The achievable fault containment coverage depends on the integration level. For example, due to the physical proximity of IP cores on a chip the fault containment coverage will be lower than the fault containment coverage between devices at the system level.

In order to ensure fault containment, the GENESYS architectural style foresees the realization of temporal and spatial partitioning [70]. Temporal partitioning ensures that a component cannot affect the guaranteed availability of communication resources (e.g., time of availability, duration or jitter of availability) to other components. Spatial partitioning ensures that a third component cannot affect the integrity of information exchanged between any other two components

Error propagation can be avoided, if erroneous messages are detected at the component boundaries by an independent fault containment region. The term error containment region is used to describe this set of fault-containment regions that are responsible for detection and/or masking of the error. An error-detection region must be comprised of at least two independent FCRs, one FCR that is affected by the fault and another independent FCR that detects and isolates the consequences of this fault. If the error detector would be the same fault-containment unit, it could also be affected by the fault. Furthermore, each safety-critical component must belong to an error-containment region (ECR).

The GENESYS architecture enables the implementation of efficient fault and error containment mechanisms, e.g., a Triple Modular Redundancy (TMR) structure enables error containment and error masking in a single step. In order to minimize the complexity in realizing error containment, the GENESYS architecture has to support transparent replication. When using transparent replication, hardware redundancy is invisible to the application and the operating system programmers. A prerequisite for transparent replication (e.g., using TMR) is that the core services of GENESYS are deterministic.

4.6.2 Integrated Security

The GENESYS architecture comprises cross-domain security solutions, since security is an important cross-domain concern in many embedded applications. The cross-domain security mechanisms address different attributes of security, such as authenticity, integrity, availability and confidentiality. Examples in the different application domains demonstrating the need for security are: the prevention of chip-tuning in the automotive industry or the prevention of terrorist attacks by a soft bomb in the avionic domain. Furthermore, the connection of the embedded systems to the Internet (Internet of Things) opens security threats that must be addressed by a generic architecture.

The GENESYS cross-domain architectural style includes the following well-accepted strategies of the security research community:

- The security mechanisms are based on open design: The principle of open design states that the security of a mechanism should not depend on the secrecy of its design or implementation [71]. An example of a protocol that follows this principle is the Secure Sockets Layer (SSL).

- Multiple layers of defense: This principle states that the attributes of security should not depend on a single mechanism.

- Alignment of security with all modes of operation: The information that is accessible by a specific architectural service determines the necessary trust level of this service. An example is the alignment of the trust level of the diagnosis services and the trust level of the security services. The diagnostic services either need a minimum trustworthiness or it is necessary to constrain the information that is made available to the diagnostic services.

- Traceability of Origin: Components and/or software modules introduced into the system should be from an authentic and authorized source and means for the verification must be supported. This principle requires the non-repudiability of the sending component. Thereby, spoofing due to intentional faults and chance events can be prevented. This principle is essential for security, but it is also important for diagnosis and robustness. A communication protocol that violates this principle is the Controller Area Network (CAN). At the chip-level, every SoC has unique tamper-proof credentials as a basis for the implementation of these security mechanisms. An example would be the use of manufacturing tolerances to derive a key and One-Time Programmable (OTP) cells.

- Adequacy of security measures: Computer systems always exhibit a tradeoff between the potential damage of an attack and cost of the prevention of attacks.

- Psychological acceptability: This principle states that security mechanisms should be as simple as possible. The security services minimize the additional user effort in order to reduce by-passing of the services by the user [71].

4.6.3 State Awareness and Robustness

Shrinking geometries, lower power voltages and higher frequencies result in a significant increase of transient failure rates. Furthermore, due to semiconductor process variations and manufacturing residuals the likelihood of internal faults leading to transient failures is growing.

Since many transient faults corrupt the component state without an effect on the component hardware, the robustness of a system can be increased significantly if the component state is monitored by an external observer and reset in case of an error. Thus, the reset of components after a transient fault is a suitable solution to deal with increasing transient failure rates. In this context, a state aware design is required for making explicit the state of components

4.6. ROBUSTNESS AND SECURITY

and providing support for the restoring of state (e.g., restoration from replicas or environment). Currently prevalent techniques, such as check-pointing, are of limited usefulness in real-time system that exhibit an invalidation of real-time images through the progression of time.

We assume that each component regularly reaches a so-called reintegration point, at which the component state is clearly defined and can be restored (e.g., from replicas). The designer of an application has to ensure that every component visits regularly such a reintegration point. The component state at the reintegration point contains all application-specific information about the past history of the component that is relevant for the future operation. We call this state the ground state. The ground state should be a minimal state of a component that is explicitly defined during system design. In case of a cyclic ground state, we call the period of the ground state the ground state cycle.

In order to simplify component restart, the ground state needs to be externalized at the LIF. An example for an externalization is a periodic ground state message. The ground state (e.g., stored at replicas) can be relayed back to the component when performing a restart. We speak of a restart message to denote the message that carries the externalized ground state back to the original component. Also, an external diagnostic component can force a component into a given ground state in order to perform application-specific component recovery. Furthermore, forcing a component into a certain ground state facilitates testing and debugging. Such a message can also be received by a diagnosis component in order to perform component diagnosis without the probe effect.

In order to handle transient faults in the communication infrastructure, the principle of fate sharing is employed. No connection state is stored in the communication infrastructure, e.g., in intermediate packet switching nodes. The connection state is only stored in components, i.e., at the endpoint of the networks. Fate sharing is also a fundamental design principle of the Internet to achieve robustness and scalability.

4.6.4 Diagnosis

The design of the diagnostic services of the GENESYS architecture will differentiate between active and passive diagnosis. In passive diagnosis, the detected errors are only logged (e.g., for later maintenance actions). Passive diagnosis cannot interfere with the application behavior and is thus not safety-critical even if the monitored application is safety-critical. The multi-cast capability of the transport service supports the independent observations of the behavior of components. Special emphasis is placed on architecture-based mechanisms on the diagnosis of transient faults.

In active diagnostic information about detected errors is used to trigger component restart and system reconfigurations (e.g., restart after a transient fault). Active diagnostic mechanisms have the same criticality as the application services that are diagnosed.

Another essential diagnostic principle is to ensure the traceability of system behavior. This principle involves the establishment of a view of consistent distributed system state despite independence of components.

4.7 System Design and Evolution

In order to be applicable in all considered application domains, the GENESYS architecture supports the coexistence of multiple design methodologies. The design and evaluation is possible at different abstraction and integration levels. Also, design decisions are traceable between abstraction levels and integration levels.

4.7.1 Model-based Design

A model-based design strategy separates cleanly the logic of an application from implementation decisions that may change over a system's lifetime. Therefore, GENESYS applications can be developed according to the model-based design paradigm, e.g., based on the MDA by distinguishing between a Platform Independent Model (PIM) and a Platform Specific Model (PSM). The PIM captures all behavioral (i.e., value and timing) and non functional (e.g., dependability, energy) aspects of an application without concern for the concrete execution platform. The PSM is expressed in terms of the specification model of the target platform. The PSM is expressed with respect to specific programming models (e.g., supported by run-time libraries on the target platform).

4.7.2 Name Space Design

The name space design influences the system structure and must be aligned with the general architectural style. Therefore, the logical and the physical system structure are described by separate namespaces. Furthermore, the GENESYS architecture is developed to support location transparency of components. Location transparency requires that the identifier of an entity does not necessarily reflect the physical location of the entity or the user. For this reason, we perform a clear distinction between addressing and identification. In particular, all communication primitives are identical regardless of the physical position of the communication partners.

It is also possible to map the GENESYS name space to the name space of legacy systems or to the IP name space by gateway components.

4.7.3 Modular Certification

Certification is a significant cost factor in the development of safety-critical systems, e.g., in the avionic domain. Consequently, there is a need for systems that are designed to simplify the certification process. Modular certification supports this requirement by separating the certification of different subsystems. Modular certification is of particular importance for mixed criticality systems. In these systems, the overall system can be subdivided into subsystems with different levels of criticality. Each subsystem can then be individually certified to the appropriate level of criticality. This modular certification allows to reduce cost and to focus assurance effort on the most critical parts of a system.

A fundamental requirement for modular certification is the provision of effective fault containment mechanisms. Therefore, the GENESYS architecture introduces well-defined fault containment regions. In the absence of effective

4.7. SYSTEM DESIGN AND EVOLUTION

fault containment mechanisms, all functions would have to be assured and certified to the highest criticality level of a subsystem in the computer system.

4.7.4 Legacy Integration and Technology Obsolescence

Legacy systems can represent major investments and a complete redevelopment of these systems is often unacceptable due to cost and time constraints. The effortless integration of existing legacy systems into a new application environment is thus of utmost concern. Many large systems consist of a combination of existing legacy subsystems and newly developed subsystems. The component structure of GENESYS is designed to support the integration of legacy systems. Firstly, a local interface of a component can be used to implement the interface to the legacy world (legacy-specific gateway component). Secondly, using optional services legacy protocols can be implemented transparently to the legacy component.

In addition to changes to the application, many long-lived systems must maintain their functionality despite a technology change of the hardware base. In order to handle this technology obsolescence challenge, a GENESYS design (i.e., a PIM) can be translated into different implementation technologies. The component-based style of GENESYS makes it possible to modify the technology of a component implementation without a redesign of the component PIM and its environment. However, the introduction of a new hardware base requires a new tool set to translate the PIM onto the new target hardware.

4.7.5 Evolvability

Every successful system changes its context and must adapt to this changing context. Over time, new requirements emerge and new implementation technologies become available. Open systems must adapt to dynamically changing system configurations and environments. Therefore, the GENESYS architecture supports the modification, extension and portability of application services. It is possible to perform dynamic run-time introduction, activation/deactivation and removal of services as well as dynamic binding of applications to services. Service discovery mechanisms are available for service announcement, registration and discovery. These mechanisms are identical for both local and remote services.

As a basis to identify dynamically introduced services in open systems, the GENESYS methodology supports the ontology-based specification of service semantics. Ontologies can be dynamically modified, e.g., by constructing a database of semantics of interfaces that can be queried online. As a basis for tool-support, the service semantics will be expressed in a machine-readable format in addition to concise natural language descriptions. The service descriptions will provide the knowledge what is required and provided, where and when the service is available, what quality level is guaranteed and what access rights are granted over the service. In addition, the description includes information about the service interaction between a service provider, a service requestor, and service registry. Thereby, it is defined how to access and interact with the service.

For several domains (e.g., the mobile domain), the portability of applications is also of importance. Mechanisms for the hand-over of services are required to enable the portability of applications between devices that support the needed functionality. Also, automatic means to adapt applications to device platforms with different service interfaces are required. For example, a mobile phone is connected to a base station and reconfigured to use Internet in case a WLAN access point becomes accessible.

A further principle is the support for the integration of functionality developed by the user community. The architecture requires means to develop functionality for new use cases in a device independent manner (without the need to standardize interfaces). Furthermore, security implications of malicious end-users must be considered and suitable abstraction levels or view points are needed for the end-users.

Five

Reference Architecture Template

THE REFERENCE ARCHITECTURE TEMPLATE is a template for building a concrete instantiation of the GENESYS architecture. The reference architecture template provides specifications for a comprehensive set of platform services. These platform services can be partitioned into the following three service categories:

1. the core services, which are mandatory and are thus part of any instantiation of the GENESYS architecture. The core services are minimal in the sense that only those services that are absolutely indispensable to build higher-level services or to maintain the desired properties of the architecture are included in the set of core services. In GENESYS the core services must be amenable to certification. For this reason they must be deterministic and simple. In many cases, the implementation of a powerful dynamic system service is partitioned into a small basic core service and a more intricate optional service, since in a static safety-critical system only the basic core service maybe needed and is therefore the subject of certification. Consider, for example a dynamic message scheduler, which must be part of any dynamic resource management. Such a dynamic scheduler is not included in the core services. However a much simpler checker that checks the properties of a schedule and ascertains that the constraints of a static safety critical schedule have not been violated by the dynamic scheduler is part of the core services.

2. the optional services, which build on these core services. This is an open set of services that can be extended as needed. All or only a subset of these optional services can be selected for any particular instantiation of the architecture. Most of the optional services are implemented in self-contained system components that interact with the generic middleware (GEM) of the application components by the exchange of messages. In case an optional service is mature and stable it can be implemented in the form of a hardware component, which leads to a significant improvement in the energy efficiency. Examples for optional services are a security service, an external memory manager or an Internet gateway service.

3. the domain specific services, which are formed by a domain-specific subset of the optional services, and are augmented by special services that are

characteristic for the domain under consideration. For example, in the automotive domain a CAN overlay network will be a domain-specific service, since most automotive applications use the CAN protocol.

The selection and implementation of the platform services is part of the instantiation of the template used to arrive at a concrete architecture (e.g., a particular chip or a network platform running a distributed application).

5.1 Core Services

The core services of GENESYS are implemented by a trusted subsystem at each integration level. Of special importance is the lowest integration level, the chip level, where components, i.e. self-contained IP-cores, are formed on an MPSoC. At the higher levels the services provided by a GENESYS MPSoC (e.g., security services) can be used to implement the services at this level.

At the chip level, a GENESYS MPSoC consists of one or more components (self-contained IP cores) and a trusted subsystem. A chip-level component, consists of a host and a communication interface that connects the host to the Network on Chip (NoC). The host is formed by the host-hardware and the allocated software, the job. A job, i.e, the core image for the host-hardware, may contain a local operating system, but must contain the relevant GENESYS middleware (GEM) and the application software. The services of the GEM of a component can be accessed from outside of the component via the message-based TII (Technology Independent Interface) and from the inside of a component via commands that are part of the API (application programmer interface).

The trusted subsystem consists of the Trusted Resource Manger (TRM), the NoC and the communication interfaces to the components. The communication interfaces must be parameterized to establish knowledge in the interface about the permitted temporal behavior of the host. The TRM performs this parametrization. A host cannot modify the parameters of its communication interface, such as the instants when a message is sent and how long a message transmission may last. It is impossible for a faulty host (caused by a hardware or software fault within a host) to modify the communication schedule set by the TRM.

At the chip-level, the core services of GENESYS are implemented by the trusted subsystem of the GENESYS MPSoC. Any fault (hardware fault or design fault) in this trusted subsystem has the potential to cause a failure of the entire chip.

5.1.1 Basic Configuration Services

The basic configuration services are provided to load the jobs to the available hardware units of the MPSoC, thus forming the components (IP-cores) of the MPSoC. In case of a static configuration, the allocation of jobs to the hardware units maybe outside the scope of architectural considerations – the jobs are already permanently assigned to the hardware units (e.g., in case of an ASIC implementation of a component, where the software is part of the hardware). The basic configuration services are also needed if a dynamic reconfiguration of an MPSoC is performed by reassigning a job to a different hardware unit,

5.1. CORE SERVICES

because the original hardware unit has failed. The basic configuration service at the chip level takes into consideration the unique hardware properties of an MPSoC. In particular, the following assumptions are made about the GENESYS MPSoC:

- The GENESYS MPSoC is internally structured into independent fault-containment regions, where the trusted subsystem forms one fault containment region and each component (IP-core) forms its own fault containment region. All temporal message errors of faulty IP-cores are contained by the communication system.

- Fault containment regions within a chip communicate with each other exclusively by unencrypted messages. It is assumed that the physical construction of the MPSoC precludes that an intruder can eavesdrop the internal communication within the MPSoC.

- All messages that leave (or enter) the chip can be encrypted, if so desired. This encryption/decryption is performed by a special optional component (IP-core), the security component. If, for example, a secure boot is desired then a security component must be present in the MPSoC to encrypt/decrypt the boot messages.

- From the perspective of safety-criticality, a whole GENESYS MPSoC may fail with a probability of 10^3 FIT. Safety-critical functions which must achieve a higher reliability (e.g., 1 FIT, i.e, 10^9 hours of operation) must be implemented redundantly by deploying multiple MPSoCs, such that the failure of any single MPSoC can be tolerated. This assumption has the consequence that special fault-tolerant services within an MPSoC–e.g., a fault-tolerant clock synchronization, are not meaningful, since the total MPSoC may fail without disrupting the system service.

Identification Service

The identification service provides a unique identifier of the hardware under consideration (e.g., chip at L1, device at L2). This identification is needed

- to inform the boot service about the type of available hardware and the attributes of the unit under consideration

- to distinguish individual manufactured physical units from each other

The implementation of the hardware identification within the MPSoC must be tamper resistant, i.e., it should be impossible to modify the unique chip identification without physically destroying the chip.

Basic Boot Service

A basic boot service is the primitive configuration service that assigns a job to a hardware unit of the MPSoC, thus creating a component or IP-core of the MPSoC. Every hardware unit must have a priori established boot access ports for the boot messages (i.e., access ports that are physically associated with the hardware) as part of their TII interface. The boot protocol links the development system, where the job images are generated with the physical runtime systems. By associating the logical names of jobs with the physical names of hardware units, this service establishes a logical name-space such that the components of the platform can be uniquely identified and addressed on the basis of their role in the given application.

The basic boot service can be extended to a Secure Boot service by an optional security service (see Section 5.2.3).

Inter-Component Channel Configurator

In a first step, the Inter-Component Channel Configurator, which is part of the TRM of the MPSoC, configures the chip-local inter-component communication system by establishing, naming, connecting, and disconnecting the ports and communication channels of the IP-cores of the MPSoC according to a schedule that is provided to the TRM by a scheduler. The TRM checks the validity of the supplied time-triggered schedule by evaluating a set of safety assertions before setting the protected communication parameters of the LIFs of the involved components. These protected communication parameters designate the cycle and phase of the time-triggered message transmissions, the maximum duration of a transmission, the type of message and the address of the receivers/sender. At any instant, only a single message is sent/received at a port. If concurrent sending or receiving of messages is desired, multiple ports must be configured. The allocation and sizing of the message buffers is performed in the memory space of the component by a cooperation between the GEM and the TRM.

Communication links to the outside of the MPSoC are provided by gateway components. A gateway component supports two interfaces, an inner interface to the Network-on-Chip and an outer interface to the chip environment. Viewed from the chip level, the inner interface is a chip-level LIF, while the outer interface is an (unspecified) local interface of the gateway component. Viewed from the device level, this outer interface is a LIF at the device level, while the inner interface of the gateway component is seen as an (unspecified) local interface. The gateway components connects the respective interfaces, performs a name translation and resolves further property mismatches that may exist between the chip-level LIF (inner interface) and the device-level LIF (outer interface).

5.1.2 Basic Execution Control Services

The basic execution control services are used to control the execution of a component. Execution control is realized by sending an appropriate message to the respective TII port of the component. It is assumed that in every component there is a local resource manager (LRM) that accepts and executes these messages. The LRM is part of the GEM of a component.

The basic execution control consists of the following three commands:

- ExecuteRequests is a message to the respective TII port of the component requesting a component to start its execution at the next restart instant with the restart state that is contained in this message. In case this restart state is empty, the component will restart with the static restart-data that are contained in its core image.

5.1. CORE SERVICES

- TerminateRequest is a message to the respective TII port of the component requesting a component to terminate its execution. The execution can be restarted with an Execute Request.

- ResetRequest is a message that is interpreted directly by the component hardware without any control by the GEM. It resets the component hardware and starts the execution of the GEM until the point where an ExecuteRequest is awaited.

These three commands must be part of every component implementation. Depending on the sophistication of the available component hardware and the LRM inside the GEM, more detailed execution control commands may be supported by a given instantiation. These commands can relate to power management (e.g., power gating, voltage level), time-management, scheduling and other execution control issues.

5.1.3 Basic Time Services

At the chip level the communication infrastructure is deterministic. A system behaves *deterministically if and only if, given a full set of initial conditions (the initial state) at the initial instant, and a sequence of future timed inputs, the outputs at any future instant t are entailed* [26]. This determinism is achieved by providing a time-triggered NoC at the chip-level of GENESYS. Such a time-triggered communication service requires a common notion of time, a global time, among all components. This global time is established by the basic time service.

We can distinguish between two different representations of time, the *linear time representation* and the *cyclic time representation*. The linear time representation follows the arrow of time, starting at a defined starting point, the epoch, and counting the number of seconds up to instant now and beyond.

In the cyclic model of time, the continuum of time is portioned into an infinite set of cycles. A cycle is a period of physical time between the repetitions of regular (equidistant) events. A cycle is specified by the duration of its period and the position of its start, the cycle start phase relative to the global time. Since many embedded systems exhibit a cyclic behavior (e.g., control systems, signal processing systems, multimedia systems) the cyclic model of time is well suited to designate progress in these systems. The cyclic model of time is also most appropriate for the description of the behavior of time-triggered systems. In a time-triggered system a cycle is associated with every time-triggered process. Whenever the cycle-start instant occurs, a control-signal is generated to start the time-triggered process.

GENESYS restricts the duration of cycles such that all cycles are in a harmonic relationship to each other. Every cycle must be a power-of-two product of a smallest cycle, with the additional restriction that the duration of one of the cycles must be exactly the duration of the physical second. These restrictions are introduced in order to simplify the interleaving of cycles, the generation of cyclic schedules and the synchronization of the activity of a system with an external time reference.

The time format of GENESYS supports these harmonic cycles. It takes the TAI second as its starting point (which is also in agreement with the IEEE 1588 time standard). The full second can readily be synchronized with an

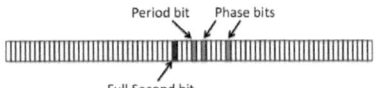

Specification of a period of $1/2^4$ (i.e 1/16) second with a phase (i.e. the offset from the periodic 1/16 second instant) of $1/2^6 + 1/2^{11} = 16113$ μseconds.

Figure 5.1: Time Format of the TTA [38]

external time reference, such as GPS time. The GENESYS time format is a binary format that counts full second in two arithmetic and subdivides the second in fractions of two arithmetic, as shown in Fig. 5.1. This time format is extensible in both directions, the instant when the time wraps around (left limit in Fig. 5.1) and the granularity of the time measurement (right limit of Fig. 5.1). This time format has been standardized by the OMG [60].

In this time format, the duration of a GENESYS cycle can be specified by pointing to the position of the bit in the binary time format (Fig. 5.1) that denotes the period of the cycle. We call this bit the period bit. The bits to the right of the period bit, the phase bits, specify the phase of a cycle.

Common Time Service

The common time base allows the temporal coordination of distributed activities (e.g., synchronized messages), as well as to interrelate timestamps assigned at different components.

The GENESYS common time service provides to each component a counter value that is globally synchronized within the given integration level. If the counter value is read by a component at a particular point in time, it is guaranteed that this value can only differ by one tick from the value that is read at any other correct component at the same point in time. This property is also known as the reasonableness of the common time, which states that the precision of the local clocks at the components is lower than the granularity of the common time base. Optionally the common time base can also be synchronized with an external time source (e.g., GPS or common time base of another integration level). In this case, the accuracy denotes the maximum deviation of any local clock of the integration level to the external reference time.

In order to enable the temporal coordination of distributed activities within the system services are provided that can trigger application activities at specified periodic instances.

Timer Interrupt Service

In order to enable the temporal coordination of distributed activities within the system, services are provided that can trigger application activities at specified periodic instances.

The platform provides a capability to the components to request an interrupt at a selected future instant of the global time.

5.1. CORE SERVICES

5.1.4 Basic Communication Services

The GENESYS architecture specifies three services for the communication among components: periodic message exchange, sporadic message exchange and real-time streaming communication.

Periodic Exchange of Messages

The periodic message exchange service, also called the time-triggered message service sends a message at its period and phase, the start instant, from one sending component to one or more receiving components, i.e. this service provides multicasting communication. The data that is disseminated with this service is state information.

Messages are associated with ports. During establishment of a port by the TRM, the configuration parameters are assigned to a port, such as the period and phase of a time-triggered message, the size of the message and the set of receivers of the message.

Before sending a message, the sender updates the state variable associated with the respective port by overwriting the state variable's previous content. The multicasting of the message is performed autonomously by the communication infrastructure at the previously configured period and phase (i.e., without any start transmission trigger from the service user). The contents of the state-variable are not consumed on reading by the communication system.

At the receiver side the communication infrastructure overwrites the state variable associated with the receiving port with the data contained in the message. This mechanism is denoted as update-in-place. For reading a message, the service user retrieves the actual value of the state variable at the specific port of a receiver (non-consuming read).

Since the transmission of messages is triggered by the progression of the common time, this service relies on the availability of the common time service.

Sporadic Exchange of Messages

The sporadic message exchange service, also called event-triggered message service, supports the exchange of event-information at arbitrary instants only constrained by a minimum inter-arrival time of events.

The sending component places the message in the specified event-triggered output port. An event-triggered output port includes an outgoing message queue that resides in the memory space of the sender. As soon as the communication is ready to accept the next message, it will fetch the message from this queue (consumable read) and transport the message to the receivers that are associated with the sending port. At the chip level, the message transport is realized via a time-triggered channel. As soon as the message arrives at the receiver(s), it will be placed in the input queue(s) associated with the receiver's ports. The size of the message queues – outgoing message queues at sending components as well as incoming message queues at receiving components – is determined by the respective component itself. If the message queue is already full and the component tries to place a new message in the queue, an error is reported via the TII.

Message reception is realized by retrieving a message from the incoming message queue (consuming read operation). For handling empty incoming message queues, the sporadic message exchange service supports two types of read operations: If non-blocking read is chosen, the read call returns instantly and signals the caller that no message has been retrieved. If blocking read is chosen, the read operation waits until a new message arrives. During normal operation this message service supports an exactly once semantics, i.e., every message is delivered exactly once.

Primitive Real-Time Streaming

The primitive real-time streaming service can be utilized for the transmission of a sequence of variable-size data elements (e.g., frames in a video stream) with corresponding temporal properties (e.g., average data rate with bursts). Similar to the sporadic message exchange service, this service uses queues at the sender and receiver side. Queues compensate for irregular data rates that are typical for streaming applications (e.g., MPEG4). For retrieving a data element out of the queue, a blocking and a non-blocking mode of operation is supported. The primitive streaming service does not exercise any flow-control from the receiver to the sender.

5.2 Optional Services

An optional service encapsulates a well-defined supportive functionality into a self-contained system component that interacts with the GEM (generic middleware) of the application components by the exchange of messages. Alternatively, an optional service can be implemented directly in the GEM of an application component. The optional services are useful across many application domains and may be needed on many different occasions. They simplify the system development process by providing ready building blocks that can be reused on the basis of their linking interface message specification without the need to know the internals of the component implementation.

Some of the optional services can become central services for a particular application domain (i.e., the services become mandatory in this domain). The set of optional services is an open set that can be extended and modified as new services are identified and conceptualized into a self-contained entity.

The partitioning of the software on a GENESYS MPSoC into a set of self-contained system and application components that interact with each other solely by the exchange of messages, takes advantage of the enormous and cheap bandwidth of the deterministic NoC that connects the components. It is thus possible to partition the software cleanly according to functional and fault-containment criteria without causing an undue performance penalty because of the distributed nature of the implementation.

As any other component, a system component forms its own fault-containment region that interacts with the application components or other system components exclusively by the exchange of messages. If a transient fault hits a system component without internal state, the component can be reset immediately. If the component contains internal state, then this internal state must be repaired before the component can continue to provide its services.

It is one of the major contributions of GENESYS that a large monolithic operating system for an MPSoC is partitioned into the core services and a

5.2. OPTIONAL SERVICES

set of optional system components, which can be implemented and tested in isolation and can be distributed. If some of these optional services become stable, the respective component can be implemented as an ASIC, thus gaining very significant power, chip area and performance advantages.

5.2.1 Diagnostic Services

The GENESYS architecture provides a number of services that relate to *diagnostics* and *robustness*. Although these services are *optional*, they should normally be included in any instantiation of the architecture. We assume that the diagnostic services are implemented in a self-contained diagnostic component, which forms its own fault-containment region. The multicast message transport service, described in Section 5.1.4, is used for the support of the nonintrusive observation of a component's behavior by the diagnostic component.

In *passive diagnostics*, where the diagnostic components monitors the operation of other components without interfering in the operation of the observed components, the diagnostic component will analyze and record the observed anomalies and store them in order to support the maintenance engineer. In such a system, a failure of the diagnostic component will discontinue the diagnostics services, but will have no effect on the operation of the other components that provide the user services.

In *active diagnostics*, where the diagnostic component can bring about a change in the operation and possible configuration of the observed system, a failure of the diagnostic component can be critical because it can bring down the whole system. The dependability of an active diagnostic service has thus a critical influence of the total system dependability and must be designed and analyzed with the appropriate care.

State Externalization

For various reasons, such as state validity checking, state exchange, logging purposes, global state snapshot, and power gating for energy saving, components should periodically externalize their internal state at predefined cyclic recovery instants. State externalization is very important for the fast recovery of platforms/components affected by transient faults. The externalized information can be used to 1) allow error detection and/or 2) enable checkpointing and retry mechanisms.

In a time-triggered system, the state externalization can be synchronized with the processing cycle within the component as shown in Figure 5.2. After the component has entered its ground state at its ground state instant (at (1) in Fig. 5.2), i.e., an instant where the internal tasks of the last component cycle have been completed and all data that is relevant for the next cycle is stored in a ground-state data structure, the ground state can be sent in a ground-state message to the diagnostic component (at (2) in Fig. 5.2).

Membership Service

The *membership service* provides a coherent global view of the operational state of components. At the chip and device level, the membership service is provided by the diagnostic component on the basis of the periodic ground state

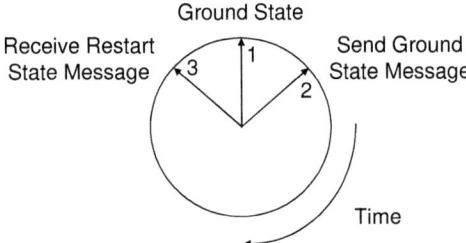

Figure 5.2: A job's state cycle. 1) The job is in a ground state and the externalization service acquires the image of the state. 2) A message with the state is sent. 3) A message with restart state is possibly received and the job restores its state during the interval (3, 1).

messages that are received from the components. The diagnostic component sends periodically a membership message to all components. In this membership message, the operational state of each component at its last membership instant (i.e., the instant when the ground-state message from this component has been sent) is contained.

At the system level, the membership service may be provided by a fault-tolerant membership protocol that is part of the inter-device communication protocol. For example, the TTP protocol [39] provides such a fault-tolerant membership service.

Analysis of Diagnostic Information

The diagnostic component checks the incoming ground state messages to find anomalies and records these anomalies in a local database. Additionally, error messages that are received from the components are examined. The application component implementations must ensure that all errors, even if they are masked by redundancy, are faithfully reported to the diagnostic component. An application specific diagnostic model analyzes all this data base information to assist the maintenance engineer in finding faulty components. Particular emphasis is placed to find out whether a *transient*, an *intermittent* or a *permanent* failure is present in a component, since the maintenance strategy is different for each one of these faults.

Component Restart Service

In systems where active diagnosis is allowed, the diagnostic component will reset and restart a failed component by sending a restart message (at (3) in Fig. 5.2) to the TII interface of a failed component, with an internal state that is expected to be acceptable at the next future restart instant in order to force the component into a restart. The component restart service is also used to restart and perform state restoration in case of power gating.

5.2.2 External Memory Management Service

In many GENESYS instantiations there may be the need to provide, in addition to the internal scratch-pad memory of a component a (large) external memory. While the organization and attributes of the component-internal memory is a local issue of the component and of no relevance at the architecture level, the external memory that is provided in the form of a system component and accessed by many application components must be properly managed from the point of view of inter-component data integrity. Access to the external memory is controlled by this memory component which acts as an intelligent memory controller that communicates with the application components exclusively by the exchange of messages.

Access Control of Memory Partitions

This service partitions the external memory into memory regions with different access attributes and manages the access to these memory regions such that the global integrity constraints of an application are maintained.

If an external memory region is solely an extension of the internal memory of a component and is accessed sequentially by a single component only, then the access control to this memory region is clear-cut.

In case of concurrent access of a memory region by different components, the memory manager must enforce a locking schema such that the integrity of the shared data is not compromised. If the external memory is organized as a *transactional memory*, then memory transactions can access the shared data in parallel. However, a permanent change of the shared data is only performed if all concurrent transaction commit. If one of the concurrent transactions aborts, all other concurrent transactions must abort as well and changes to the shared data are lost and never made visible to any other transactions.

In a multi-criticality system, where applications of different criticality co-operate, it must be ensured that only a process that has the proper safety classification is allowed to update the safety-critical data. Processes of lower criticality may read the data by a non-blocking protocol, but may not modify the data. From a security point of view, the access privileges to data are determined by the given security policy. For example, a confidential process may read data from a lower security process but may not write data to this process.

Stable Storage

In many applications *stable storage (non-volatile memory)* is required such that persistent data remains intact even if the system goes through power-down/power-up cycles. If this stable storage is provided by the hardware inside a component, it is not visible at the architectural level. However, hardware-technological considerations suggest that it is more economical to provide only a single stable storage component on an MPSoC, e.g., an IP-core that has control over a FLASH memory. This FLASH-memory controller has to communicate with the other components of the chip by the exchange of messages and must manage the access to the stable storage.

Since it is more difficult to recover after a transient fault if the affected component has an internal state than if the component is without an internal state it is recommended that components store their internal state redundantly in the stable-storage component, such that after the reset of a component the most recent internal state can be recovered from the stable storage component.

Secure Storage

Secure storage keeps data in an encrypted form and ensures that only authorized processes, services and applications get access to the data. Secure storage can be implemented as pure software but hardware protection may be required to get a high enough level of security. Non-volatile memory is also often required. The security services described in the next Section will be used to implement secure storage.

5.2.3 Security Services

The GENESYS architecture provides *by design* mechanisms for the security related isolation of a job. The physical separation of the IP cores together with the one-to-one mapping between IP cores and jobs ensure data separation of different jobs. The restriction of the inter-component communication exclusively to message passing ensures *by design* that no hidden channels among components of different confidentiality can exist that bypass the message passing mechanisms.

A basic identification service – the provision of a tamper-resistant unique identification of any GENESYS MPSoC is part of the core services. Using this core service, a dedicated optional security component can be provided that makes available enhanced security services, such as secure key management, encryption and decryption of all messages that leave or enter the MPSoC and a secure boot service. Depending on the application requirements, symmetric or asymmetric ciphers can be supported.

Secure Key Management

Secure key management is an optional service for GENESYS integration levels L1, L2 and L3. The objective of this service is to establish a *chain of trust*. Keys are required for many cryptographic functions. In most cases the security of the system depends on the secrecy of the employed keys. Therefore, the keys should not be stored in plain text in the memory or on a disc, but have to be sealed in a *cryptographic envelope*. To operate on such an envelope a non-encrypted key is required, which is usually called the root key. The root key serves as the starting point for the chain of trust.

The security management service embeds the *root key* in a tamper resistant memory which guarantees that no other service or job can access it in plain text. Whenever a job or any optional service wants to access a key contained in an envelope (protected by the root key) it has to issue a decryption request to the secure key management services for that specific key. If the request is granted, the security key management service will decrypt the requested key in a protected region that can only be accessed by the security key management service itself. In the next step it delivers the decrypted key securely to the requester. The granting of decryption requests depends on the employed

5.2. OPTIONAL SERVICES

security policies (e.g., one possibility would be that only jobs authenticated by the secure boot service may have access).

Encryption and Decryption

This security service provides the basic algorithms for the encryption and decryption of messages given that the trusted keys are available. These algorithms may be implemented in the security component with substantial hardware support, in order to take advantage of the performance gain and energy efficiency of a hardware implementation. Any application component can send an outgoing unencrypted message to the security component. The security component will encrypt the message using the provided keys and pass the message to the gateway component that sends the message to the component environment. In the other direction an encrypted incoming message will be sent from the gateway component to the security component that decrypts the messages and passes it on to the intended receiver.

Random Number Generation

In addition to the ciphers for encryption and decryption the security component contains a random number generator. A true random number generator is a device that generates random numbers from a physical process. A major requirement is that this process is completely unpredictable. Thus, such devices can be based on quantum phenomena or chaos theory.

Random numbers are required in both symmetric and asymmetric cryptography as a way of generating keys. A random number generator which does not have adequate randomness may compromise the security, since the integrity of the communication between any two parties is conditional on the continued secrecy of these keys.

The security mechanisms can be used to build a *secure execution environment*. A secure execution environment is a hardware protected execution environment for critical functions that offers protection against SW based attacks and also to some extent against hardware tampering. It enforces properties including system integrity, device identity and control over built-in R&D features. Lower level security services are used to provide the following higher level services.

Service Authentication

Service authentication is an optional service for GENESYS integration levels L1, L2 and L3. It is performed when there is a request to register a service to the service manager (see service registration/deregistration).

Secure Boot Service

The secure boot service ensures that the binary image of the job itself that is downloaded from a trusted server has not been modified by an intruder. It performs an authentication and integrity check on the job and it admits the job's execution only if the checks succeed.

Service Access Control

Service access control is an optional service for GENESYS integration levels L1, L2 and L3. It involves granting and controlling access rights to use a particular service.

5.2.4 Resource Management Services

In addition to the basic configuration services described in Section 5.1.1 more advanced dynamic resource management services can be provided by dedicated resource management components. In GENESYS integrated resource management takes a holistic view on the management of the diverse resources, such as:

- *Power management:* which is concerned with the instantaneous power consumption of a unit

- *Energy management:* which is concerned with the most efficient use of energy to expand the life-time of battery operated devices

- *Time management:* which is concerned with the allocation of computing resources to time-critical tasks such that deadlines are not missed. Scheduling is an important aspect of time management.

- *Memory management:* which is concerned with the optimal allocation of memory

- *Quality of service (QoS) management:* which is taking a comprehensive view on the services of a system in order to provide utmost utility

- *Quality of Experience (QoE) management:* which is taking account of the subjective expectations of the end user in order to optimize the personal experience of using the system

The resource management services of GENESYS cover resource management at the *chip level*, at the *device level* and at the *system level*.

Local Resource Management

Each component (IP-core) at the *chip level* must have its own local resource management (LRM) that is part of the GEM of the IP-core. Each LRM encapsulates the local policies and mechanisms used to initiate, monitor, and control computations on the corresponding IP core. The capabilities of this LRM depend on the hardware characteristics of the respective IP-core and the functionality of the chip-local operating system. For example, if the IP-core hardware supports *power gating* and *dynamic voltage and frequency scaling*, then these capabilities must be controlled by the LRM and offered to the next level of resource management, the chip-global resource manager (GRM) by messages across the TII (technology independent interface).

5.2. OPTIONAL SERVICES

Global Resource Management

The Global Resource Management (GRM) consists of two parts, the Trusted resource manager (TRM) and the Un-trusted Resource Manager (URM). The functionality of the TRM, which is part of the core services, has been presented in Section 5.1.1. Only the TRM that is part of the trusted subsystem may directly interact with the LRM via the TII interface. This restriction is introduced in order to avoid that a faulty component sends an incorrect message to the TII of a healthy component and thus causes fault-propagation. It is the responsibility of the TRM to check messages that are intended for the TII of another component with respect to provided safety assertions. The *resource management proper* is done by the URM which is a normal component, such as any other component in the system. The URM will include the resource management software, such as a dynamic message scheduler and a dynamic energy scheduler.

Device Level Resource Management

At the device level (level L2) where a number of devices are integrated, a dedicated system component, the device-level resource manager (DRM) takes a global resource management view of all chips that form the device, develops a resource management strategy and interacts with the URM on each chip to instantiate this strategy. The DRM is an un-trusted component, just like any other system component. The resource management decisions of the DRM are checked by the local TRMs to ensure that none of its decision is violating a safety assertion.

Configuration and Reconfiguration

In a dynamic system, it is the responsibility of the DRM to detect and configure a new component that has been introduced into the platform at run time. In a second step the application services must be reconfigured to take advantage of the services that are offered by this new component. Furthermore, the presence of this new component must be advertised to the other components of the platform.

From the point of dependability, reconfiguration is a very sensitive topic. Any fault in a component that has the authority to reconfigure a system can cause a correct configuration to be reconfigured to a faulty configuration and thus lead to a total system failure. For this reason, the DRM of a safety-critical system may be triplicated to mask the failure of any one of the three DRMs that form the triade. Each URM is then receiving three messages and votes on these three messages in order to mask the failures of any faulty DRM. In GENESYS we do assume that the failure rate of a chip is larger than the failure rate of a safety-critical service in a safety-critical system. It follows that a failure of a URM, which is hosted on a chip, is non-critical, since it will be masked by the replicated chips that must be available in any case to achieve the required overall dependability of the safety-critical service.

5.2.5 Gateway Services

Viewed from the chip-level, a gateway component is a component that has an *inner interface, the LIF* to the NoC of the chip, and a *local outer interface* to the environment of the chip. Viewed from the device level, the *local outer interface* becomes the *device level LIF* and the *inner interface* to the NoC becomes the *local interface*.

The gateway component establishes a link between two worlds – the inner world of the MPSoC and the outer world of the environment of the MPSoC. Since the information representations and the protocols in the environment of the chip, i.e., the outer world, are wide-ranging the set of gateway components is open-ended.

In general a gateway component has to resolve all *property mismatches* that exist between the internal world of the MPSoC and the environment. In particular a gateway component has to provide one or more of the following services:

- *Provision of the physical interface* (mechanical and electrical) to the outside.

- *Protocol translation:* The protocol at the outer interface has to conform to the give LIF standards of the environment, while the protocol at the inner interface is determined by the chip-level LIF.

- *Address mapping:* The address space of the chip-level is constrained by the number of IP cores on the chip, the name space of the environment, e.g., the Internet is wide open. The gateway component has to map internal address to outer addresses.

- *Name translation:* The name-spaces within the MPSoC and the outside world are in many cases incoherent. The gateway component must resolve this incoherency.

- *External clock synchronization:* The outer interface of a gateway component may have access to an external time reference (e.g., GPS time) that must be brought into the GENESYS MPSoC.

- *Firewall erection:* The gateway component must protect the inside of the MPSoC from malicious outside intruders.

In the following we will describe some few typical gateway components realizing that this is an unbounded open set.

Wireless connection

In open systems of level 3 where mobile devices interact with base stations and with each other by the exchange of wireless messages, the gateway component must contain the physical sender and receiver for these messages. It must control the parameters such that a tolerable error-rate is maintained while minimizing the energy consumption. The detection of new partners that dynamically enter the scenario is in the responsibility of this gateway component.

5.2. OPTIONAL SERVICES

Internet Connection

A standard gateway component can be provided to establish a link to the Internet. This gateway component may use the services of the *wireless connection* discussed above to physically gain access to an Internet base station. The internet connection component will perform address translation, protocol translation and will erect a firewall such that malicious intruders are not able to enter the MPSoC. Since the unidirectional message transmission that is part of the GENESYS core services is fully compatible with the design philosophy of the Internet, the *fate-sharing principle*, the integration of a GENESYS subsystem into the Internet is straight forward.

Legacy Integration

The integration of legacy applications into the GENESYS architecture is performed by gateway components. The behavior at the outer interface of a gateway component corresponds fully with the architectural style of the legacy system, while the behavior at the inner interface corresponds with the architectural style of GENESYS. The property mismatches between these two interfaces are resolved by this legacy specific gateway component.

Fault-tolerant Clock Synchronization

In a safety-relevant system, a high availability of the global time base must be assured by a distributed fault-tolerant clock synchronization. This synchronization service must not depend on the correct functioning of any particular clock.

Synchronization theory [46] requires that at least four clocks are present in order to mask a Byzantine failure of any one clock. This implies that in a system that provides fault-tolerant clock synchronization at least four MPSoC, each one with its independent oscillator must be present and these four MPSoCs must be connected by redundant communication links in order to tolerate the loss of a communication link. The distributed fault-tolerant clock synchronization algorithm will be executed in each one of these four gateway nodes in order to arrive at a fault-tolerant global time base.

Inside an MPSoC fault-tolerant clock synchronization is not an issue, since the probability that the oscillator fails is smaller than the probability that the whole MPSoC fails for other reasons.

Process Input Output

Gateway components are also used to interconnect analog and digital sensors and transducers to the GENESYS system. Such a process input/output component will read the raw data, will perform reasonableness checks and will convert the data into the standard engineering units that are used in GENESYS. The I/O data will then be packed into GENESYS messages and distributed to the other components of the system.

The process I/O component can be used to monitor a process to detect significant events that need attention by other components. These events are distributed to the other components by the event-message mechanism that is provided as a basic GENESYS service.

5.2.6 Mobility Services

Mobility is an important aspect of open systems, e.g., a smart mobile device. The technical solution supporting mobility is often based on some kind of cellular network infrastructure. This is a much more general concept than the generally known cellular networks for mobile phones or WLAN. It can be applied,e.g., for body area networks. In commercial operated networks mobility is managed mainly by the network infrastructure, but in many other cases the mobile device does most of the mobility management.

One basic need is to continue sessions when devices are moving around. Another basic capability is the routing of incoming communication to the targeted mobile device. Services supporting mobility are built on top of basic communication mechanisms specified as core services.

Component/Service Detection

The fundamental property of open systems is that their configuration changes dynamically and is not known at design time. Any platform intended for open systems must provide the basic mechanisms for the detection of components that are introduced to the system ad-hoc. Typically, these mechanisms include protocols for advertisement and registration. If the system is built around one central unit that is always present, the mechanisms can be centralized, but in the general case they have to be distributed. Component detection is often useful for static systems too. For example, it is often necessary for the device to detect its configuration at boot time.

The platform should also provide application developers the basic mechanisms to access the services provided by the platform as well as the application services built on top of the platform. These mechanisms should be quite generic to facilitate application portability across different platforms and implementation technologies. For this purpose the platform needs some kind of service manager. The service manager can be combined with the resource manager because the availability of certain services can depend on the availability of associated resources. There is also a connection to platform security due to the need to handle authorization and access rights.

Connectivity Management

One basic need is to continue sessions when devices are moving around. Another basic capability is the routing of incoming communication to the targeted mobile device. Services supporting mobility and connection management are built on top of basic communication mechanisms specified as core services and implemented by special gateway components.

Mobile Device Controlled Mobility: Mobile Device Controlled Mobility is an optional service for GENESYS integration level L3. With this service the mobile device is actively controlling the connection to the cellular network infrastructure. All the subservices of this service are running on the mobile device. Its subservices are as follows:

- Cell Detection: This subservice informs the mobile device about reachable cells in the network infrastructure. It can be used when

5.2. OPTIONAL SERVICES

the mobile device and the network infrastructure are operating and it returns information of the set of cells reachable in the network infrastructure.

- Connect: This subservice establishes connection between mobile device and a cell. It also passes identity information to the cell if needed by the system (this may be needed to track the location of the mobile device if the system supports such capability). It can be used when the mobile device is within the reach of at least one cell of the network infrastructure, but not connected to the network. As a result the mobile device is connected to the network via a selected cell.

- Cell Changeover Notification: This subservice notifies the mobile device that it has to change the communication to another cell in order to avoid interrupting the on-going session. It activates when the mobile device is connected to the network and about to move out of the reach of the current cell and generates a notification that the connection to the current cell is about to break.

Infrastructure Controlled Mobility: Infrastructure Controlled Mobility is an optional service for GENESYS integration level L3. With this service the cellular network infrastructure is responsible of the mobility management functions. There is a network controller that can be either centralized or distributed. Its subservices are as follows:

- Mobile Communication Service: This subservice runs on the mobile device. It gives information of connection status and notifies of incoming communication. It can be used when the mobile device is connected to the network.

- Connect: This subservice establishes the connection between the mobile device and a cell. It also informs the network controller about the new mobile device in the network. It is activated when the mobile device enters within the reach of the cellular network infrastructure (either switched on inside the network or moves inside the network) and connects the mobile device to the network.

- Hand-Over: This subservice moves the mobile device connection to a new cell. It is activated when the cell connected to the mobile device detects that the mobile device is about to move out of the cell. It determines the new target cell and informs the new cell that it has to take care of the communication of the mobile device. It also hands-over all the application relevant information to the new cell and triggers the Mobile Communication Service to notify the mobile device about the hand-over.

Additionally to the Connection Management the Session Management Service is an optional service for GENESYS integration level L3. It manages the optimal (e.g., in terms of energy or QoS) execution of sessions in a distributed computing environment. It also supports session mobility (moving the execution of sessions between devices without disrupting the service).

80   CHAPTER 5. REFERENCE ARCHITECTURE TEMPLATE

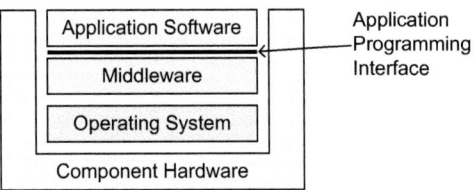

Figure 5.3: Structure of a job

5.2.7 Generic Middleware Services

In Section 5.1.1 we have introduced the notion of a *job* as the core image that is loaded onto a hardware unit in order to form a component (or IP-core). From an architectural point of view, the internal structure of the job is of no avail, provided the message interfaces of the component, as outlined in Section 4.2.1, are well-specified. However, in order to make it is easier to define these message interfaces it is expedient to provide a model of the component-internal structure, in particular of the software elements that form a job.

We consider a job to be structured into a component-local operating system, a middleware, and the application software as outlined in Fig. 5.3. The software interface between the operating system/middleware and the application software is called the API (application program interface). At this interface commands are provided that control the execution of the hardware.

At the API inside a component the message passing interface (MPI) between the GEM and the application software can adhere to established software standards for message passing [18]. However at the LIF, only the architecturally visible three unidirectional message communication services established in Section 5.1.4 are of relevance.

The middleware can be further partitioned into GEM and application-specific middleware. From the architectural point of view, the services of the GEM are of significance. These services are offered across the component LIF if they relate to the operational aspects of a component and across the TII if they relate to the meta-level aspects of a component, such as component configuration. In this Section we focus on the operational services of the GEM that are offered at the LIF of a component.

Voting Service

The voting service supports the implementation of triple modular redundancy (TMR). The integration level at which this services is applied has an important impact on the achieved reliability. Since a chip is considered as a fault containment region of an ultra-dependable system, this services should be employed at integration levels higher than the chip-level in such an application. Nevertheless, such services are possible and useful at all the levels of the system hierarchy.

The voting service takes the results of three independent replica deterministic fault-containment regions as an input and delivers a voted result as an output for further processing.

5.2. OPTIONAL SERVICES

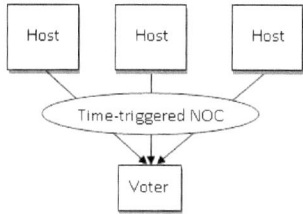

Figure 5.4: Voting Service – Chip-level TMR

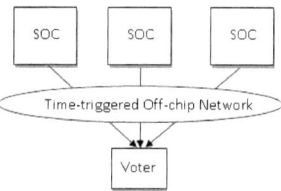

Figure 5.5: Voting Service – Device-Level TMR

The voting service can be used for two main purposes: 1) Voting-on-value - where the correctness of a job output is checked and 2) voting-on-state - where the correctness of a job state is checked [58]. The period of voting-on-state, which in general is different from the period of voting on value, determines the size of the vulnerability window. A vulnerability window is created when voting-on-value becomes impossible because a critical number of jobs (single job in the case of TMR) are already affected by errors. Since an error will manifest itself in the state of a job, it will be discovered during the next voting-on-state and recovered thereafter which in turn will end the vulnerability window. Thus, the voting-on-state period determines the length of the vulnerability window.

Event Recognition and Handling

After recognition of one or more events, the information about the events is made available according to prioritization rules regarding the event and the interesting parties, if known. *EventHandling* is a central service for dynamic applications at L2 and L3.

High-Level Protocol Implementation

The core communication mechanism of GENESYS supports the exchange of unidirectional deterministic multicast messages. In many scenarios it is advantageous if a bidirectional sequence of such message exchanges is captured in the abstraction of a higher-level protocol that can be invoked at the API by a single command.

A simple example of such a higher-level protocol is a client-server protocol. The client initiates the communication, requesting that the server performs a service, transferring a parameter set if necessary. The server waits for incoming communication requests from a client, performs the requested service and dispatches a response to the client's request. In order to execute such a client-server request, first the necessary communication channels must be configured, either statically within the MPSoC or dynamically. All these actions can be performed in the GEM of a component without user involvement at the API.

The MPI standard can be implemented in the GEM of a component to support a standardized communication pattern among remote and local components that conform to this standard.

Receiver Controlled Streaming

In Section 5.1.4 *Primitive Real-Time Streaming* has been introduced as a core service. The *receiver controlled streaming* service extends this primitive streaming service by introducing bi-directional flow control in order to handle irregular data dependant streaming traffic. High and low watermarks at the queues are introduced in order to inform the application when a minimum or maximum queue level is reached. The queue sizes (incoming and outgoing queue) and the high and low watermarks can be configured by the service user.

5.3 Domain Specific Services

The domain specific services presented in this section relate mainly to the consumer electronics domain. Most of the services that are needed in the industrial domain have already been covered in the *optional service* section.

5.3.1 Data Management Services

Among the domain-independent services of the GENESYS platform is stable (non-volatile) storage (see in Section 5.2.2). This is a primitive core service to store permanent data. The services specified in this section are higher level services built on top of this core service.

File system is an optional service for GENESYS integration levels L1 and L2. It provides the basic file system capabilities such as naming, hierarchical organization and meta-data as well as the necessary security mechanisms (e.g., access control).

Database management system is an optional service for GENESYS integration levels L1 and L2. It provides advanced data organization and retrieval capabilities, such as data modeling language, schemas, database query language and transaction mechanism. It also supports concurrency, integrity, and recovery. Similar to the file system, it provides the necessary security mechanisms.

5.3.2 Combined Quality-of-Service and Resource Awareness

In many systems, services depend on restricted or limited resources. As there may be several services competing over these resources, optimal system performance, measured in Quality-of-Service (QoS), relies thus on smart resource al-

5.3. DOMAIN SPECIFIC SERVICES

location. For systems of higher complexity that depend and interact with their environment, built-in mechanisms are needed to adapt this resource allocation to the systems status and the requested services in order to optimize performance. In this regard, it seems appropriate to picture a negotiation between several bidders (the services) for restricted goods (the resources) to understand the flexible processes of resource allocation in such systems. Such negotiations benefit from information, here from awareness about services, their QoS, and resources, from knowledge about the dependencies between resources offered to a service and the QoS achievable with it, and the ability to plan, using and providing information from and to L1, L2, and L3.

For the later, the following two optional services are required in addition to the respective domain-independent services (see sections 5.1 and 5.2) that relate to the previous items.

Service & Resource Predictor

Service & Resource Predictor is an optional service for GENESYS integration levels L2 and L3. It provides access to information about a system's future status regarding resources, running services, and QoS of services. It informs about services scheduled for a period of time, their expected QoS, and their allocated resources, about resources expected to be available at a period of time, and accepts and handles requests to schedule the execution of services or to remove services from the schedule or to reconfigure scheduled services to update its information base. Altogether, it answers what QoS will likely be available from service S at time t, what QoS progression is expected from service S in the time period $[t1, t2]$, what resources will likely be available at time t, and what resources progression is expected in the time period $[t1, t2]$.

Service & Resource Planner

Service & Resource Planner is an optional service for GENESYS integration levels L2 and L3. It provides knowledge about how to optimize the future execution of multiple services on bounded resources. Knowledge becomes available to other services that might change the services execution. Given access to information about services (including their QoS attributes) and resources, this service infers the optimal resource allocation in regard to the value of services under the given constraints and infers the optimal resource allocation schedule in regard to the value of services under the given constraints. It also handles requests to schedule the execution of services or to remove services from the schedule or to reconfigure scheduled services to update its information base. Altogether, it answers what is the optimal resource distribution in regard to the value to the system or the user given constraints on services / resources and what is the optimal resource distribution strategy in regard to the value to the system or the user given constraints on services / resources and actual predictions.

5.3.3 Multimedia and Graphics

This is a rather mature domain, where solutions, standards and APIs exist that can be translated to GENESYS services. There is no reason to reinvent the wheel. However, the core services of the GENESYS platform have to be available such that the higher level multimedia and graphics application services can be easily implemented.

For multimedia data streaming is important. Platform core services are needed for source and sink ends of push and pull streams as well as synchronization of multiple streams. Synchronization of multimedia streams (e.g., lip sync) is typically based on time stamps created at the time of content creation and embedded in the streams.

For concretizing the kind of core services needed for multimedia, consider the standards created by the Khronos Group[1], and in particular the OpenMAX standards. The OpenMAX includes APIs at three abstraction levels:

- AL (Application Layer) facilitates the capture and presentation of audio, video and images in multimedia applications on embedded and mobile devices. It includes the ability to create and control player and recorder objects and to connect them to configurable inputs and output objects including content readers/writers, audio inputs and outputs, display windows, cameras, analog radios, LEDs, and vibra devices.

- IL (Integration Layer) defines a media component interface to enable developers and platform providers to integrate and communicate with multimedia codecs implemented in hardware or software.

- DL (Development Layer) contains a comprehensive set of audio, video and imaging functions that can be implemented and optimized on new CPUs, hardware engines, and DSPs and then used for a wide range of accelerated codec functionality such as MPEG-4, H.264, MP3, AAC and JPEG.

Figure 5.6 illustrates the software landscape for the OpenMAX. The OpenMAX IL is the most relevant layer for GENESYS. It is a component-based media API that consists of two main segments: the core API and the component API.

The OpenMAX IL core is used for dynamically loading and unloading components and for facilitating component communication. Once loaded, the API allows the user to communicate directly with the component, which eliminates any overhead for high commands. Similarly, the core allows a user to establish a communication tunnel between two components. Once established, the core API is no longer used and communications flow directly between components.

OpenMAX IL components represent individual blocks of functionality. Components can be sources, sinks, codecs, filters, splitters, mixers, or any other data operator. Depending on the implementation, a component could possibly represent a piece of hardware, a software codec, another processor, or a combination thereof. It should be noted that the OpenMAX definition of component is different from GENESYS definition. In some cases an OpenMAX component can be a GENESYS component (e.g., in the case of a pure hardware implementation), but in other cases it can be part of a GENESYS job. It is also possible to create OpenMAX components dynamically. Therefore the concept of OpenMAX component is closer to GENESYS application service rather than GENESYS component.

---

[1]more information available at http://www.khronos.org

5.3. DOMAIN SPECIFIC SERVICES

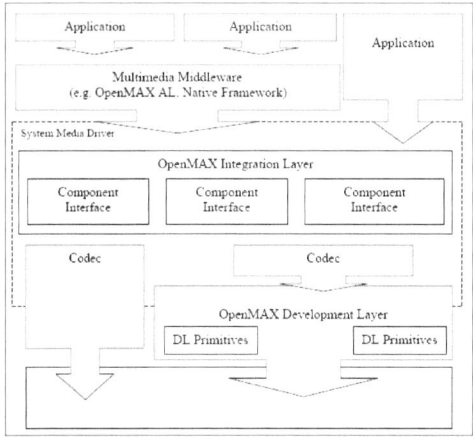

Figure 5.6: Software landscape for OpenMAX AL, IL and DL standards (source The Khronos Group Inc.)

The individual parameters of a component can be set or retrieved through a set of associated data structures, enumerations, and interfaces. The parameters include data relevant to the component's operation (i.e., codec options) or the actual execution state of the component. Buffer status, errors, and other time-sensitive data are relayed to the application via a set of callback functions. These are set via the normal parameter facilities and allow the API to expose more of the asynchronous nature of system architectures.

Data communication to and from a component is conducted through interfaces called ports. Ports represent both the connection for components to the data stream and the buffers needed to maintain the connection. Users may send data to components through input ports of the components or receive data through output ports. Similarly, a communication tunnel between two components can be established by connecting the output port of one component to a similarly formatted input port of another component.

Figure 5.7 depicts the component architecture. There is only one entry point for the component (through its handle to an array of standard functions) but there are multiple possible outgoing calls that depend on how many ports the component has.

Synchronization is enabled by the use of synchronization (sync) ports on a clock component. The clock component also implements all rate control by exposing a set of configurations for controlling its media clock. The clock may be controlled by the IL client (application). A real-time reference (global clock) is needed, anyhow.

Component registration and discovery is outside the scope of OpenMAX IL (implementation dependent) but these mechanisms are obviously needed. There is a need for resource management, since several components can share

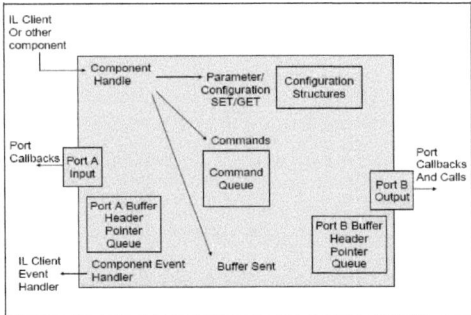

Figure 5.7: OpenMAX IL component architecture

processor, memory and/or communication resources. OpenMAX IL does not fully address resource management, but has hooks for both resource management and policy. They include component priorities and behavioral rules.

The control communication between the client (application), core and components has been described in the OpenMAX IL in terms of calls and callbacks. In GENESYS a more natural communication style is by using messages. In most cases the command-response communication pattern is used, but not always (For example, there is a need to subscribe to events).

Below we list some basic generic services that are needed as building blocks for an OpenMAX IL compliant system.

OpenMAX IL is an optional service for GENESYS integration levels L1 and L2. It provides the basic capabilities of the OpenMAX IL media component interface for dynamically loading and unloading components and for facilitating component communication. Its subservices are as follows:

- Allocate OpenMAX IL component: This subservice is provided by the OpenMAX IL core. It allocates a specific OpenMAX IL component as requested by an OpenMAX IL client. This is in principle analogous to the (sub)service provided by the service manager to get access to an application service, and can be seen as a special case of application service discovery with multimedia specific service properties and ontology.

- Setup OpenMAX IL communication tunnel: This subservice is provided by the OpenMAX IL core. It sets up a communication tunnel to connect given OpenMAX IL components as requested by an OpenMAX IL client. This is closely related to the basic streaming core services of the GENESYS platform. However, since the concept of OpenMAX IL component is different form the GENESYS component, the associated communication services are also different. In particular, the communication between OpenMAX IL components can happen strictly within a single GENESYS component.

- Send command to OpenMAX IL component: This subservice conveys

5.3. DOMAIN SPECIFIC SERVICES

commands sent by an OpenMAX IL client to specific OpenMAX IL component. This is similar to the basic message based communication of the GENESYS platform, except that it can happen also strictly within a single GENESYS component.

- Subscribe to OpenMAX IL event: This subservice allows an OpenMAX IL client to subscribe to a named event of a specific OpenMAX IL component. The subservice ensures that the component is aware that the client is interested in the named event and will send indications of each occurrence of the event. Sending indications is similar to the basic message based communication of the GENESYS platform, except that it can happen also strictly within a single GENESYS component.

5.3.4 Trust and Privacy

Trust and privacy are important security aspects of personal communication systems. The issue is complicated by the fact that privacy is sometimes in conflict with security. Especially this is the case if privacy requires anonymity and this is not allowed in a highly secure operation. Therefore privacy services are always optional.

Identity Management

Identity management is an optional service for GENESYS integration level L3. It manages the identity of different users of the system. System supported user identity is necessary for security, trust management and privacy protection. Its subservices are as follows:

- Identity creation: This subservice creates a logical user identity known by the system and maintains identity structures, such as aliases and groups.

- Sign in: This subservice verifies the identity of a physical user, links the physical user to a logical user known by the system and maintains this information while the physical user is connected to the system. It supports single sign in for multiple usage sessions. The user has to provide the necessary means for identity verification (e.g., a password or biometrical data). As a result, the physical user is associated with logical user identity and granted access to the system with the rights defined for the logical user.

Trust Management

Trust management is an optional service for GENESYS integration level L3. It allocates trust to users or services. The origin of the trust can be the local identity management or a trusted third party. Its subservices are as follows:

- Trust allocation: This subservice creates a trust token and allocates the trust level. The link between the identity and trust token is protected by the trust management service and hidden from normal (unauthorized) users and services.

- Trust query: This subservice verifies the validity of a trust token and handles queries of the trust level.

Privacy protection

Privacy protection is an optional service for GENESYS integration level L3. Privacy protection has two main aspects. One is to provide the support for anonymity of the user in service execution. Anonymity is in principle in conflict with security, but with appropriate trust mechanisms anonymity can be ensured within an acceptable security level. The other privacy aspect is the protection of sensitive personal information. Its subservices are as follows:

- Privacy protected service execution: This subservice provides mechanisms to hide user identity and other private data when accessing a service while still providing the necessary trust information. It allows a user to access a service without disclosing her identity even when the service has to maintain a defined security level. For this purpose the service is provided with the means to verify that the user can be trusted at the required level.

- Privacy protected personal information: This subservice prevents privacy breach when accessing personal information. Privacy metadata is associated with the data for this purpose. When a user wants to access sensitive personal information of herself or another user, she is given access to the information only if the owner of the information has allowed it.

5.3.5 Open Systems and Ambient Intelligence

In ubiquitous computing environments like smart spaces and ambient intelligence environments, a number of advanced functions are needed to adapt the system to the context and user preferences as well as help users and other entities to utilize the system. These services, all of them optional at L3, address a wide range of topics like situation awareness, personalization, or service composition.

Situation Reasoner

Situation Reasoner is an optional service for GENESYS integration level L3. It interprets the contextual state of an entity as a situation. In a smart space this entity might be a user but it can also be any component of the system. The Situation Reasoner is a general-purpose reasoner and thus provides the means to deduce new contextual information based on available information. The process of achieving this new information is based on AI techniques and a local repository of explicit rules or knowledge, which can be configured either by an administrator of the smart space or by another component or service.

Dialog Manager

Dialog Manager is an optional service for GENESYS integration level L3. It provides dialogs appropriate for current situation and context that facilitate the user to access the application services of the smart space. To achieve this, it associates situational events with the appropriate system reactions and chooses the appropriate content and form. One task of the Dialog Manager is to provide access to system services for the user of a smart space via system

5.3. DOMAIN SPECIFIC SERVICES

dialogs. Additionally, it provides system reactivity, i.e. methods to define reactions of the system based on contextual events.

Service Orchestrator

Service Orchestrator is an optional service for GENESYS integration level L3. It provides facilities for dynamic composition of application services from other services, managing of a corresponding service repository, and plays the role of a workflow engine for executing the composite application services.

User Profiler

User Profiler is an optional service for GENESYS integration level L3. It supports personalization and adaptation of a system or an application to the specific needs of the user according to the user's usage patterns. Depending on the application or system, it might depend on the Situation Reasoner to infer a classification of the user, use learning to build the user's profile, or provide the user with the facilities to define the preferences.

Context Archiver

Context Archiver is an optional service for GENESYS integration level L3. It gathers all context events and provides a context querying service.

Smart Space Gateway

Smart Space Gateway is an optional service for GENESYS integration level L3. It facilitates remote access to smart spaces and enables bridging between them. Furthermore, it provides a possibility for external systems to advertise their application services to the nodes of smart spaces.

Six

Development Methodology

THIS CHAPTER introduces the GENESYS methodology framework described in more detail in [63]. The methodology framework is based on three main building blocks; the process model, the modeling language, and a set of evaluation methods. An integrated development environment is also introduced, upon which the selected modeling and evaluation tools can be integrated to.

The objective of this chapter is to define a methodology framework for developing embedded systems according to the GENESYS cross-domain architecture style and reference architecture template. The methodology framework is composed of a set of key artefacts, which provide the basis for building specific methodology instances.

The first key artefact of the methodology framework (Figure 6.1) is the modeling process; the Y-chart model that separates application, platform and system architecture design phases. Each design phase defines the input, output and trigger definitions.

The second key artefact is the primary modeling language; the Unified modeling Language (UML) adapted to embedded systems engineering with the MARTE (Modeling and Analysis of Real-time and Embedded systems) profile. Other modeling languages are allowed, if proper model transformations between the primary language and specific ones are supported. A set of architectural views are also defined for each design phase.

The third contribution of the methodology framework is the quality evaluation part that defines an extensive set of evaluation methods and tools that are integrated together by a tooling platform, introduced as an integrated development environment. The defined tool environment shall support tracing modeling artefacts between process phases, transforming and extending modeling capabilities according to the needs of designers and work at hand, and providing commercial and open source tools for executing an instance of the methodology framework.

6.1 Principles

The methodology framework is based on seven principles which are introduced next with the supporting parts of the methodology framework.

CHAPTER 6. DEVELOPMENT METHODOLOGY

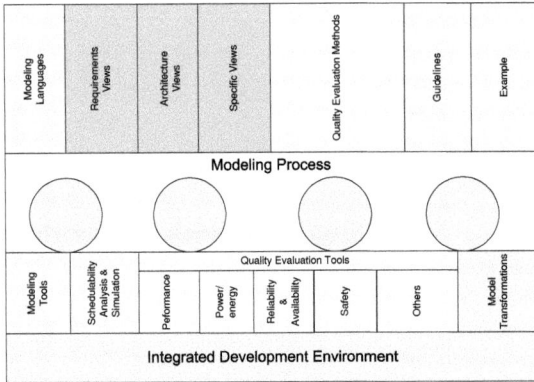

Figure 6.1: The Methodology Framework

6.1.1 Embedded Systems Engineering Process

The methodology framework supports the full lifecycle of embedded systems with the top-down and bottom-up approaches. The top-down development model assists in developing new embedded systems according to the cross-domain architecture style and the reference architecture template providing support for design and evaluation. The bottom-up development model supports the adoption of the style and template by providing support for integrating legacy components to the system design models and upgrading an old platform to conform with the cross-domain architecture style and the reference architecture template.

To make it easy to adopt the process model it has been divided into a set of independent development phases, which are smoothly interoperable.

Support: The process model, the defined methods, techniques, tools and guidelines.

6.1.2 Model Driven Development

The methodology framework supports the development of embedded systems based on the cross-domain architecture style and reference architecture template. The approach follows the model driven development; models are primary artifacts which are represented on two abstraction levels as platform independent models (PIM) and platform specific models (PSM). Three kinds of model transformations are supported: vertical, horizontal and hybrid.

The top-down vertical transformation is used to convert requirements to PIM, PIM to heterogeneous computation models and code. Reverse engineering supports code-to-models transformation.

Horizontal transformations provide support for transforming a model to another model at the same abstraction level. Models for performance analysis and reliability prediction are extracted from the PSM.

6.1. PRINCIPLES   93

Hybrid transformation supports an activity, which includes several development phases in a loop and requires models at multiple abstraction levels, e.g., test modeling, test generation, test execution, and design updates based on test results.

Support: PIM and PSM modeling practice for embedded systems engineering. Some transformations have been identified, supported by existing tools or/and specified as part of the defined integrated engineering environment.

6.1.3 Model Representation

The methodology framework supports different model representations. A view provides a projection of the related entities of the architecture, e.g., a structural view and a behavioral view. Textual languages are used for describing the intended behavior of services, a modeling language for describing structure and behavior and a specific interface language for service interface descriptions. The selected languages are extended for describing non-functional properties and service semantics. Mappings from requirements to models and from models to computing resources are supported, as well as model consistency checking.

Support: Views, languages, mappings and appropriate model verification techniques.

6.1.4 Modeling Semantics

Semantics is defined at two levels: interface semantics at all integration levels (L1-L3) and service semantics of open systems on Level 3. Semantic models allow extending the meaning of services at design time. Service semantics is expressed in a machine readable format for dynamically introduced services of open systems on Level 3.

Support: Service categories, interdependencies of services, rules for usage of services defined by the cross-domain architecture style and reference architecture template.

6.1.5 Formal Methods

The framework provides a formal modeling language which allows a precise definition of system behavior, model checking capabilities, modular proofing, i.e. module or subsystem based proofing, interactive proving of theorems, and verification of causal and temporal behavior in a limited scope.

Support: A formal language for modeling behavior of critical parts of embedded systems, a model checking tool, guidance for interactive proofing of modular systems, and a method and tool for verification of causal and temporal behavior.

6.1.6 Quality and Non-Functional Properties

The framework supports modeling and evaluating non-functional (NF) and quality properties at the model level:

- scalability required due to the diversity of used technologies and application domains, related to other NF/quality properties, e.g., performance

- composability which is related to miss-match identification of service interfaces and semantics
- performance and power/ energy
- dependability, including reliability, availability, safety and security
- evolvability by focusing on checking the use of 'standard' design practices and variability management
- trade-off analysis between the above mentioned NF/quality properties

Support: Methods and tools for designing and evaluating the defined NF/quality properties

6.1.7 Integrated Development Environment

The framework provides an integrated development environment, which automates the early V&V process flow and supports repetitive design and V&V tasks and unit test generation. Early V&V supports HW/SW partitioning, simulation and (virtual) prototyping, and heterogeneous simulation including models and code. The tool environment automates mappings by providing support for vertical transformations between abstraction levels and horizontal transformations at the same abstraction level. Moreover, the environment allows the user to control the design flow.

Support: Tools for semiautomatic development and integration of GENESYS systems.

6.2 Process Model

Figure 6.2 represents the main phases of the embedded systems development based on the cross-domain architecture style and the reference architecture template. Despite of phases, the process model is iterative and incremental, illustrated by the bidirectional arrows between the System Allocation-/Configuration/Refinement, Quality Evaluation and Realization phases. The links backward to Application Architecture Design and Platform Architecture Design from Quality Evaluation and Realization are also illustrated.

System engineering starts with the requirements specification phase, which results in the definition of the functional properties, non-functional properties, quality requirements and constraints of a system. The evaluation criteria are derived from the defined quality requirements and prioritized according to the scope and importance of the requirements. Evaluation criteria define goals for quality evaluation. Scoping helps in classifying the requirements into two categories: application specific and platform specific requirements, which form the input for application architecture design and platform architecture design.

The application architecture design phase follows the principles defined by the cross-domain architecture style and takes into account the existing services available at the application service repository and the platform module library. Application architecture design results in a platform independent model (PIM) of the application architecture.

Platform architecture design is done according to the cross-domain architecture style and the reference architecture template. The reference architecture

6.2. PROCESS MODEL

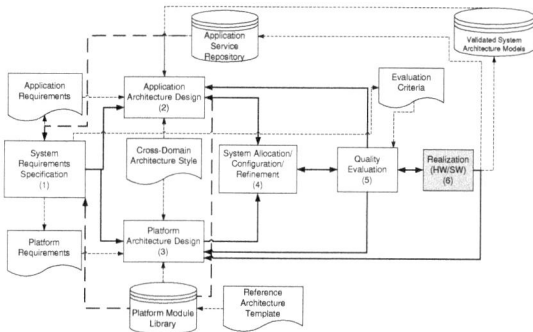

Figure 6.2: Overview of the Process Model

template defines the structure and behavior of the platform core services, classified according to the integration levels they belong to. The cross-domain style defines three integration levels: chip (Level 1), device (Level 2) and (open-/closed) system (Level 3). The module library provide core and optional services at two abstraction levels: model level and code level (if the realization is available). If a particular service is missing from the platform module library, a new optional service is defined at the PSM (Platform Specific Model) level. The platform architecture design phase outputs an instance of the PIM at a specific integration level that is further used as a system-platform model upon which the application-PIM is transformed and allocated to.

The system allocation/configuration/refinement phase associates/maps the application architecture design model onto the platform architecture design model resulting in the system architecture model, which consists of a set of views: structure, behavior, and allocation (deployment), which are required for the next phase: quality evaluation. In the system architecture design phase, the platform architecture is configured for the use of a specific platform. In fact, in this phase the whole system architecture is the first time described as a whole, and therefore, several refinements are typically needed. These refinements may be required before and after performing the quality evaluation phase. Architecture modeling and evaluation is a highly iterative and incremental process, and what steps need to be performed depends on the improvements defined as the results of quality evaluation.

Depending on the used evaluation methods, specific models may be needed for quality evaluation purposes. Thus, the diagrams of the defined views are transformed horizontally for the specific case at hand.

The evaluation process is iterative; it starts from the quality requirements of the highest priority and ends up to the quality properties of low priority. Each quality property is evaluated separately, and thereafter the tradeoffs analysis is conducted. If conflicts are encountered, a new iteration is to be taken (i.e. System Allocation/Configuration/Refinement and Quality Evaluation phases). When quality requirements are met, the realization of the system is made by

96   CHAPTER 6. DEVELOPMENT METHODOLOGY

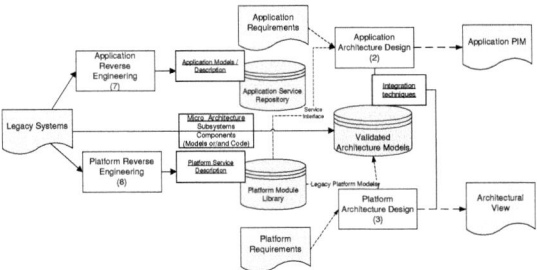

Figure 6.3: Legacy Integration Process

manufacturing hardware and implementing software. Realization includes a set of refinement and testing phases, which are not discussed here. The assumption is that after unit, integration and validation tests, a new application and an optional (domain-specific) service are accepted. Thereafter, the new application can be included to the application service repository as a new reusable service and the validated architecture into the repository of validated system architecture models. The focus is on how to develop applications on top of platforms that follow the principles defined the cross-domain style and reference architecture template.

6.2.1 Legacy Integration Process

The reference architecture template must provide support for the integration of legacy components in embedded systems engineering. In order to do so, the methodology framework provides the following process models, covering legacy systems capture, reuse and integration. This general process is depicted in Figure 6.3.

The legacy integration capture process model foresees two different integration paths, one related to legacy applications and their interfaces, and another one related to legacy platforms. Both of the phases take as input the legacy system to be introduced to the methodology framework.

Despite the proposed process model being similar in case of legacy integration of application and platform elements, these two tasks must deal with two very different problems that have to be treated separately with very different tooling.

On the one hand, the application reverse engineering phase takes the legacy system source code, in the best cases accompanied by application designs, as input. Therefore, the work to be done consists of identifying the jobs and interfaces in the system in order to create GENESYS compatible components that could be afterwards reused in future designs. This phase can be partially automated by using reverse engineering tools and source code analyzers.

On the other hand, the platform reverse design phase uses the specification of the software/hardware platform as input. These specifications might be described in a formatted natural language (e.g., datasheets), UML or a more

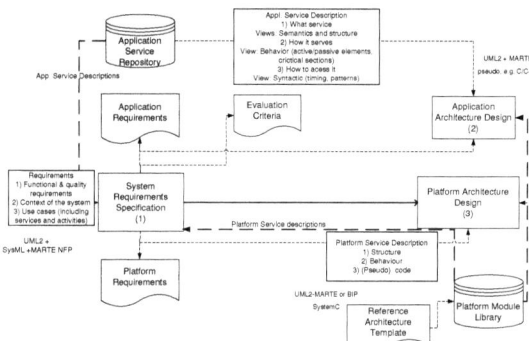

Figure 6.4: Overview of the System Requirements Specification Phase

formal language (e.g., SystemC, VHDL, PSpice) or as a combination of these two. Therefore, the automation of this phase depends on the used input formats. As output both phases will provide a set of models and views compatible with the methodology framework that will be included to the repositories to enable an efficient reuse of the legacy services.

6.3 System Requirements Specification

The System Requirements Specification phase (Figure 6.4) produces the requirements documents for the development of applications and platforms of the cross-domain style enabled embedded systems. This phase also specifies the evaluation criteria to be applied in the Quality Evaluation phase.

Requirements engineering is the task of identifying which functionality a system-to-be should implement. Additionally, non-functional requirements have to be addressed that define characteristics concerning the development (e.g., composability and evolvability) and properties of the system (e.g., reliability and performance) beyond the pure functionality. Due to the special characteristics of the embedded systems domain, a requirements engineering method is required that takes care that the specified functional as well as the non-functional requirements can be verified on the implemented system. This is important to achieve certification and assure safety and other quality aspects for humans and machines interacting with the system.

With regard to the methodology framework, the requirement engineering activities involved in the System Requirement Specification phase are the ones related to the elicitation, analysis and documentation of requirements. Meanwhile, verification and validation activities of the requirements engineering are covered during the quality evaluation phase, where the system design is evaluated against its non-functional requirements, and the system realization where the system design is transformed to simulations and target code of the system. Requirements management activities, such as versioning and traceability of the requirements, are activities transverse to all phases of the methodology; i.e. are not covered on specific phases but are handled all along the lifecycle.

Requirements Elicitation. The objective of this activity is to build and understand the problem that the system-to-be is supposed to solve. Elicitation seeks to discover all potential sources of requirements including:

- Goals: high level objectives that the system needs to satisfy.

- Domain knowledge: is necessary in order to allow requirement engineers to obtain specific knowledge not directly provided by the stakeholders.

- Stakeholders: provide different viewpoints with regard to the functionality that the system must provide.

- Operational environment: the system-to-be will be restricted by several factors, among them are, for example, the restrictions with regard to software or hardware where it should be deployed or the interfaces that it must provide in order to interact with legacy systems.

- Organizational environment: impact of the structure, culture and internal policies of the organizations involved needs to be assessed in determining requirements. Thus, there will be project and process related requirements caused, for example, by the need of following a certain project management standard like the V-Model XT or by the need of a certain certification, this is especially relevant for safety critical systems.

- Laws or regulations: usually a system is constrained by the fulfilment of specific constraints related to regulations or laws such as safety regulations, data protection laws and similar.

The most common techniques for capturing requirements are: interviews, questionnaires, scenarios, prototypes or facilitated meetings.

Requirements Analysis. The aim of requirement analysis is to structure and prioritize requirements. The activity results in a model of the business requirements, the application requirements, a model of the requirements and constraints for the platform and a set of quality criteria. This activity involves the following tasks:

- Classifying requirements: grouping requirements into logical entities. Different criteria can be used: priority, architecture/application, functional/non-functional, associated risk, etc.

- Prioritizing requirements: establishing the relative importance and risk of each requirement and establishing an implementation priority.

- Conceptual modeling: abstract behavior and structure models of the system are designed in order to get understanding of the problem and transfer this understanding to the developers involved on the system architecture design.

6.3. SYSTEM REQUIREMENTS SPECIFICATION

Requirements Negotiation: addresses problems within the requirements where conflicts occur between stakeholders' needs, between requirements and resources, or between system capabilities and constraints.

Requirements Documentation: In this activity, each requirement is described by the following fields:

- Id: a unique identifier

- Text: a textual description that describes the requirement

- Source: states the origin of this requirement. The following categories are considered: customer / operational environment / organizational environment / law / regulation.

- Kind (Functional / Non-Functional / Quality): states if the requirement is related to the fulfilment of a certain functional capability or if it is related to the fulfilment of a certain quantitative or qualitative constraint or quality attribute. An example of a constraint is a time deadline and an example of a quality attribute is performance, e.g., responsiveness of the system.

- Scope (Application / Platform / System): states if the requirement imposes a constraint on the application or on the architecture.

- Development phase: this information is used in order to trace the model elements from other artifacts during the development phase that contribute to satisfying the requirement.

- Status: this field will describe the current state of the requirement. There are four possible states for a requirement: feasible (the requirement has been considered valid by a requirements engineer or a checking engine), unfeasible (an opposite case), satisfied (it has been already satisfied) or undetermined (the requirement has not been analyzed yet).

- Risk: associated to this requirement

- Priority: assigned to this requirement

The most important fields for quality requirements are: Id, Kind, Scope, and Priority. Moreover, the requirements of the execution qualities, e.g., reliability, need an attribute including the required, estimated, predicted and measured values.

As a method the goal-oriented requirement engineering approach is proposed together with the usage of use case and scenario analysis. A goal expresses some objective to be achieved by the system. High level goals, such as business or user requirements, can be gradually refined into more concrete sub-goals by asking how the requirement is supposed to be fulfilled; thus, those sub-goals will contribute to the fulfilment of the higher level goal. This refinement process can be repeated until a suitable granularity is achieved. If the refinement and subdivision of requirements is performed correctly, it is sufficient for the system to fulfil those primitive requirements, as all other requirements are fulfilled by composition. In the methodology framework requirements are described as SysML diagrams by using the hierarchical relation that is established among requirements.

Use cases are used especially in order to document application architecture requirements. A use case defines a system-level capability without revealing or implying any particular implementation or even design of that capability. Each use case is related to a certain amount of requirements. A use case is associated with pre and post conditions that constrain its activation. Use cases describe the context where the system is used, including the system and associated actors. An actor is an object outside the scope of the system which interacts with it. A stick figure in UML2 and SysML use case diagrams illustrates an actor that can also be any entity, which provides information or requests information such as control outputs from the system.

A use case should be detailed by relating them to some scenarios. A scenario is a particular actor-system interaction corresponding to a use case. A scenario models message sequences among object roles collaborating to produce system behavior in its operational environment. Additionally state machines are used for describing the operation modes of a system. The set of use cases and related scenarios define the initial usage profile of the system that is further refined in the system refinement phase.

6.4 Architecture Design

This section defines the three phases of architecture design: the application architecture design, platform architecture design and system architecture design, the last being the result of the System Allocation/Configuration/Refinement phase. First, an overview related to these phases is given including the commonalities, e.g., the selected modeling languages and models with their justifications. Thereafter, each architecture design phase is presented separately.

6.4.1 Modeling Languages

Application, platform and system architecture descriptions are a combination of textual and graphical descriptions. English is used for textual descriptions. Graphical models are described by a selected set of languages defined in Figure 6.5.

The service interface descriptions have to define the following information: syntax for accessing a service, service semantics (i.e. the goal of a service) and behavior of a service (i.e. how the purpose of the service is achieved).

Based on a short experimentation, the UML-MARTE [62] was selected as a common modeling language. Moreover, SystemC is needed for platform architecture design. The BIP (Behavior, Interaction, Priority) model is applied to L1 core services. The following sub-profiles of MARTE are applied to architecture modeling.

- NFP - Non-Functional Properties: for defining non-functional and quality properties

- HLAM - High Level Application modeling: for application architecture modeling

6.4. ARCHITECTURE DESIGN

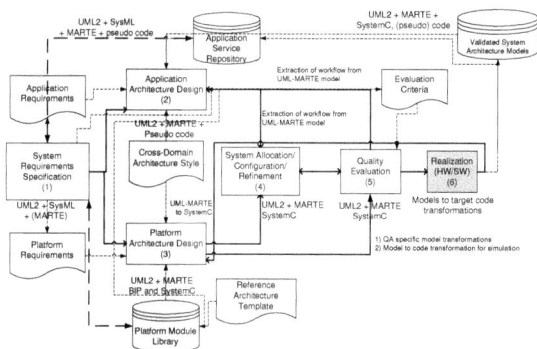

Figure 6.5: Architecture design phases and the selected modeling languages

- GCM - Generic Component Model: for defining the structure of applications
- GRM - Generic Resource modeling: for platform architecture modeling
- Alloc - Allocation modeling: for allocating applications to platform services
- SRM - Software Resources modeling: for modeling operating systems, concurrency and interactions of applications.
- HRM - Hardware resources modeling: for detailed hardware modeling
- GQAM - Generic Quantitative Analysis Modeling: platform modeling for analysis

6.4.2 Views, Models and Transformations

Figure 6.6 gives an overview of the required architectural descriptions; application service description, platform service description, system architecture description and micro architectures. The two last mentioned descriptions are based on the application and platform service descriptions but include some extra views or models required for completing the architectural description of that specific phase.

Because quality evaluation is the next phase after architecture design, it has strong influence on which views and models are required. Typically, structure, behavior and allocation views are necessary for quality evaluation. Structure can be presented in different abstraction levels; for example, an application service can be modeled as a Distributed Application Subsystem (DAS) composed of a set of jobs or as a job, and therefore, the structural view includes two models; one for defining the structure of DASes and one for defining the structure of involved jobs. They both belong to the structural view but can be modeled by using different constructs of the modeling language. Moreover,

102   CHAPTER 6. DEVELOPMENT METHODOLOGY

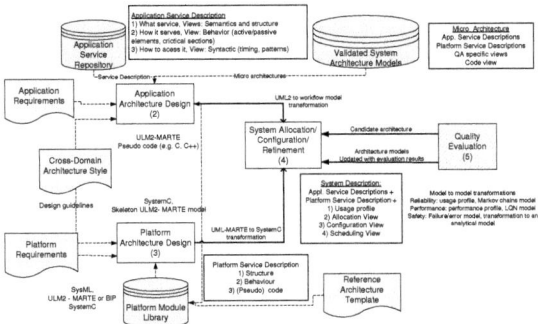

Figure 6.6: Architecture modeling phases including views, models and transformations

design information of interfaces is required for evaluating composability and evolvability of the system architecture. If the specific information required for quality evaluation is not available, the architectural models are to be transferred into another model that is suitable for the evaluation purposes at hand.

6.4.3   Application Architecture Design

The Application Architecture Design phase is concerned with the design of the applications from both functional and non-functional points of view. One of the most important challenges regarding the methodology framework is to enable service based development of embedded applications by using the core and optional services provided by the architecture template as the basis. The most important artifacts of the applications are jobs that interact with each other via unidirectional messages. The interface of a certain job is composed by the definition of those messages. In order to be able to perform this composition, the services provided by the different jobs have to be defined, not only from a syntactical point of view, but also from a behavioral point of view.

In order to provide developers with models that are expressive enough, it is important to present the structures of the services and jobs in the application architecture model. The next sub-sections will cover the modeling of these views using UML-MARTE. MARTE is a UML profile and, therefore, it cannot be used without it. It is important to note that UML provides several ways to describe some aspects of the system models. This fact makes it difficult to provide a unique method to create the models as many different diagrams can be used to specify the same aspects in the models. For example, in many cases state machines and activity diagrams can address the same behavior.

The goal of the Application Architecture Design phase is to produce a platform independent model of an embedded application. The phase produces the following views:

Structural view: The structural view contains the definition of DASes (i.e.

6.4. ARCHITECTURE DESIGN

interaction between jobs), the jobs, LIFs and messages that take part in the application under design.

Syntactical view: The syntactical view contains the description of the protocols that manage the access to a certain service. The interface description is partly defined by the structural view and the syntactical view.

behavioral view: The behavioral view defines the behavior of the application at two levels: as behavior of the application and as behavior of the jobs involved in the application.

Non-functional view: The non-functional view provides information about non-functional aspects of the application models, such as timing constraints, performance, reliability, etc.

Structural view

The structural view describes the application as a whole and the building blocks, i.e. jobs and interfaces, which it is combined of. The structural view of an application provides information regarding the construction of the service. Services are defined by their interfaces. Therefore, the structural view is described as follows:

- Describe the jobs involved in the application under design.

- Describe the service interfaces of each job and messages passed through each interface.

- Describe the application as a composite of jobs. Reuse the available application service descriptions.

- Describe platform services accessed by the jobs.

The structural view has to describe the applications in terms of jobs. Moreover, the different services involved in the application must be defined in terms of their interfaces and the kind of messages they request/provide. Lastly, structural descriptions also include passive elements that help different jobs to communicate. The MARTE profile provides two specific sub-profiles for this kind of view: High-Level Application modeling (HLAM) sub-profile and Generic Component Model (GCM) sub-profile. These two sub-profiles along with the UML2 constructs allow a rich description of applications, services, and their interactions.

Descriptions of the jobs and their LIFs of an application are given in a UML class diagram. The goal of this diagram is to describe each of the jobs of an application along with all the messages that job produces/accepts (i.e. the LIF). Since jobs represent an active component of an application, each job will be represented by a single UML active class. The semantics of the UML active class will be extended using the specific <<RtUnit>> stereotype from the MARTE HLAM sub-profile to match the definition of a job. The stereotype gives a class the semantics of a task or a set of tasks that are executed in some computing resource of the underlying platform. The stereotype includes properties that may increase expressivity of a class. In the case of programmable processors, there may be the need to decompose jobs to finer

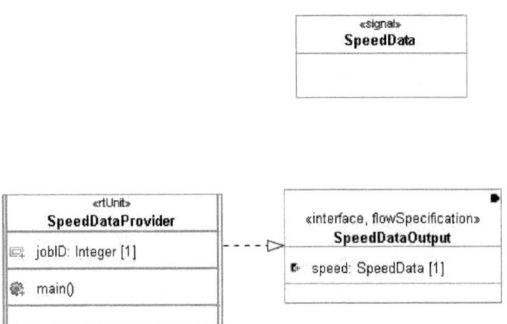

Figure 6.7: Example job and LIF

grain tasks that are scheduled by e.g., an operating system. The <<RtUnit>> stereotype serves also this modeling purpose.

The job description is completed with the definition of the messages accepted and produced by each of the defined jobs. This message list will compose a job's linking interface (LIF). Following the cross-domain architecture style, the LIF of a job will be composed of a list of input and output unidirectional messages, each of which will be represented in our class diagram as a UML interface element. To link interfaces and jobs, the class defining a job implements all the interfaces that compose its LIF. The semantics of the UML interface are further refined by the application of the <<FlowSpecification>> stereotype from the MARTE GCM sub-profile. This stereotype provides the interface the semantics of a unidirectional messages gateway and specifies whether the interface will produce or consume a message. Note that bidirectional interfaces are not allowed since each interface addresses a single interaction. Figure 6.7 shows an example description of a job that provides an output message. The produced message is specified by a UML property defined in the interface and stereotyped with the <<FlowProperty>> stereotype from the MARTE GCM sub-profile. This stereotype gives the property the semantics of the message produced or consumed by that interaction interface. Note that this property must always be typed as a UML signal.

Input interfaces, similarly to output interfaces must always specify the message they will consume. Additionally, input interfaces must declare a UML signal reception element that will be also included in the class implementing that interface.

Once jobs and interfaces have been defined, the job classes of interaction ports are to be defined to enable application composition. Therefore, a UML port element is created for each interface in each job. These ports are stereotyped with the <<FlowPort>> stereotype from the MARTE GCM profile to provide them with the GENESYS semantics. Note that the directions defined in the <<FlowSpecification>>, <<FlowProperty>> and <<FlowPort>>

6.4. ARCHITECTURE DESIGN

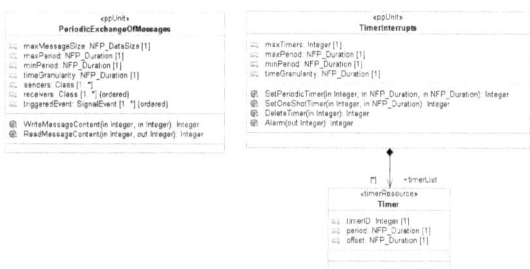

Figure 6.8: Service interfaces of the platform services

stereotypes for the same interface must always be coherent.

Lastly, the platform services used by the deployed jobs in the system are to be defined. The platform services have been specified by implementation independent interfaces. Therefore, UML classes will be used to represent the service interfaces of the platform services. These classes are stereotyped with the <<PpUnit>> stereotype from the MARTE HLAM sub-profile. This stereotype refines a UML class by giving it the semantics of a protected passive element of the system.

An instantiation of the methodology framework should provide a model package including the definitions of all service interfaces of the platform services. These definitions are stored in the Application Services Repository. Figure 6.8 depicts two definitions of two different front-ends of platform services. These services are then instantiated in our application models via UML associations from the client jobs to the accessed platform services.

Applications (DASs) are compositions of jobs that further use application and platform services for achieving the desired functionality/capability of a system. A UML composite diagram is used for composing DASs. Using this diagram we will create a class that will host the whole application and we will create a property in the class for each of the jobs previously defined. Then we will link the input and output ports of the jobs via UML connectors. To achieve multi-level composability, it is possible to leave outer ports to the hosting class. Figure 6.9 shows a cruise control system using UML2 and MARTE.

Syntactical view

The syntactical view of the application describes how the services are accessed. A syntactical description includes

- a description of the messages involved in the access of a certain service, and
- a description of the communication protocols used.

The syntactical view of a service is often mixed with its structural view since service syntaxes are tightly coupled to structural elements. For example, messages are coupled to LIFs.

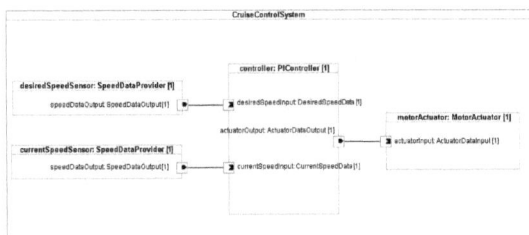

Figure 6.9: A cruise control system composite diagram example

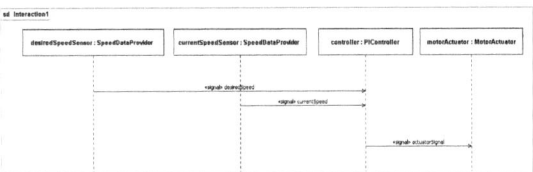

Figure 6.10: Example sequence diagram showing the interactions between GENESYS jobs

In order for clients to be able to access GENESYS services it is mandatory that the service-users are aware of the syntax the services understand. In this kind of applications the syntax of a service is defined by the messages that are exchanged by service-users and services and by the order in which these signals and messages are sent from service-users to services and vice-versa. Since the GENESYS architectural style states that all the GENESYS messages must be unidirectional all the protocols have to be implemented in the behavior of the jobs. As we previously said, messages are introduced in application models as UML signal elements. The data included in a message is described using UML properties.

The fact that communication protocols have to be embedded in each job's behavior makes it difficult for GENESYS application designers to reuse (third party) applications/services/modules. To cope with this issue, the syntactical view of a job must somehow provide application designers this information. If the behavioral view of the job is provided, the communication protocol can be inferred from it. However, if behavioral views are not available, the GENESYS methodology framework assumes that third party module developers provide a UML sequence diagram specifying the interactions between their reusable elements and GENESYS jobs. An example is provided in Figure 6.10.

behavioral view

The behavioral view of an application describes the control flow between jobs and applications. It is possible that many implementation details appear in

6.4. ARCHITECTURE DESIGN

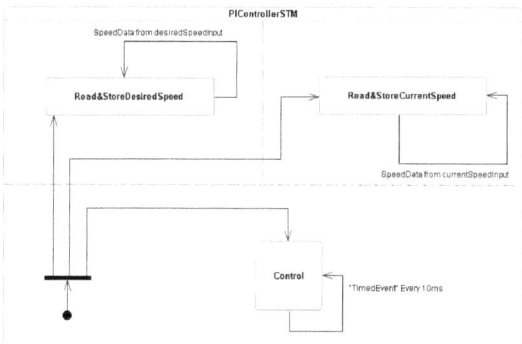

Figure 6.11: Example of a UML state machine diagram

behavioral views, since it is common to use variables, function-calls and even code in them. The behavioral view is very important in the early validation phase since it provides a means to test the system's functionality and evaluate that the system fulfils its quality requirements related to applications. The behavioral view is also crucial in the system realization phase, since the behavior described in this view is what the developers will implement in the final product.

The behavioral view is defined in two different granularity levels. In the coarser grained definition, the behavior of the jobs is defined using UML state machine diagrams. State machines allow the designers to specify the number of tasks that compose a single job and also specify the communication protocols followed by the application jobs. Figure 6.11 shows a simple state machine of a job composed of three tasks.

UML regions in the state machine diagram represent different tasks inside a single job. The cross-domain architectural style states that the jobs must react to interactions on their LIFs. However, some jobs (e.g., sensors) may need to do their work periodically based on a time event. Therefore, the only transition triggers permitted are based on messages (represented by UML signal events) and based on time (represented by UML time events). To complete the descriptions of these triggers we will need to specify:

- For signal events (i.e. message arrivals), the port in which the message has been received.

- For time events, a <<TimedEvent>> stereotype from the MARTE Time sub-profile will be applied to the event to formalize the timing specification.

Finer grain behavioral descriptions will further refine these top level behavioral descriptions. The methodology assumes that behavioral refinements are made by linking UML activity diagrams or UML opaque behaviors to the "Effect"

108   CHAPTER 6. DEVELOPMENT METHODOLOGY

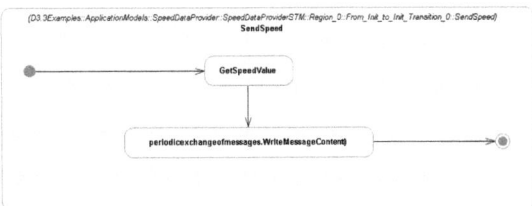

Figure 6.12: Activity diagram example for fine grain behavioral descriptions

fields on state machine transitions. An example of a UML activity diagram is provided in Figure 6.12.

GENESYS jobs will access the platform services to complete their functionality. These interactions between the application and the platform services will be introduced in the fine grain behavioral descriptions via API calls.

Non-functional view

Embedded systems are complex hardware/software systems often constrained by strict functional and non-functional requirements. From this requirements set, non-functional requirements are often the most important ones and also the most difficult to specify in design models. The GENESYS methodology framework introduces the non-functional view in the application models that allows the designer to specify as many non-functional properties as necessary for their application domain.

Non-functional properties are represented as UML properties stereotyped with the <<NFP>> stereotype from the MARTE NFPs sub-profile. A non-functional property must always be typed with a UML data type element stereotyped with <<NfpType>>. The used data type can be extracted from the MARTE BasicNFP_Types library or created extending the NFP_CommonType data type in the same library. Moreover, constraints can be applied to the elements owning the non-functional properties. In case a constraint that affects a non-functional property is applied to an element it must always be stereotyped with the <<NfpConstraint>> stereotype from the MARTE NFPs sub-profile. Note that UML state machines, opaque behaviors and activities are also classes, and therefore they may own non-functional properties.

Any instantiation of the methodology framework in a concrete application domain should always define the non-functional property set applicable to that domain, as well as a set of application guidelines in order to keep the model transformations coherent

6.4.4 Platform Architecture Design

The Platform Architecture Design phase deals with the modeling of the platform architecture that supports the applications designed during the Applica-

6.4. ARCHITECTURE DESIGN

tion Architecture Design phase. The platform architecture is a logical architecture that is later realized as hardware and software.

The GENESYS architectural principles define three integration levels at which applications might be developed: System Level (L3), Device Level (L2) and Chip Level (L1). Each of these levels addresses different application description challenges through the use of modeling techniques.

Chip level applications focus on developing hardware systems that will be implemented on single chips (e.g., Multi-Processor SoCs). Platform components at this integration level consist of IP cores. These IP cores implement computation, storage and communication resources that are either taken from IP core libraries or developed/acquired if non existent. Software consists typically of RTOS, device drivers and middleware on top of which services and applications are designed at the chip level.

Device level applications focus on creating complete embedded devices. They make use of platforms that can, for example, be composed of a set of chip level platforms providing services to device level applications. Additional middleware and services may be used on top to facilitate efficient interface to applications.

System level applications are composed of a set of distributed devices that interact with each other. At this integration level only software platforms may need to be considered since the devices composing the application already have their hardware/software architecture defined.

The platform architecture modeling produces the models of the following views:

Structural view: The view describes the platform architecture from its structural point of view. The platform architecture model is composed of resources (both SW and HW) at various level of granularity (e.g., processor, computing node, multiple interconnected computing nodes). Resources provide services described by using the core and optional services provided by the GENESYS template and/or new services if proper platform services are not available.

behavioral view: The behavioral view describes the behavior of the services included in the platform structural view. Basically, the behavioral descriptions of the high-level services are taken from the Platform Module Library that includes the descriptions of the core and optional services defined by the GENESYS reference architecture template.

Non-functional view: Similarly to the non-functional view defined in the application design phase, the non-functional view in the platform architecture design phase allows the platform designers to specify non-functional properties and constraints applicable to each platform element. This view follows the same methodological patterns as the non-functional view of application architecture.

Structural view

The structural view is meant to describe the elements that compose the execution platform of a GENESYS application. These elements can be both hardware elements (e.g., CPU, buses, memory, etc.) and/or software elements (e.g., threads, semaphores, etc.). MARTE provides the Generic Resource modeling (GRM) sub-profile to model the resources of an execution platform from a high abstraction level, and the more specific Software Resources modeling (SRM) and Hardware Resources modeling (HRM) sub-profiles for finer grain resources modeling.

An important aspect of the platform structural view models is that it must include references to the GENESYS platform services. The platform structural model will be crucial for the further allocation and quality analysis steps.

behavior view

According to MARTE GRM, resources are used to model the execution platform from a structural point of view, while the resource services supply the behavioral point of view.

In addition to the behavior descriptions of core and optional services of GENESYS, there are various execution support services like transferring data, sharing resources, communications and synchronization of tasks. The behavioral view is presented as the interfaces and their state machine descriptions (i.e. protocol) of the above mentioned services.

Regarding the methodology framework, in order to model the behavior of the platforms, UML behaviors (i.e. activity, sequence and state machine diagrams) could be useful to model interactions within the platforms.

In order to ease a link between the models and the analysis/simulation tools, the GENESYS methodology provides the option of using opaque behavior UML model elements. Opaque behaviors are defined by pieces of code or pseudo-code regarding its specification; therefore, using this approach, it is very simple to establish a link between the UML+MARTE models and other modeling languages like SystemC or BIP.

Platform Module Library

The Platform Module Library provides the ready-made services defined by the reference architecture template. The definitions of platform services have three dimensions: abstraction, integration and aggregation. These dimensions have different purposes. Each service has two abstraction levels: model and code/implementation, which are intended for the use of different stakeholders. The integration level defines the scope of a service; the platform can be applicable on one, two or all integration levels. The definition of the integration level is a property of a service that guides the architect to select a proper service for the platform architecture under work. The aggregation dimension is used for separating common services from variable services and managing their relationships. Thus, the dependencies between services are defined by the aggregation dimension implemented as a taxonomy of services.

The service taxonomy categorizes services into groups of correlated services, which makes it easy for the platform architect to find a service that fit to a platform architecture design. Core services are used in each GENESYS compatible system, i.e. it is to be checked that all core services have been used in the platform architecture design. Other services are generic and domain specific optional services, which embody variability that has to be managed by the module library management mechanisms. Optional services need defini-

6.4. ARCHITECTURE DESIGN

Figure 6.13: Periodic Exchange of Messages Service API

tions of their relationships with core and other optional services, service specific properties and rules that help in selecting, configuring and using a service in architecture design and evaluation phases. These definitions specify explicitly how to deal with variability, i.e. they define facts and rules for variability management. The implementation of variability mechanisms depends on the organization who instantiates the platform module library. Thus, there can be different kinds of taxonomies, depending on the usage of the platform module library.

System designers using the GENESYS architecture template are provided with a set of services that simplify the design and implementation tasks. These services are instantiated as part of the platform architecture that supports applications. Following the approach described above, GENESYS services can be seen as black boxes that provide the designer with higher level views. Figure 6.13 shows an example GENESYS service, the Periodic Exchange of Messages Service.

The service model includes a service interface description with the available interfaces of the service as well as the inputs and outputs. This representation is sufficient for platform designs but in order to perform non-functional analyses on the system models level a more detailed description is needed. The service interface operations are stereotyped with MARTE::GRM <<GRService>>, which denotes the definition of the service interfaces for the clients.

Each of the GENESYS platform services is treated from the architect's point of view as a black box that provides him/her the desired functionality. A complete description needs a behavioral description. behavioral representation which is the most widely used by analysis tools is the state machine. MARTE also provides some stereotypes for adding non-functional properties to the behavioral diagrams.

From the designer's point of view, a new GENESYS service does not differ as a concept from the development of a concrete application within the scope of GENESYS. The design of a new service must go through the six phases of the GENESYS development process. However, the application models must clearly state the service interface under design using the <<GRService>> stereotype. Figure 6.14 shows an example.

6.4.5 System Allocation/Configuration/Refinement

The System Allocation phase of the GENESYS process model is related to the mapping of the applications to the platform architecture elements that will support their execution.

112   CHAPTER 6. DEVELOPMENT METHODOLOGY

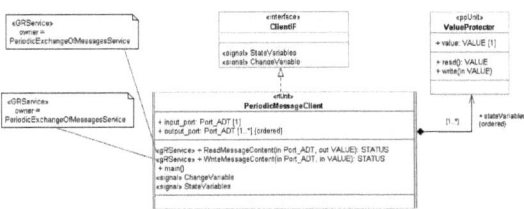

Figure 6.14: The <<GRService>> stereotype in new service design models

This phase includes an allocation view, platform architecture configuration view, scheduling view and additional information, e.g., probabilities of state transactions, needed for quality evaluation purposes.

The allocation view defines how applications and services are deployed on the computing and communication resources provided by the execution platform. Typically platform architecture elements need to be configured through configuration parameters. Additional information required for specific evaluation methods is provided by adding the required information to the models provided by the earlier design phases. An allocated system contains all the necessary information to implement the final product. If the vertical model transformation is supported, simulation and target code can be generated from the validated system architecture models.

The MARTE profile includes a specific sub-profile Alloc that allows a designer to specify which application elements will be associated to which platform resources. In this section we will use again the cruise control system (CCS) example to illustrate allocation modeling in MARTE.

The platform model of the cruise control system controller consists of a CPU managed by a system fixed priority scheduler. Three threads have been defined, all of them hosted by the system scheduler. Lastly, two shared protected variables have been defined, each of them with a blocking call for acquiring and releasing the variable lock (i.e. a mutex).

The allocation is performed using the structural views of both application and platform models and using the <<Allocate>> stereotype on UML abstraction dependencies. The <<Allocate>> stereotype allows further describing the nature and kind of the allocation as well as any constraints to be applied during the allocation process. Additionally both application and platform elements are stereotyped with <<Allocated>>.

Figure 6.15 shows the structural view of the application model allocated on top of the structural view of the platform model. Each of the operations and receptions in the controller has been allocated on the three threads and the passive protected units have been mapped to mutex-protected variables.

The system refinement includes schedulability analysis that tries to assure that a system meets its real-time requirements. This evaluation can be addressed through various simulation and analytical methods. Many of the latter mentioned quality evaluation methods have been implemented by different

6.4. ARCHITECTURE DESIGN

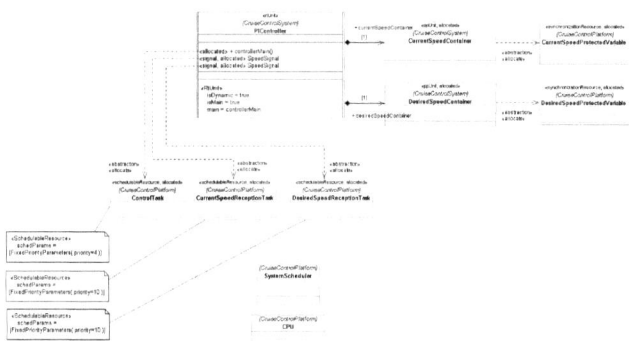

Figure 6.15: Allocated model of the CCS controller

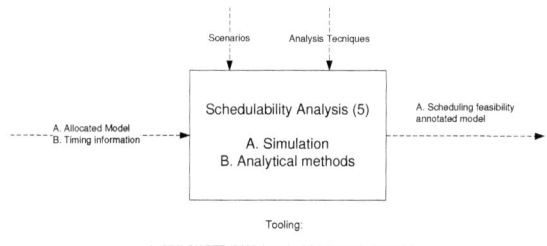

Figure 6.16: Overview of the schedulability analysis support

schedulability analysis tools such as Cheddar [74], MAST[1] and TIMES [7].

These tools use allocated models as input with some extra information regarding execution times, periods, deadlines, etc. These models can be extracted from the scheduling view. MARTE provides the Schedulability Analysis modeling (SAM) sub-profile for further annotating allocated models with scheduling information.

Figure 6.16 outlines two different approaches for schedulability analysis. The first one focuses on is feasibility analysis by using schedulability analysis models. The second one aims at application-platform performance analysis using transaction level simulations.

---

[1]modeling and Analysis Suite for Real-Time applications. httpp://mast.unican.es

6.5 Quality Evaluation

The Quality Evaluation methods give support for evaluating the following quality properties: performance, power/energy efficiency, dependability including reliability, availability and safety, composability, and evolvability. Please, see [63] for more elaborate descriptions.

Quality attributes can be classified into two categories; functional qualities, which are observable at execution time (i.e. execution qualities), and non-functional qualities, which are observable during the product life cycle (i.e. evolution qualities). Functional qualities, e.g. performance and dependability, express themselves in the behavior of the system, while non-functional qualities, e.g. composability and evolvability, are embodied in the static structures of systems.

The interest of the quality attributes for system architecture is in how quality attributes interact with, and constrain, each other, and how they affect the achievement of other quality attributes. Therefore, a set of quality attributes is to be handled at the same time and tradeoffs between quality attributes are to be calculated and managed. For example, dependability is a concept that includes four quality attributes: reliability, availability, safety and security. Moreover, a new concept 'trustworthiness' focuses on a holistic view of quality including the following attributes: correctness, safety, availability, reliability, performance, security and privacy. The holistic approach aims at applying multidimensional optimization techniques on a set of quality attributes that can have intrinsic and/or extrinsic relationships on other quality attributes. An intrinsic relationship exists if one quality attribute affects another. For example, models to predict reliability depend on a system's anticipated performance. This relation between reliability and performance is intrinsic. Extrinsic relationships occur when attributes behave in an opposing way, e.g. an increase in reliability decreases performance. In this case, the relation between reliability and performance is extrinsic. However, the relations between two attributes do not exist per se but they are properties of system architecture [23].

In the following sections, the quality evaluation methods specific for each quality attribute (QA) are outlined.

6.5.1 Performance Evaluation

Performance evaluation means a process of estimating through using performance models in quantitative terms what would the performance properties of the system being designed when implemented, whereas after implementation it is more of measuring the values of properties (the latter is not addressed in the sequel).

Performance evaluation in the context of real-time embedded systems development tries to provide insight to three main issues:

- Responsiveness: Is the system capable of producing responses to user (external) service requests in defined response times or at defined throughput?

- Resource adequacy/utilization: Does the system have resources and their capacity enough for the currently planned applications? How efficiently are the resources utilized?

6.5. QUALITY EVALUATION

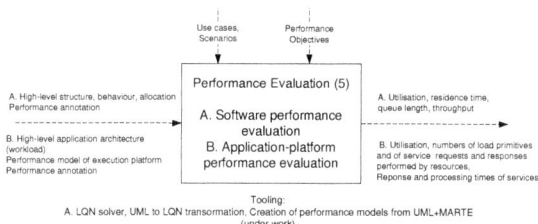

Figure 6.17: Input, output and support for performance evaluation

- Scalability: Does the system facilitate extensions/reductions and scale up/down resources and their capacity enough to accommodate future applications/changes in applications?

Performance evaluation methods can be classified to three main classes: analytical methods, simulation methods and monitoring methods [33]. Future embedded systems integrate an increasing number of concurrent applications on MPSoCs. Therefore, performance evaluation is taking more and more importance in the industry, while it is unfortunately becoming increasingly complex.

In many cases, what the developers of complex applications need is an evaluation of performance with a coarse, but guaranteed, error margin. The key issue there is on the existence and capabilities of appropriate tools, and on whether the assumptions that they put on the behavior of platforms and applications are valid for the system under test. The GENESYS architecture principles on complexity management, component-based design, composability, etc., will allow raising the abstraction level at which performance modeling and evaluation is performed, and should have a significant impact on this situation.

Figure 6.17 outlines two different approaches as examples where the main focus of the first is software architecture performance analysis/evaluation using Layered Queueing Network (LQN) performance models; and the second is aimed at application-platform performance analysis/evaluation using transaction level simulation of workload models of an application mapped on capacity models of an execution platform.

6.5.2 Power/Energy Evaluation

It is obvious that to be able to manage power/energy issues, trade-offs, often dynamic, with respect to performance are needed. Applications that are usually considered to transform to embedded software do not consume power/energy per se, but their execution on a MPSoC causes power/energy consumption in the various components of the platform (processors, memories, interfaces, interconnects, power supply/conversion itself etc.). Therefore, there is an interaction of application architecture and platform architecture in handling power/energy issues and an assumption is made that the MPSoC platform contains appropriate means for planning/deciding (e.g. some kind of power-energy/resource manager) and for controlling (e.g. DVFS controls, clock-gating and/or power-gating).

In the era of MPSoCs, the power/energy estimation needs to be done at system-level, i.e. effects of both the application and platform should be included. When executing the application functionality in the form of embedded software, as well as system (platform) software, on a platform causes power to be consumed in the hardware resources and their interactions: processing elements, various memory elements and interconnections. The amount of energy spent depends on the internal state of each element.

In addition to spreadsheet and analytical models of power/energy, system-level simulation is the most researched technique.

6.5.3 Reliability and Availability Evaluation

Reliability is defined as the probability of the failure-free operation of a system for a specified period of time in a specified environment. Service reliability extends the traditional reliability definition, requiring in turn that either the system does not fail at all for a given period or it successfully recovers state information after a failure of a system to resume its service as if it was not interrupted. Availability is measured as the probability of a software service or system being available when needed. Reliability and availability are often defined as attributes of dependability, which is "the ability to deliver a service that can justifiably be trusted". From an architecture point of view, reliability and availability are execution qualities of a system.

In [22] architecture-based reliability evaluation methods are categorized into state-based, path-based and additive models. All of them are analytical methods. The state-based models use the probabilities of the transfer of control between components to predict the system reliability, whereas the path-based models compute the reliability of composite components based on the possible execution paths of the system. The additive models address the failure intensity of composite components, assuming that the system failure intensity can be calculated from component failure intensities.

Simulation models are used in testing and operational phases [21]. The aim of simulation is to identify components' criticality to the reliability of an application and detect faults and the number of failures in applications. Thus, simulation models are domain specific and can be regarded as optional approaches in the GENESYS methodology. Monitoring methods use a running system as a source and therefore they are considered only if they give support for architecture-based reliability prediction.

The GENESYS methodology supports the reliability and availability evaluation by defining methods and techniques that help to consider reliability and availability at three levels: system, architecture and components. Therefore, reliability and availability evaluation is based on the following works: reliability prediction of component-based architectures [68], reliability prediction in model-driven development [69], reliability evaluation of service architectures and software families [29] and trustworthiness evaluation and testing of open source components [17]. These approaches have been selected for the starting point based on their contradictory contributions to reliability evaluation concerning scope of evaluation, modeling languages, abstraction levels, evaluation techniques and tool support. Except the last one, the methods are analytical

6.5. QUALITY EVALUATION

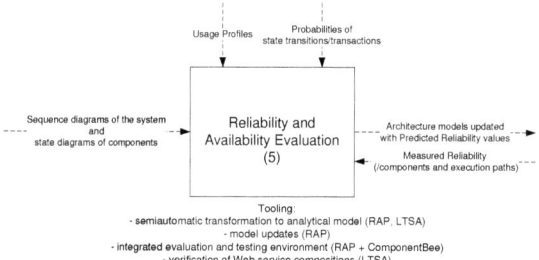

Figure 6.18: Input, output and support for reliability/availability evaluation

methods based on architecture models. The last one is an integrated approach that exploits reliability measurements in order to improve the accuracy of prediction.

Figure 6.18 depicts the overview of the phase where the reliability and availability of the components, architecture and the whole system are predicted based on analytical models and measured reliability values of existing components. The overview is based on three prediction approaches which will be introduced next. All these approaches are model-driven. Thereafter, a couple of mature commercial tools that support different kinds of analysis are introduced.

6.5.4 Safety Analysis

A safety critical system is a system that an action incidence (not performed, or performed incorrectly in logic or in time), could result in danger, injury, death, or property damages. An intrinsically safe system, on the other hand, cannot cause harmful exposures or damages under normal or abnormal conditions even when the equipment and personnel are in their most vulnerable condition [50, 51].

Safety properties are normally defined by using two factors: hazard and its risk. Hazard is a system state potentially causing accidents, the risk is concerned with the degree of acceptance of the hazard in certain environmental conditions, determined by severity, probability, exposure time, operation modes and possible mitigation of the hazard's effect.

A safety assessment process provides analytic evidence showing compliance with system requirements. The process includes specific assessments conducted and updated during system development; both processes interact along the product life-cycle. A general safety assessment processes is structured as follows [16]: Functional Hazard Assessment (FHA), Preliminary System Safety Assessment (PSSA), System Safety Assessment (SSA), Common Cause Analysis (CCA).

The inherent properties of the GENESYS architectural style and its domain specific instantiations, allows a modular certification approach. For the instantiated systems (aligned with the GENESYS architectural style and ser-

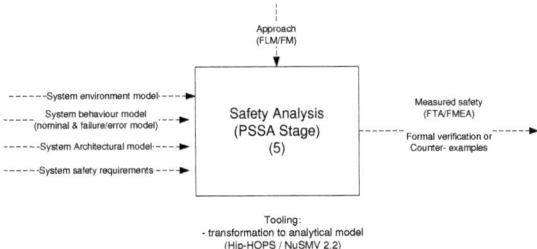

Figure 6.19: Input, output and support of safety analysis (PSSA Stage)

vice template), the overall system can be subdivided into subsystems with different levels of criticality; each of them can then be individually certified to the appropriate level of criticality, avoiding the full product certification to the highest criticality level of all subsystems, reducing cost and simplifying the complexity of certification effort [56]. Overview of the safety analysis in depicted in Figure 6.19.

Composability Evaluation

Composability is a concept that refers to integrability and interoperability of components and services. Integrability is the ability to make separately developed components and services of the system to work correctly together. Systems are based on integrated components, when the components are used as building blocks in product development. However, the black-box nature of components and insufficient component documentation make the integration of components difficult. Successful component integration requires that the component matches the functional and quality requirements of a system and interoperates with other components of the system.

Two approaches have been suggested to be used together to estimate and to avoid integration mismatches in these two cases: model-based integration and component-based integration. The approaches are different, but their results are complementary. The purpose of both approaches is to identify clashes, which yield mismatches. Corresponding with the approaches, two types of clashes/mismatches can be detected:

- Model-based integration yields model constraint and rule clashes/mismatches

- Component-based integration yields component feature clashes/mismatches.

The model-based integration approach tries to combine information from different views to allow precise reasoning. Integrating architectural views means that problems and faults are still relatively easy (and inexpensive) to fix, because architectural issues are considered early in the development life-cycle.

The component-based integration approach can be used early for risk assessment of existing components/services while little information is available. The

6.6. INTEGRATED TOOL ENVIRONMENT

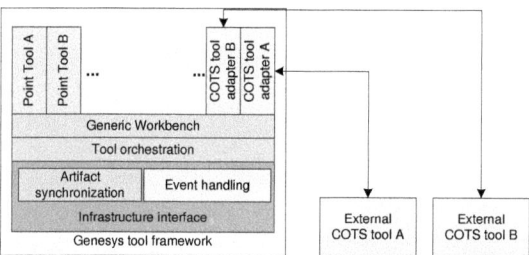

Figure 6.20: High level architecture of the tool environment

approach uses a set of conceptual features for describing components and the connections between the components. When composing systems, many potential architectural mismatches can be detected by analyzing their various choices for conceptual features. Feature mismatches may occur when components have different or same (collision) characteristics for some particular feature, such as concurrency, distribution, dynamism, layering, encapsulation, supported data transfers, triggering or capability. Component features can be derived through observation and assumptions of their external behavior (black-box analysis) without knowing their internal workings.

6.5.5 Evolvability Evaluation

Evolvability is a concept related to several quality attributes, e.g. flexibility, adaptability, extensibility, maintainability, and modifiability. Therefore, many evaluation methods cover one or more quality attributes of evolvability. Most of these methods are scenario based methods, and thus the first step in evolvability evaluation is to define what to evaluate and why. The idea is to first concentrate on the part of the system architecture that influences the most on quality (e.g. size, criticality, complexity), and when that part is proofed to be correct, the evaluation focuses on the other parts that have lower impact on quality.

6.6 Integrated Tool Environment

This section introduces the proposed architecture for the GENESYS design environment. The high level architecture of the tool environment is illustrated by Figure 6.20.

The basis of the tool environment is the interface to the development infrastructure server that manages all the assets (models, source code, documents, etc.) required during the development process. It should support team collaboration and versioning for all kinds of artifacts. This storage layer also incorporates traceability and navigation support by allowing the inter-artefact link creation and traversal.

The tool orchestration layer support the tool interactions on the client side. Its main purpose is to organize the information flow between the tools and to offer a tool automation environment for the automatic execution of point tools triggered by the design workflow.

The generic workbench offers integration interfaces for the point tools and implements a generic user interface (GUI) that gives access to the lower layers of the framework (design artefact handling, queries, transformations, navigation, design workflow).

Point tools (performing a specific step in the development process) can be either integrated on the top of the core design environment or (in case of COTS tools) can be interfaced with custom tool adapters. Point tools are invoked either by the user or (in case of automatic tools, like code generators, or some analysis tools) by the tool orchestration layer.

The design artefact store supports the management of various development artifacts like models, source code, documents, reports, and so on. The design artefact store is a server component that stores the design artifacts in a central (versioning) repository. It also contains an artefact catalogue (project tree for all development projects) and user rights management in order to support the access control rule definition on the various design artifacts. The query engine supports the definition of custom queries/views on the repository or on different models. The navigation and traceability support module implements a uniform inter-element trace definition, maintenance, and navigation framework that allows the tracing of concepts throughout design steps. The model transformation module executes automatic transformations on the various elements in order to synchronize various models or to derive analysis models from engineering ones.

The communication and event layer serves as an interface for the developer PCs (clients) that run the GENESYS Development Environment. The client-server architecture allows for real-time team collaboration both on models and textual documents and the immediate synchronization of models between developers on model changes.

The GENESYS tool environment has to support several different model transformations in order to provide all the functionalities described in the earlier chapters. In the following, a brief outline of the most important transformations will be given. Figure 6.21 illustrates the key transformation paths in the development workflow. Only some important models and modeling languages are shown. Dashed lines represent manual or semi-automatic transformations, continuous lines represent automatic ones. Bidirectional arrows represent bidirectional (or synchronization-like) transformations.

The MARTE to BIP transformation is exemplarily summarized in Table 6.1. Due to the fact the UML-MARTE and BIP are two different languages they focus on different aspects of embedded systems. Thus, there are issues that prevent a full transformation without making assumptions. Many of these issues occur due to the great degree of semantics that MARTE stereotypes introduce in the annotated models. The issues located during the MARTE to BIP transformation development suggest that making a backward transformation could be difficult since BIP does not store any kind of MARTE semantics annotations. This problem could be resolved by identifying behavioral patterns and associating them with concrete MARTE concepts.

The IBM Jazz platform[2] is a novel integrated collaboration enablement

---

[2]IBM Jazz Platform Information Portal, http://www.jazz.net/

6.6. INTEGRATED TOOL ENVIRONMENT

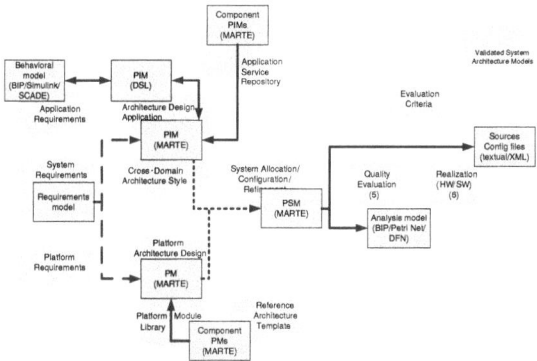

Figure 6.21: Overview of transformations in the development workflow

technology. It is still under development, but it supports nearly all the features required for the Infrastructure Server of the GENESYS tool chain. It contains a versioning artefact store (only on the file level), collaboration utilities, requirements management and traceability framework, and a customizable design workflow. Its main drawback is the lack of central model management and transformation support, and the lack of tool automation support. As it has an open, extensible architecture, these missing functions can be added by integrating other tools to it.

Eclipse EMF CDO[3] is a distributed implementation of the industry standard Eclipse Modeling Framework (EMF). It features a central model repository stored in a standard relational database that can be reached by multiple clients simultaneously. Although some important features are still missing (e.g. model versioning) it can be a solid foundation for the model artefact store. Given its open architecture, the integration of versioning and query/transformation support should be feasible.

One of the key technologies is the selection of an appropriate model transformation technique. The complexity and diversity of transformations during the development process necessitates the selection of a powerful tool. There are several proposals, like VIATRA2[4] and ATL[5] from the Eclipse project, but none of them has all required features (live and batch transformations, EMF integration, incremental pattern matching, etc.).

In case of client side technologies, the selection is straightforward. The Eclipse Framework is the most widespread tool integration framework nowadays, and its importance is still growing. It contains several components that can be easily reused by the tool environment.

As a summary, we can state that most of the important technologies are

---

[3]Eclipse EMF CDO Project Home Page, http://www.eclipse.org/modeling/emf/?project=cdo#cdo
[4]VIATRA2 Model Transformation Framework, http://www.eclipse.org/gmt
[5]Atlas Transformation Language, http://www.eclipse.org/m2m/atl

Concept in MARTE	BIP equivalent
<<GaAnalysisContext>>	BIP System
Property in a <<GaAnalysisContext>>	BIP Compound Type
Signal	BIP Port Type + BIP Data Type
Regions in <<RtUnit>>	BIP Atomic Component Type
<<PpUnit>>	BIP Atomic Component Type
State in a Region	BIP Petri Net State
First State in a Region	BIP Petri Net Initial State
Transition in a Region	BIP Petri Net Transition
TimeEvent trigger in a Transition	BIP Timed Data + BIP Transition Guard
SignalEvent trigger in a Transition	BIP Transition Trigger
<<GaAcqStep>> and <<GaRelStep>> in Transitions	BIP Connector Type + BIP Ports in atomic components
SendSignalAction in a Region	BIP Port in atomic component
SignalEvent in a Region	BIP Port in atomic component
Connector in <<GaAnalysisContext>>	BIP Connector Type

Table 6.1: Summary of mapping from MARTE to BIP

present currently, but there are several missing elements that should be created in order to achieve a complete model-driven tool chain that will be capable of handling real size development projects.

6.7 Conclusion

The definition of the GENESYS methodology framework is based on seven principles which were derived from the requirements identified and defined by the authors with the help of industrial partners involved in the GENESYS project. To summarize, we justify the completeness of the GENESYS methodology framework by illustrating how these principles are supported by the methodology framework.

Principle 1: Embedded systems engineering process The methodology framework provides the following support for the whole life-cycle of embedded systems engineering:

- A process model with appropriate modeling and evaluation methods that support modeling and early verification and validation from requirements specification to validated system architecture models (top-down approach).

- Each modeling and evaluation phase is supported by a set of tools which can be integrated by means of the platform of the integrated tool environment.

6.7. CONCLUSION

- Adoption of the UML-MARTE modeling language is supported by guidelines and a set of examples.

- A process model defines how the existing services and components (models or code) from the application service repository and the platform module library could be used in application and platform architecture design. Appropriate integration techniques have been introduced (bottom-up approach).

It should be noted that the methodology framework allows for exploration, refinement and iteration. For example, the approach can be applied with more abstract (and less detailed) models for feasibility assessment at an early stage of development. Later on, the drawn conclusions can be validated with more mature (and more detailed) models until finally signed off for realization.

Principle 2: Model driven architecture development The model driven architecture design is supported as follows:

- The process model follows the Y-chart model by separating application and platform architecture design at the abstract (logical/PIM) level. The PSM model is achieved by allocating application models to platform models and transforming and configuring the combined models for a specific system model. These three architecture design phases (application, platform and system allocation/configuration/refinement) are separate and provide models at different abstraction levels.

- A set of identified model transformations (horizontal and vertical) have been defined as part of the integrated development environment.

The top-down vertical transformation is supported by the selection of a language suite, i.e. UML2, SysML and MARTE. Horizontal transformation, i.e. model-to-model transformations are needed for quality evaluation. The defined MARTE-BIP transformation is an example of such a needed transformation. That is to be supported by the interactive development and integration environment. Hybrid transformation is supported only in one case, where model-based reliability testing is integrated with reliability prediction. As summary, all transformations, i.e. vertical, horizontal and hybrid need improvements and further research activities.

Principle 3: Model representation The model representation is supported by defining:

- the views required in each modeling phase,

- a primary modeling language and possible extensions needed in different phases of the modeling process,

- how applications are to be mapped to the platform model, and

- schedulability analysis techniques and tools for checking architectural models before the quality evaluation phase.

Although the model representation is covered to a large extent, we anticipate that representation of quality properties and model consistency checking still need further studies, at least in applying MARTE in real industrial cases and making existing tools smoothly applicable in instances of the GENESYS methodology framework.

Principle 4: Modeling semantics Semantics modeling is covered only to the extent supported by the UML2 modeling language, e.g. semantics of exchanged data and interface types. However, in order to fully exploit semantics modeling, much more should be defined. For example, service semantics as part of the platform module library and application service repository, 'standardization' of linking interfaces and technology independent interfaces by means of interface ontologies, and defining rules for instantiation and run-time usage of platform services and developing (semi)automatic tool support for design time and mechanisms for run-time management. Thus, modeling the semantics of embedded systems services will be one of the key research items of future ARTEMIS projects.

Principle 5: Formal methods The use of formal methods for modeling platform services for safety critical systems is supported by:

- Theory of formal modeling based on user functionality hierarchy and logical component architecture
- Verification by model checking and/or interactive theorem proving
- Verification tools for model checking and manipulation and evaluation of timed automata

The use of the BIP framework for composability evaluation is possible by implementing the defined model transformation. The use of existing model checking tools will be possible through the integrated development environment but further studies are needed on the development of appropriate adapters for commercial, proprietary and/or open source tools.

Principle 6: Evaluation of quality and non-functional properties. The evaluation methods, techniques and tools introduced in this book cover most of the quality and non-functional properties that were defined to be of high importance in embedded systems engineering in the ARTEMIS Strategic Research Agenda (SRA).

The only exception is information security. Information security evaluation was intended to be covered by the results of the ITEA/Eureka project €-Confidential, which was running concurrently with GENESYS and a trusted security platform as its focus. However, the results available were not mature enough to be included in this document.

The draft version of the €-Confidential methodology introduces an overview of the Secure Software Development Lifecycle (SSDL) methodology with a set of phases and activities. These activities can be merged to the GENESYS process model in the similar way as the safety analysis activities have been done. For example, in €-Confidential the architecture design phase includes 'Create threat model' and 'Secure architecture review'. The Create threat model activity is part of the system allocation/refinement/configuration phase and the secure architecture review activity should be part of the quality evaluation phase in the **GENESYS** process model. Because any evaluation method or technique was not introduced in SSDL, we decided not to provide a partial non validated evaluation method for one important quality attribute. However, we assume that security evaluation could exploit and adapt many of the existing safety evaluation techniques and methods.

Principle 7: Interactive development and integration environment.
The methodology framework should facilitate early validation and verification by supporting HW and SW partitioning, simulation and (virtual) prototyping, and heterogeneous simulations including models and code. This principle is covered by the integrated development environment to the following extend:

- Model transformations in the development workflow have been identified and shortly specified. The MARTE-BIP transformation is introduced as an example.

- Live, bidirectional and incremental model transformations between DSLs and MARTE are considered as a solution for integrating domain specific design with standard based model based early V&V.

The support for integrated, automated model-to-model and model-to-text transformations is a key to the success of the model-driven development approach. Therefore, an initial specification of an interactive development and integration environment has been defined. However, further research and experimental studies are required in order to make it possible to orchestrate model based embedded systems engineering based on diverse models, methods and tools and provide forward and backward traceability for the whole design flow. Especially there are two research items that needs further investigations: a) integration of distributed model storage and model transformation support and b) creation of a uniform and extensible solution for tracing artifacts throughout the life cycle of embedded systems.

Seven

Prototype Implementation

THIS CHAPTER describes a prototype for the industrial domain, which focuses on composability, networking, and integrated resource management at chip-level. By means of a time-triggered network-on-a-chip, this prototype supports the integration of heterogeneous IP cores. The prototype implements selected services of the reference architecture template and complies to the GENESYS cross-domain architectural style.

7.1 Introduction

The central element of the prototype is a Time-Triggered Network-on-Chip (TTNoC). It serves for the interconnection of multiple, possibly heterogeneous IP cores called micro components. Figure 7.1 illustrates the structure of the GENESYS prototype.

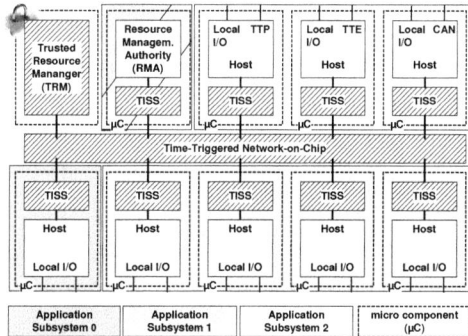

Figure 7.1: Overall structure of the GENESYS Prototype

Micro components (MCs) are made up of a host and the *Trusted Interface Subsystem (TISS)*. The purpose of the TISS is to ensure that a fault of a host cannot lead to a violation of the micro component's temporal interface specification. Besides this, special purpose micro components for integrated resource management and reconfiguration, e.g. the *Trusted Resource Manager (TRM)* and *Resource Management Authority (RMA)*, are included. The TRM and the RMA are used for integrated resource management and realize parts of the functionality of the Global Resource Management (GRM). The RMA is responsible for computing new allocations of communication resources, which are written into the TISSes by the TRM.

7.1.1 Implemented Architectural Services

The prototype implements selected core services, namely periodic communication, sporadic communication, common time and reconfiguration. Furthermore, the optional service for voting is implemented.

Periodic Communication

The NoC transports *periodic* messages from one sender port of a micro component to a set of receiver ports at distinct micro components. The periodicity stems from the specification of periods and phases (temporal offset with reference to the begin of a period). The instant of transmission, which is expressed in the notion of periods and phases in a time-triggered communication schedule, is known a priori at each participant of communication. Consequently, communication is predictable and deterministic with respect to timing, latency, and arrival time. Periodic messages are transported in encapsulated communication channels, which assure that a fault, e.g., a software fault, in the micro component cannot disrupt the communication between other micro components or local computation in unrelated micro components. By design, encapsulation entails error containment. That is, encapsulation prevents temporal interference, e.g., stalling messages or delaying computations in another micro component, and spatial interference, e.g., overwriting a message produced by another micro component. As a result of encapsulation, we avoid dealing with interfering subsystems, which is more difficult to understand than to reason about the behavior of clearly encapsulated subsystems. In other words, encapsulation facilitates complexity reduction and composability. In the GENESYS prototype, the Trusted Subsystem is the architectural element that enforce encapsulation and error containment among micro components.

Sporadic Communication

Similar to periodic messages, the NoC supports sporadic messages. For sporadic messages, the constraint of periodicity of messages is relaxed. That is, a sporadic message need not necessarily be sent in each period. The sending micro component makes the decision, whether a message is sent or not, depending on the application semantics of the software executed in that micro component.

Common Time

The NoC maintains a global notion of time. The purpose of the common time in GENESYS is to synchronize communication activities between micro components. For this purpose, each micro component contains a local replication

7.1. INTRODUCTION 129

of that common time, whereas these replications are internally synchronized to a precision of one macro tick (approximately 953 ns in the current prototype implementation). Additionally, this core service establishes accuracy to an external reference time. For instance, the reference time is supplied by an external, deterministic communication network, which also entails a common time, such as Time-Triggered Ethernet (TTE) [37], or an external time synchronization technologies such as GPS, DCF77, or NTP.

Voting

To detect and tolerate single-core failures in a dependable system, Triple Modular Redundancy (TMR) can be implemented. When using Triple Modular Redundancy, a core is replicated and a voter is used to perform a majority vote over the results of the replicated cores. Thus, the intended service can be provided even in case of a failure of one of the replicated cores. Such a voter has been implemented in the scope of the prototype in the form of a hardware middleware module (coded in VHDL) named the Voter Plug-In. The Voter Plug-In takes advantage of the time-triggered nature of the communication service, which allows the voter to determine exact time instances at which the input data from the three replicated cores should be valid and equal. Therefore, the Voter Plug-In operation is organized in time slices, starting with the first state data sent by one of the replicated cores and lasting until the correct result is provided by the voter. Such a time slice is called a voting round. Since voting is performed only on state data, a Voter Plug-In round consists of receiving three state ports of equal length from the three replicated cores, determining the correct voting result, and forwarding this result and the current state port status (valid data/corrupted data) to the attached host.

Reconfiguration

Reconfiguration denotes the process, when resource allocations (e.g., the time-triggered communication schedule, introducing new periodic and sporadic messages) are modified in the NoC. New resource allocations can be calculated by a general purpose micro component at run-time, or can be determined offline before deployment and fetched at run-time. The reconfiguration core service investigates new resource allocations by checking the compliance with constraints in the time-triggered communication schedule, it also tracks potential collisions in the NoC, and approves it for distribution.

7.1.2 Outline

Section 7.2 describes the hardware, on which the GENESYS prototype has been built. Furthermore, it reveals the internal design of micro components used in that prototype. Section 7.3 explains features and functions of the implemented demonstration application. The results of this implementation are summarized in the following section 7.4. Finally, we validate the implementation concerning the architectural core services in section 7.5.

7.2 Prototype Hardware

An MPSoC development kit depicted in Figure 7.2 has been used for the prototype implementation. This MPSoC development kit consists of several PCB devices equipped with FPGAs of the Altera Cyclone II^{TM} series and different CPUs. The board serves as an emulation of an MPSoC, where the FPGA implements the NoC and the CPU boards represent the micro components.

Figure 7.2: The MPSoC Development Kit equipped as used in the prototype

7.2.1 Mainboard

The basis of this prototype set-up is a mainboard (see Figure 7.3) that provides 9 Powerlink extension slots, on which the other PCB devices can be mounted as add-on boards. Furthermore, the PCB devices can be stacked vertically beginning at the Powerlink extension slots on the mainboard. Besides the Powerlink extension slots, the mainboard possesses one Cyclone II EP2C70 FPGA.

7.2.2 FPGA Board

An FPGA board as shown in Figure 7.4 is assembled with an Altera Cyclone II EP2C35. This FPGA is free to take particular entities of the GENESYS prototype. On the one hand, an FPGA board can be used to hold a Generic Middleware (GEM) in order to wrap the physical signals of the uniform network interface to the interface of the CPU board that is used to realize application functionality (i.e., that hosts the implementation of a job). On the other hand, an FPGA board can also contain a GEM plus a "soft-core" CPU (e.g., a LEON3 SPARC V8 Processor core, an Altera Nios II Embedded Processor). In the latter case, the FPGA board embodies a complete host and provides the computational resources for the execution of a job itself.

7.2. PROTOTYPE HARDWARE

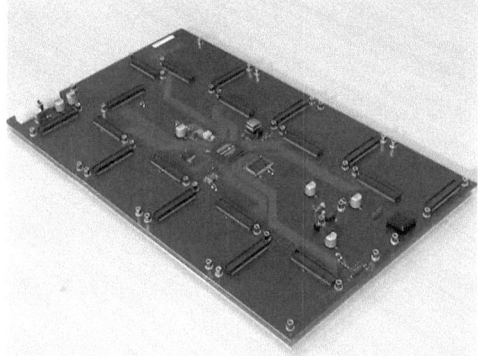

Figure 7.3: The MPSoC Mainboard

Figure 7.4: The FPGA Board

7.2.3 Basic I/O Board

The basic I/O board provides interfaces to the external environment. Usually, a basic I/O board will be stacked upon an FPGA board, so that the host in the FPGA board can operate the physical interfaces of the basic I/O board. It features a serial RS232, CAN, LIN, TTP/A, Ethernet controller, and General Purpose I/O.

Figure 7.5: The Basic I/O Board

7.2.4 Multimedia I/O Board

The multimedia board is structured similar to the basic I/O board, but the interfaces can be regarded as multimedia devices. For instance, a multimedia board is equipped with an AC97 compatible audio device. Also, a color touch screen LCD display can be driven by the basic I/O board. Moreover, the multimedia board contains an USB controller that can function as an USB host as well as an USB device.

7.2.5 Physical Constraints

Note that the MPSoC Development Kit does not provide a single FPGA to hold a whole design of the GENESYS prototype. Instead of this, all entities are spread across several FPGAs of FPGA boards. Thus, the MPSoC Development Kit "emulates" an SoC. The reason for this hardware partitioning is that no single FPGA, which would have been big enough to house a complete GENESYS prototype, had been available at that time, when the development of the GENESYS prototype started.

7.2.6 Partitioning of the Prototype

The MPSoC Development Kit is the main prototype hardware. We run the GENESYS prototype on this hardware. Figure 7.7 graphically describes the

7.2. PROTOTYPE HARDWARE

Figure 7.6: The Multimedia I/O Board with touch screen LCD display

distribution of architectural entities to the given hardware components.

The design example, i.e. the GENESYS prototype, on the MPSoC Development Kit features 9 hosts. The RMA as well as the Gateway occupy one host each. The Diagnostic Unit reserves another one (at slot 0). The 6 remaining hosts are free for the DASs of the demonstration application. The TRM is a stand-alone unit and is not realized on a host.

In total, the design example features 10 TISSes, which are connected by the TTNoC consisting of 6 Fragment Switches. The Fragment Switches are arranged into an 2x3 mesh topology in this design example.

Moreover, we learn from Figure 7.7 that the TSS (the 6 Fragment Switches, the 10 TISSes, and the TRM) resides in the EP2C70 FPGA of the mainboard. The 9 hosts are implemented in the EP2C35 FPGAs of the FPGA boards mounted on the Powerlink extension slots of the mainboard. Basic I/O boards and multimedia boards, which are required by the demonstration application.

Each host utilizes one Nios II Embedded Processor as its application computer. Besides this, a host possess memory controllers to operate the memory chips of the FPGA boards, and other peripherals such as a JTAG for debugging. All peripherals are interconnected by the Altera Avalon Memory-Mapped Interface. Considering the entities of the GENESYS prototype, a host must be equipped with a Port Memory (32 KByte on-chip memory) and a GEM suitable for the Avalon Memory-Mapped Interface. Besides this, the Gateway is a host that features an additional Time-Triggered Ethernet (TTE) controller.

In fact, the design of the TRM is similar to a host, except for the number of memory controllers, as there are not as many memory chips available on the mainboard as on an FPGA board.

7.2.7 Micro Components

In this section we examine the interiors of micro components, as they are used in the demonstration application.

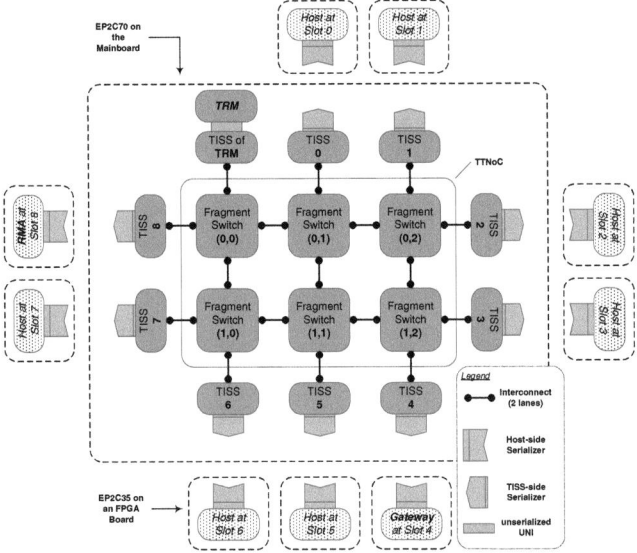

Figure 7.7: Partitioning of the GENESYS prototype on the MPSoC Development Kit

Trusted Resource Manager (TRM)

The TRM in this GENESYS prototype uses a Altera Nios II CPU and executes a custom embedded real-time operating system. Figure 7.8 lists the hardware components that make up the TRM. Moreover, Table 7.1 lists parameters of the TRM such as operation frequency and available memory.

CPU	Altera Nios II/f
	2 KB instruction cache, 2KB data cache
System Frequency	≈ 91 MHz
Memory	2 MB external SSRAM
	32 KB internal Port Memory
Local I/O	1 user LED
	"Enable" wires for all Fragment Switches

Table 7.1: Parameters of the TRM

RMA and Nios II based Hosts

The RMA and one type of host used in the demonstration application utilize the same hardware design. Consequently, the difference lays in the executed

7.2. PROTOTYPE HARDWARE

Figure 7.8: Components within the TRM

software.

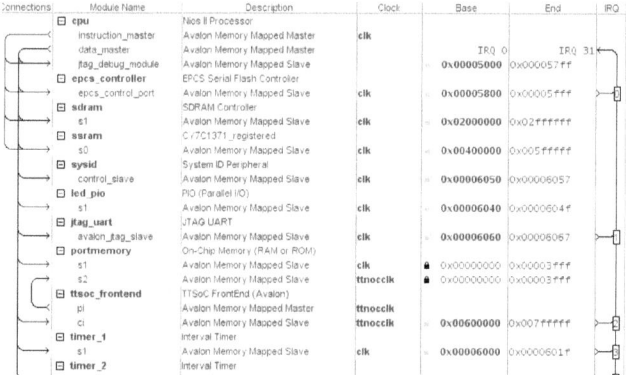

Figure 7.9: Design of the RMA and Nios II based hosts

Further information concerning this design entity are given in Table 7.2.

Time-Triggered Ethernet Gateway

Figure 7.10 shows the hardware design of the Time-Triggered Ethernet (TTE) Gateway. Apparently, its "heart" is the Time-Triggered Ethernet Controller, which realizes the connectivity to TTE networks.

CHAPTER 7. PROTOTYPE IMPLEMENTATION

CPU	Altera Nios II/f
	2 KB instruction cache, 2KB data cache
	Floating Point Unit (FPU)
System Frequency	≈ 91 MHz
Memory	16 MB external SDRAM
	2 MB external SSRAM
	16 KB internal Port Memory
Local I/O	1 user LED

Table 7.2: Parameters of the RMA and Nios II based hosts

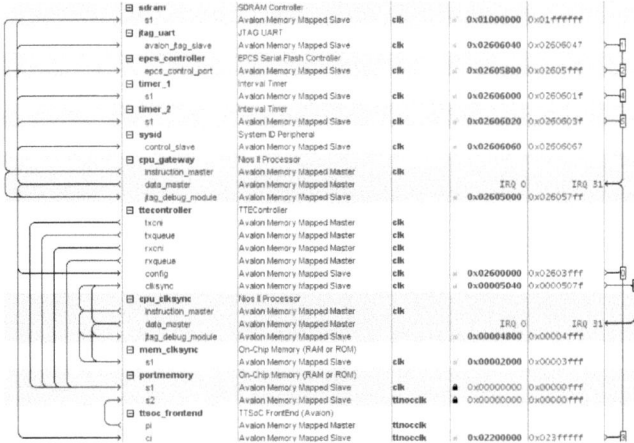

Figure 7.10: Internals of the TTE Gateway

CPU	Altera Nios II/f
	2 KB instruction cache, 2KB data cache
System Frequency	≈ 52 MHz
Memory	16 MB external SDRAM
	16 KB internal Port Memory
Local I/O	1 user LED

Table 7.3: Parameters of the TTE Gateway

7.2. PROTOTYPE HARDWARE

Aeroflex Gaisler LEON3 based Hosts

The LEON3 CPU, part of the open source Gaisler Library (GRLIB), is a SPARC V8 compliant soft-core (i.e. synthesisable) 32-bit processor. LEON3 is highly configurable by the use of VHDL generics. The main features are: there is support for MMU, FPU, symmetric multi-processor setups, instruction/data caches, on-chip debug support, hardware multiply/divide AMBA v2 is used to interconnect the CPU with periphery cores like a memory controller, a SD-card IP-core or an UART controller.

When work on this GENESYS prototype started, LEON3 had been the only soft-core CPU available for our target technology that has MMU support on Linux. Even though there are MMU-less Linux patches available, without MMU, programs need to run in physical address-space (fork restrictions) and e.g. kernel module loading is not possible. We wanted to use Linux, especially for the Multimedia host, because of the wide selection of available open-source software and drivers.

So, the LEON3 based host is the most significant design in the GENESYS prototype, as the majority of the micro components are realized this way. Accordingly, this subsection describes the design of the LEON3 user host in more detail. We focus on where GRLIB is extensively used for interfacing FPGA board hardware and the available extension boards (multimedia and I/O board).

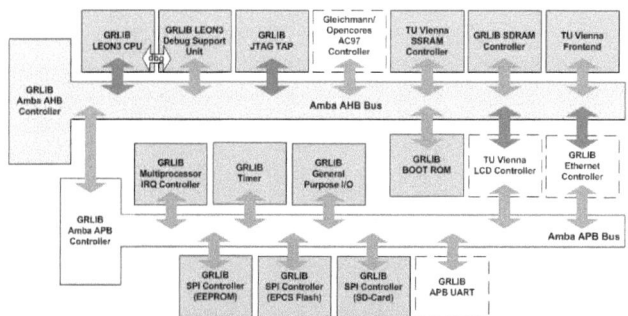

Figure 7.11: Design of the LEON3 based hosts

The LEON3 system features a high performance Amba AHB bus as well as an APB bus for low-bandwidth intensive IP cores. Figure 7.11 illustrates the design of the LEON3 user host. Cores connected with blue arrows are bus slaves, while cores connected with red arrows are bus masters. The periphery available on the extension boards is optionally controllable by the dashed IP cores.

7.3 Demonstration Application

One MPSoC Development Kit has been used for the demonstration application [57]. This demonstration application consists of two Distributed Application Subsystems (DASs): the control DAS and the multimedia DAS.

7.3.1 Overview

Figure 7.12 depicts the design of the demonstration application. The chip "TTSoC I" realizes both, the Control DAS and the Multimedia DAS. The figure shows the used micro components (MCs), as well as their physical positions on the Development Kit. Figure 7.13 further outlines the mapping of implemented functions onto the prototype hardware of the MPSoC Development Kit.

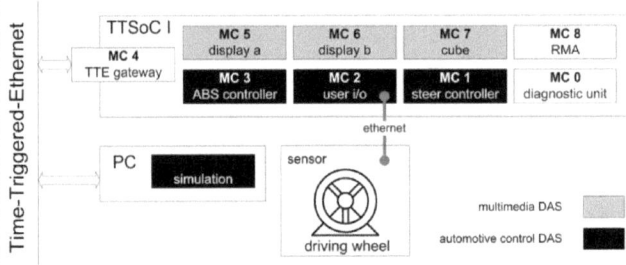

Figure 7.12: Overview of Demonstration Application

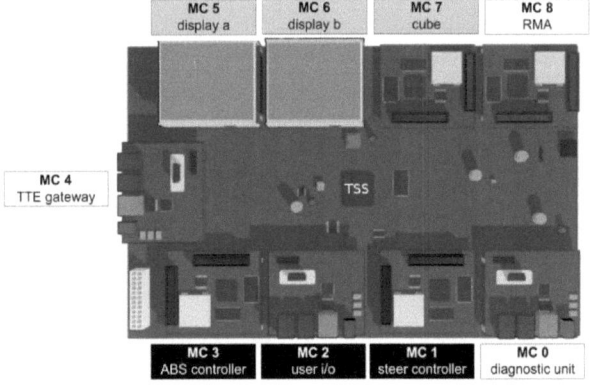

Figure 7.13: Mapping functions onto MPSoC Development Kit

7.3. DEMONSTRATION APPLICATION

A PC is used to run a racing car simulation where a simulated car provides sensor values as inputs and takes the Control-DAS output as its actuator set-values. A driving wheel sensor, which is made up of a steering wheel and a Soekris Net 4801 embedded PC, is connected via Ethernet to the MC 2 and provides wheel, gas and brake pedals sensor input to the Control-DAS. Concerning the Multimedia-DAS, a video of a spinning three dimensional cube is calculated on MC7 and sent to MC 5 and MC 6, which also demonstrates the multi-cast capabilities of the TTNoC.

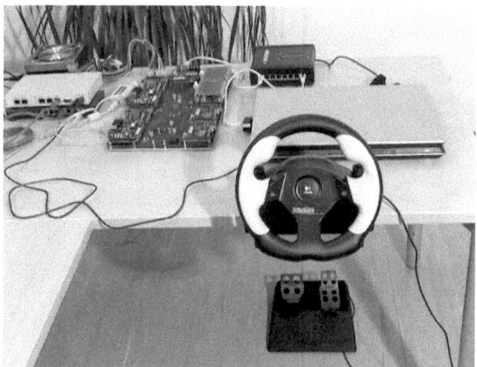

Figure 7.14: Complete hardware set-up for the demonstration application

Figure 7.14 shows the complete hardware setup that has been used for the demonstration application. This comprises the MPSoC Development Kit, a PC to run the simulation engine, and auxiliary devices such as a Time-Triggered Ethernet (TTE) switch, a Soekris Net 4801 embedded PC, and a steering wheel with pedals. The usage of each of these components is explained in the following.

7.3.2 Control Distributed Application Subsystem

The control DAS is realized on a single (emulated) chip which communicates over its Time Triggered Ethernet (TTE) gateway with the open-source racing car simulation TORCS running on a PC system. Furthermore, the (emulated) chip interfaces a steering wheel and brake and acceleration pedals on one of its MCs (i.e. MC2).

The set-up is used to control a vehicle in the racing car simulation. The actual set points for all the simulated actuators are calculated on the respective micro component in the chip by processing the simulated sensor values in a closed feedback-loop. This allows experiments with Steer-By-Wire and Brake-By-Wire applications: e.g. Anti-Lock Braking System (ABS), Electronic Stability Control (ESC), Cornering Brake Control (CBC), etc.

For the control DAS we decided to implement a simple Brake-/Steer-By-Wire based Anti-Lock Braking System (ABS). ABS helps to keep a car steerable during (emergency) braking. All wheels are prevented from getting locked, thus they do not skid uncontrollably. A typical ABS (for motor-cycles, cars, air planes, ...) consists of an Electronic Control Unit (ECU), two or more wheel speed sensors (one sensor for each wheel) and two or more actuators responsible for modifying the braking force applied on each wheel.

During a braking process, speed of the wheels is constantly checked and if one or more wheels rotate considerably slower than other wheels, a locking condition is prevented by reducing the braking force on those wheels that start to lock.

Figure 7.15: Screenhost of TORCS Racing Car Simulator

TORCS (The Open Racing Car Simulator) is an open-source (GPL) racing car simulation initially developed by Eric Espie and Christophe Guionneau in the year 2000. The simulator can be used as ordinary car racing game, as AI racing game and as research platform. For the latter use, TORCS has already been chosen multiple times because of the clean C++ design, nice graphics for visualization and adequate simulation (e.g. Northern Illinois University uses it for teaching and research, Fraunhofer ESK Research Institute for visualization, haptic feedback studies have been carried out for Nissan Motor by Kevin Roundy, ...).

Figure 7.15 shows a screenshot of TORCS. The simulation includes tire and wheel properties (tire pressure, springs, dampers, stiffness, etc.), car properties (forces, weight, transmission, suspension, engine, etc.), and aerodynamic properties (ground effect, spoilers, ...). Beside the adequate simulation model for testing brake-by-wire, the software design of TORCS features the development of so called "robots". Each car in a race is controlled by a single C++ class that may take input from physically present wheels and pedals, from an Artificial Intelligence (AI) or from the network. This will make it especially easy to directly control a car from the GENESYS prototype.

All channels of the control DAS operate in a frequency of 64 Hz, i.e. a periodicity of $15,625$ ms.

Even though messages and ports could be organized more efficiently for this

7.3. DEMONSTRATION APPLICATION

demo (e.g. to use a single port to transport all wheel speed values instead of 4), we decided to model a more realistic layout (e.g. as if each wheel speed originated from a different speed sensor).

Sensor

The sensor consists of an USB steering wheel connected to the single-board computer Soekris net4801 that operates Debian Linux 2.6. The USB steering wheel is supported by the Linux Input Drivers project, so we can sample joystick input data from the input subsystem. Furthermore, we have implemented an UDP IP streamer that opens the joystick input device, parses the joystick events for the wheel, pedals and button events and streams them to a configurable target IP address. By using a bootable 512MB compact flash card where all required data and configuration is stored on, the Soekris single-board computer starts and operates autonomously after power-up.

User I/O

The User I/O MC consists of a LEON3 based host equipped with the I/O extension board. The host's application computer runs the Snapgear Linux 2.6 distribution. The single Ethernet interface of the host is set up to receive IP packets from the sensor (driving wheel). We have implemented an UDP IP receiver (counterpart of the sensor's streamer) that maintains a shared memory with the joystick state data. We regard the shared memory as Local I/O interface.

Further, we have developed the user I/O job to interact with other jobs of the control DAS and to use Linux process synchronization mechanisms to obtain data from the Local I/O Interface (shared memory with joystick state data).

According to the communication schedule, joystick state data is periodically sent to the ABS and Steer controller. Table 7.4 summarizes the Linking Interface (LIF).

service name	service description	ports
driving_wheel	driving wheel input from the user	angle: outgoing, 4 byte, state, 64 Hz
buttons	state of 6 user input buttons	setting: outgoing, 4 byte, state, 64 Hz
pedal_gas	gas pedal input from user	gas: outgoing, 4 byte, state, 64 Hz
pedal_brake	brake pedal input from user	brake: outgoing, 4 byte, state, 64 Hz

Table 7.4: Control DAS's LIF of User I/O

Anti-Lock Braking System (ABS) Controller

This MC consist of a Nios II based host and runs a real time operating system. The ABS controller job implements a simple ABS found in one of the driver robots of The Open Racing Car Simulation (TORCS): braking force from the brake-pedal is reduced, if one or more wheels turn considerably slower than the actual car speed (see Listing 7.1).

```
void apply_abs(uint32_t car_speed, uint32_t fr_wspeed, uint32_t
    fl_wspeed, uint32_t rr_wspeed, uint32_t rl_wspeed, uint32_t*
    break_force)
{
  float slip = 0.0f;
  if (car_speed < ABS_MINSPEED) return;
  slip += fr_wspeed * WHEEL_RADIUS;
  slip += fl_wspeed * WHEEL_RADIUS;
  slip += rr_wspeed * WHEEL_RADIUS;
  slip += rl_wspeed * WHEEL_RADIUS;
  slip = car_speed - slip/4.0f;
  if (slip > ABS_SLIP)
  {
    *break_force = *brake_force - MIN(*brake_force, (slip -
       ABS_SLIP)/ABS_RANGE);
  }
}
```

Listing 7.1: Control DAS ABS Algorithm

For practical reasons, our implementation of the ABS controller also processes acceleration input (gas pedal). The job does not require a Local I/O Interface, because it only processes data exchanged via the LIF.

LIF: `pedal_brake`, `pedal_gas`, `speed_wheel`, `speed_car`, `actuator_brake`, `actuator_gas`

Steer Controller

Similar to the ABS controller, the steer controller consists of a Nios II based host. The steer controller job processes steering user input and applies a fixed driving wheel to steering translation according to:

$$steering_{output} = steering_{input} \times 0.75$$

This job does not require a Local I/O Interface, because it only processes data exchanged via the LIF.

LIF: `actuator_steer`, `driving_wheel`

User Info

This MC is made up by a LEON3 based host equipped with the multimedia extension board. For this host, we also use the Snapgear Linux 2.6 distribution. The user info job displays data from the sensors on the LCD display.

This job does not require a Local I/O Interface, because it only processes data exchanged via the LIF.

LIF: `driving_wheel`, `speed_wheel`, `speed_car`, `pedal_gas`, `pedal_brake`

Simulation

We have set up the simulation (TORCS) on a PC notebook with Debian 2.6, RTAI extensions and a TTE-PCMCIA network interface. An RTAI application kernel module writes actuator set values received from the ABS controller via

7.3. DEMONSTRATION APPLICATION

TTE into a structured shared memory, respectively reads sensor data from the shared memory and sends it to the ABS controller. TORCS offers interfaces to extend the racing simulation with robot drivers. We have implemented such a robot driver that communicates with the RTAI application kernel module by means of the structured shared memory. For practical reasons, the robot driver also implements auto-transmission. Table 7.5 describes the LIF of the Simulation job.

service name	service description	ports
speed_wheel	wheel speed sensor output from the simulation	front_left: outgoing, 4 byte, state front_right: outgoing, 4 byte, state rear_left: outgoing, 4 byte, state rear_right: outgoing, 4 byte, state
speed_car	actual car speed measured at transmission driveshaft	speed: outgoing, 4 byte, state
actuator_steer	steering actuator	angle: outgoing, 4 byte, state
actuator_brake	wheel brake actuators	front_left: incoming, 4 byte, state front_right: incoming, 4 byte, state rear_left: incoming, 4 byte, state rear_right: incoming, 4 byte, state
actuator_gas	the car's accelerator	gas: incoming, 4 bytes, state

Table 7.5: control DAS's LIF of Simulation

7.3.3 Multimedia Distributed Application Subsystem

Within this DAS there is video data exchanged between all participating MCs. We structured the video data into single frames. Each frame is represented as a bitmap, where each pixel is described by its color. The color is encoded in 8 bit sized words and the highest resolution we want to support is 240×320 pixels. We target 24 frames per second, thus the video data bandwidth totals to 1800 Kbyte/sec that we need to transfer in a single encapsulated communication channel (ECC). All ECCs operate with a period of $\frac{1}{2}$ kHz and transport 3600 Byte sized parts of a whole frame in frame packets. A frame packet can be transferred in a single message and is made up of one header word (4 byte) that describes the position of the packet data in the actual frame.

This DAS features multiple application modes that are switched during runtime (on-the-fly reconfiguration) every 4 seconds by the Diagnostic Unit (DU). The available application modes are described in Table 7.6.

144   CHAPTER 7. PROTOTYPE IMPLEMENTATION

mode	NoC bandwidth
normal	1800 Kbyte/sec
negative	
degradation level 1	900 Kbyte/sec
degradation level 2	450 Kbyte/sec

Table 7.6: Multimedia DAS application modes

Cube

MC 7 consists of a Nios II based host and runs a real time operating system with the cube job. This job uses a simple graphics library (included in one of Altera's demo designs) that calculates the video of a spinning three dimensional cube.

There are two virtual frame buffers: one active and one inactive. The active one is constantly transferred over the NoC to potential receivers.

We render the cube in accordance with the currently active application mode into the inactive virtual frame buffer. Each time the computation of the frame is finished and after the active frame buffer has been completely transferred over the NoC at least once, the two frame buffers are swapped with each other.

service name	service description	ports
spinning_cube	rendering a spinning cube	frame_data normal mode: outgoing, 3604 byte, event negative mode: outgoing, 3604 byte, event degradation level 1: outgoing, 1804 byte, event degradation level 2: outgoing, 904 byte, event

Table 7.7: Multimedia DAS's LIF of Cube

This job does not require a Local I/O interface, because it only processes data exchanged via the Linking Interface (LIF).

Display

Both MCs, where the display jobs are deployed to, consist of LEON3 based hosts equipped with the multimedia extension board We use Snapgear Linux 2.6. for each of them. According to the application mode, actually the degradation level, the received frame data is processed differently:

normal and negative mode : the frame is rebuilt in 1:1 scale and written to the display frame buffer

degradation level 1 : the frame is rebuilt in 1:2 scale and written to the display frame buffer

degradation level 2 : the frame is rebuilt in 1:3 scale and written to the display frame buffer

The display frame buffer is accessed over the job's Local I/O interface.
LIF: `spinning_cube`

7.4 Results of the Demonstration Application

In this section we try to give an impression of what the live-action demonstration application looks like. Figure 7.16 show screenshots of the control and multimedia DASs.

Figure 7.16a depicts a screenshot of TORCS, which is run on the PC notebook. We also see in the corners, how the driver / player uses the steering wheel and acceleration and brake pedals.

Figure 7.16b shows a photography of these multimedia I/O boards (with LCD display) that implement the "Display" service of the demonstration application. This set-up also proves the feasibility of multi-casting in the TTNoC, as the same bitmaps are calculated by a single micro component and sent to the two micro components equipped with the LCD displays.

7.5 Validation of implemented Architectural Services

The demonstration application extensively uses many of the GENESYS's architectural services and therefore allows an assessment about the effectiveness of the GENESYS reference architecture template.

7.5.1 Composability

In the demonstration application we organize our application into two separate and independently operating Distributed Application Subsystems (DASs) that offer their set of functionality to the user. Each DAS is composed of multiple micro components, which is the atomic unit of abstraction (and thus also the unit of distribution and fault containment) on chip level.

We execute a single job on each micro component that solely interacts with other jobs through the well-defined Linking Interface (LIF) specification (clear separation of processing and interaction). We accomplish a considerable reduction of complexity, as we have a clean partition of the whole application and also don't need to deal with implementation details within micro components, but only with their LIF when we compose them to the complete application.

By using a service-oriented model that provides a structured view on LIFs of interacting jobs, we are able to further decrease design ramifications to a cognitively easily manageable problem: the engineer just needs to define what services a job requires to be able to provide its own services - either to other jobs or the user itself.

With respect to the demo application, the GENESYS architecture provides sufficient means to manage complexity and uphold composability.

(a) Control DAS in action

(b) Spinning cubes of multimedia DAS

Figure 7.16: Impressions of demonstration application

7.5.2 Communication in the Deterministic Network-on-Chip

The demonstration application uses periodic as well as sporadic communication. Therefore, we can draw the following conclusions.

Determinism

Determinism is established by the time-triggered communication schedule according to which all communication takes place. By architectural design the demonstration application cannot violate this feature of the GENESYS architecture: The TRM only allows valid time-triggered communication schedules and the demonstration application, like any application on a chip, must obey this rule.

Encapsulation

A conflict free time-triggered communication schedule is ensured by the TRM and guarantees temporally and spatially separated communication channels that have static end-to-end latencies and guaranteed bandwidth. During transmission, messages belonging to one communication channel cannot influence messages of any other communication channel.

The demonstration application consists of two independent subsystems that coexist on the same chip. There is a total of 38 on-chip and 11 off-chip encapsulated channels. We found no evidence that one of the subsystems has any influence on the other: message delivery and functionality remained unchanged at the subsystem under test regardless whether the other subsystem is active or not. Concerning types of communication, the demonstration application successfully uses both periodic as well as sporadic messages in various channel configurations (uni- and multicast).

7.5.3 Common Time

The GENESYS architecture proposes a common global time base to synchronize communication activities. In the demonstration application we realize this feature in the following way: a common clock domain directly implements the common time for the communication service, while different, independent local clock domains drive the micro components.

The demonstration application consists of multiple hosts that not only are different with respect to their application computer, but also require different system clock frequencies. In fact, even hosts with the same hardware (and thus same system clock) are not in the same clock domain: each of them operates autonomously its own clocks.

The demonstration application fully relies on this feature of the GENESYS architecture and the implementation supports it without any noticeable problems.

7.5.4 Reconfiguration

The current implementation supports integrated resource management with respect to NoC bandwidth (re-)allocation during runtime that we call "on-the-fly reconfiguration". The multimedia part of the demonstration application relies on this feature for switching between different bandwidths to realize degradation levels. We encountered no difficulties with this core service.

7.5.5 Off-chip Gateway

In our prototype implementation we facilitate off-chip communication by means of a Time-Triggered Ethernet (TTE) gateway. In the demonstration application, we establish multiple channels from the chip to a PC notebook with a TTE PCMCIA network adapter and vice verse via that TTE gateway. Once a TTE link is established (clients are synchronized to the rate master), the communication is stable and no message is lost.

Eight

Migration Path and Relationship to Domain-Specific Architectures

8.1 Network on Terminal Architecture (NoTA)

NoTA is a modular service-based system architecture for mobile and embedded devices. It is an open architecture with the primary goal to define a unified interface for embedded devices in order to ease the development and integration of interoperable services and devices. The development of NoTA is driven by an open architecture initiative, initially started at Nokia Research Center in 2003, with the aim to provide a solution that can be used throughout the industry, academia and developer community. Since then several releases of interconnect implementations have been developed and are now open to the public. These results are currently used in industrial product implementations.

NoTA does not define services for any specific domain or products, but provides a service-oriented framework for the design of embedded applications, which is driven by end-user requirements [43]. NoTA identifies devices that consist of service nodes and application nodes. Devices communicate via the so called Device Interconnect Protocol (DIP). The DIP offers two communication modes: message-based communication and streaming communication. The message-based communication is bi-directional and used by application nodes to exert control over service nodes. The streaming communication is unidirectional and enables the transfer of data (e.g., multimedia data).

8.1.1 System Structuring

NoTA provides three distinct abstraction levels for system design, denoted as functional architecture, logical architecture, and implementation architecture [75]: The functional architecture describes the functional aspects of the system by means of application nodes (AN) and services nodes (SN) interconnected by the DIP. Application nodes interact with the user of the system and make use of the services provided by the SNs. Service nodes provide their services to ANs and utilize the services of other SNs to fulfill their specified service. Services provided by ANs and SNs are solely exploited via service interfaces. These interfaces are described by the Service Interface Specifica-

CHAPTER 8. MIGRATION PATH AND RELATIONSHIP TO DOMAIN-SPECIFIC ARCHITECTURES

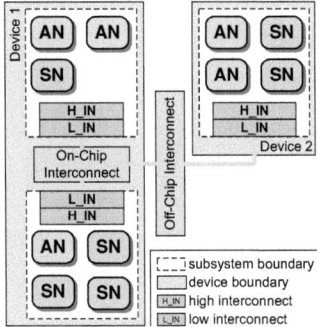

Figure 8.1: NoTA System Structure

tion (SIS), which defines the service syntax, the behavior (time-free via finite state machines) and bounds for non functional properties such as latencies, bandwidth and energy consumption [52].

The logical architecture describes the grouping of ANs and SNs to subsystems. Besides this logical viewpoint, subsystems also exhibit a physical viewpoint: All resources required for implementing the ANs and SNs are part of the hosting subsystem and are not shared with other subsystems. Hence, services of different subsystems can access shared resources solely via the service interface. Thus, the partitioning of services into subsystems is a first important design decision influencing system performance versus service independency and encapsulation.

The implementation architecture describes the physical implementation of the system. At this viewpoint, the conceptual element provided by NoTA is a device. A device is a physical entity that provides resources like processors, buses, memories, and peripherals, which can host one or more subsystems. An exemplary implementation architecture of a NoTA system is depicted in Figure 8.1.

8.1.2 Device Interconnect Protocol

The DIP represents the communication infrastructure of a NoTA system. The DIP consists of two protocol layers - the Low Interconnect (L_IN) and the High Interconnect (H_IN) (cf. Figure 8.1). Essentially, the L_IN connects subsystems by mapping the communication requests of services to the actual physical communication infrastructure. It provides uniform socket-based communication mechanisms. The L_IN is further responsible for the discovery of the physical entities that are the endpoints for the communication activities. For providing a uniform interface to the H_IN independent from the underlying physical transport protocol, the L_IN is split into two layers. While the higher layer provides stable services that are independent from the transport protocol, the services of the lower layer are tailored to the characteristics of a particular

8.1. NETWORK ON TERMINAL ARCHITECTURE (NOTA)

physical interface.

The main purpose of the H_IN is the registration, discovery, and activation/deactivation of services. Service registration and discovery is managed by one dedicated H_IN - denoted *HManager*. A new service is registered at the HManager with its service ID and its interconnect address, i.e. the information on which device and subsystem the particular service is located. For service discovery, a query containing the service ID is sent to the HManager, which resolves the according interconnect address. Service IDs are allocated based on a service ontology by a dedicated service node, the Service Level Resource Manager [48].

The DIP is nearly independent of a specific communication technology. Hence, it is possible to replace an off-chip network with an on-chip network with low overhead, e.g., when a chip is replaced by an IP core due to technological advancements. In such a case, the transport protocol specific part of the L_IN needs to be adapted, whereas the remaining parts of the DIP, in particular the interface towards the application and service nodes, remain unaffected.

8.1.3 Commonalities and Contrasts of NoTA and GENESYS

Both architectures, NoTA and GENESYS, are driven by very similar objectives: to tackle the ongoing digital convergence in modern embedded systems and the resultant challenges. This section elaborates on similarities of both architectures, but also points out the major differences.

Commonalities

Service Orientation: Both architectures focus on the identification and specification of services. In terms of GENESYS, this is the identification of cohesive subsystems, the DASs, and their further decomposition into jobs, each of which is providing a well-defined application service. In NoTA the system's functionality is described by means of service nodes and application nodes, which are logically grouped to subsystems. Furthermore, system design is concerned with a reasonable allocation of those functional entities onto physical hardware entities. In NoTA the term device is used to denote a component, i.e., the entity that represents the integration of hardware and software to implement a dedicated part of the overall system's functionality. Depending on the level of integration, the terms used in GENESYS are IP cores, chips, and devices.

Component-Based Design: Modularity, reuse, and insensitivity to technological changes are major foci of both architectures. For this purpose, both architectures push the construction of components with explicitly defined interfaces. A component is a self-contained subsystem that can be independently developed and used as a building block in the design of a larger system. It is a replaceable part of a system that encapsulates the implementation. This encapsulation of functionality facilitates the evolvability of the system: For instance, due to the explicit interface specification, components can be exchanged without the need to alter any interacting components as long as the component's behavior at its interfaces remains stable.

Interface Specification: To enable component-based design and to achieve interoperability between components, interface specifications need to precisely describe the component's behavior in the value domain and the temporal domain. This includes functional and non functional properties (e.g., dependability properties) as well as syntactic properties of the exchanged information. Furthermore, a semantic specification is required to decide on the interoperability of different component implementations.

In GENESYS components are interconnected via LIFs. A precise LIF specification includes input and output assertions, a specification of syntactic, temporal and dependability properties, semantic specification, and a periodic ground state (i.e., the interface state at the restart instant of a component). The interface specification in NoTA, denoted Service Interface Specification (SiS), is split in two parts [52]: The control interface describes the input and output messages sent or received by a service as well as the externally observable states of the service. The data interface comprises a list of data types each service supports for communicating with other services as well as a description of non functional properties for the data transfer between services.

Stable Platform Services: Both architectures define a stable set of platform services that can be utilized for the development of applications. The interface to these services is independent from the actual underlying implementation technology. This minimizes the migration effort of already implemented applications to new technologies. The platform services that are available in every instantiation of the architecture are denoted core services in GENESYS. They form the stable waist of the architecture and hide changes of the implementation technology from the application. Among the core services are basic communication services, diagnostic services, security services, and resource management services. NoTA provides a stable API to ANs and SNs to access the services provided by the DIP (e.g., service registration and discovery). The H_IN is completely independent from the underlying communication technology; thus, the application would be unaffected from technology changes.

Since particular applications (e.g., legacy software) would require additional functionality that exceeds the capabilities of the platform services, both architectures provide means for extensibility: The GENESYS waistline architecture serves exactly for this reason. While the set of core services remains stable, optional services can be used to extend the architecture and provide higher-level services to an application developer. Similarly, the basic services provided by NoTA can be extended using proxy layers upon the H_IN, which enable the provision of higher-level services (e.g., the Khronos protocol stack) upon the NoTA communication infrastructure.

Differences

Architecture Extent and Focus: NoTA is a framework for the development and integration of applications, mainly targeted to the needs of the consumer applications industry. It provides well-specified interfaces and a standardized interconnect protocol in order to facilitate the integra-

8.1. NETWORK ON TERMINAL ARCHITECTURE (NOTA)

tion of independently developed services. The GENESYS architecture goes beyond this core functionality. It defines architectural principles; each instantiation of the GENESYS architecture needs to adhere to, i.e., a guideline how to develop a concrete instantiation of the architecture. In addition, it describes a concrete set of services: core services (e.g., communication services, diagnostic services) and optional services (e.g., security services).

Guarantees for Architectural Properties: It is the intention of NoTA to provide an interface to the applications that abstracts completely from the implementation technology, i.e., from the transport layer that is accessed by the L_IN to connect different components. Although functional and non-functional properties of component interactions are included in the SiS (e.g., communication latency, energy efficiency), it is hard to guarantee those properties, since they very much depend on the actual implementation of the underlying platform. For instance, if Ethernet is used for data transport, a maximum transmission latency between components A and B cannot be guaranteed in case a (perhaps faulty) component C monopolizes the communication link to component B.

Also GENESYS abstracts from the concrete implementation technology. However, the architectural style enforces characteristics of the used platform that ensure that important properties of the architecture can be guaranteed. For instance, the periodic message transport service ensures the timely transport of messages with respect to guaranteed bandwidth, transmission latency and latency jitter. Also, fault isolation between components is provided by encapsulation mechanisms of the GENESYS architecture. Thus, only platforms that ensure those properties are suitable technologies for GENESYS.

Multiple Integration Levels: For the design and integration of embedded applications with NoTA a single level of abstraction is used: Multiple devices, each of which is hosting one or more subsystems, are integrated via the DIP. The internal physical structure of a device is only of minimal relevance for NoTA: The device is required to provide adequate resources for the implementation of the hosted subsystem(s) and if multiple subsystems are located on a single device, the only way subsystems can interact is via the service interfaces. So NoTA does not explicitly state at which level the integration of ANs and SNs takes place, i.e., a NoTA application can be implemented on a single chip, on multiple chips, or on a set of physical devices.

GENESYS rigorously distinguishes multiple integration levels. At each integration level the only way components can interact is via the LIFs of the component. At the system level devices are integrated, which are interconnected by an inter-device LIF. If the internal structure of the devices is of relevance for the system designer, a device is decomposed into a set of chips, interacting via inter-chip LIFs. If relevant, chips are further decomposed into a set of IP cores interacting via inter IP core LIFs. The interface specification is identical at each integration level. However, the functional and non-functional properties of the LIFs may differ at the individual integration levels depending on the deployed communication infrastructure.

8.1.4 Instantiation of NoTA as Middleware on top of GENESYS

The similarities between NoTA and GENESYS, as discovered in the previous section, raise the question, whether it might be possible to combine the benefits of both architecture and instantiate NoTA as optional service on top of the GENESYS architecture. It is the purpose of this section to provide a theoretical evaluation of this matter.

Compatibility in System Structure

The first question to be answered is, whether the way to structure systems in both architectures matches. In NoTA, applications are described in terms of service nodes (SNs) and application nodes (ANs), which interact via strictly defined interfaces. The counterparts hereto are jobs in the GENESYS terminology.

In NoTA, subsystems are used to group SNs and ANs that belong together to larger functional units. Subsystems in the terminology of NoTA are not only logical constructs, but also represent a physical entity that provides adequate resources to implement the hosted services. Hence, subsystems also consist of physical interfaces to the physical interconnect. If interacting subsystems are located on the same device, this interface might connect the subsystem to an intra-device interconnect, whereas subsystems located on different devices communicate via an inter-device interconnect. The GENESYS architecture provides the concept of DASs to perform a logical integration of multiple jobs to a single logical entity. A direct equivalent to the concept of subsystems is not provided, since the physical structuring of a system depends on the integration level in GENESYS: At the chip-level, the GENESYS architectural styles enforces a strict one-to-one mapping of jobs to IP cores. Thus, multiple jobs that form a logical unit and require spatial proximity for an efficient implementation due to their interaction patterns are implemented as IP cores on the same chip. This corresponds to the representation of NoTA subsystems.

In order to implement the physical interface of a NoTA subsystem, a dedicated gateway IP core can be used in the GENESYS architecture to interconnect each chip to a chip-external network. The next integration level in GENESYS, the device level, provides the encapsulation of several chips into one device. This is analog to the integration of multiple NoTA subsystems into a single NoTA device. The physical interconnection of NoTA devices to the overall system is represented by the system level in GENESYS.

NoTA on top of GENESYS

The GENESYS architecture is devised by experts from industry, research institutes, and academia of many different domains to ensure that important requirements of all targeted domains are covered in the resulting architecture template. That is, the GENESYS architecture comprises know-how and experience of different fields of application, to facilitate its deployment across domain boundaries. In particular with respect to temporal guarantees for communication and encapsulation of applications, the GENESYS architecture could improve the existing platforms for consumer applications, since those properties

8.1. NETWORK ON TERMINAL ARCHITECTURE (NOTA)

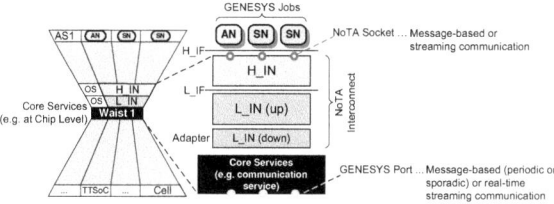

Figure 8.2: Placing NoTA as Optional Service in the GENESYS Waistline Architecture

are key requirements for component-oriented design, component integration, and reuse.

To broaden the applicability of the GENESYS architecture for consumer applications, the provision of the NoTA application programming interface as optional service on top of the GENESYS core services would be highly advantageous. This could ease the change for consumer applications from their specialized hardware platforms towards GENESYS and would increase the acceptance of the GENESYS architecture in this high-volume domain.

To facilitate this instantiation, mainly the DIP of NoTA needs to be realized as optional service for GENESYS. Firstly, the DIP provides a stable interface to the applications; secondly, parts of the lower layer of the DIP are used to adapt the interconnect implementation to the actual transport protocol. The examples described in [47, 65] use such adapters to stack the DIP on top of the MIPI UniPro protocol. Likewise it is reasonable to build the DIP as an optional service on top of the GENESYS core services and to develop an adapter that connects the NoTA interconnect to the core communication services of GENESYS.

The GENESYS architecture seems to be well-suited as an implementation platform for NoTA: The DIP provides message-based communication and streaming communication. Both types of communication are also natively provided by GENESYS (via periodic or sporadic message based communication as well as real-time streaming). The example outlined in Figure 8.2 depicts a GENESYS system at the chip level using, e.g., the TTSoC architecture [40] as platform to provide the core services at this level. The main extensions of NoTA compared to the GENESYS core services are service registration/discovery and NoTA-specific resource management. In NoTA, the so-called resource management service node (RMSN), is used to implement this functionality. The RMSN is realized as a dedicated node in one subsystem. The same strategy can be followed when implementing NoTA as optional service for GENESYS, i.e., to use a dedicated job for implementing the functionality of the RMSN.

8.1.5 Résumé

The development of NoTA and GENESYS is inspired by very similar challenges. For solving those challenges many commonalities between both architectures can be found. The main similarity is the component-orientation and that both architectures take the achievement of composability and interoperability as an objective with top priority. As a consequence, both architectures are based on service specifications which include rigorous specifications of interfaces.

In contrast to GENESYS, NoTA is tailored to applications of the consumer domain. Therefore, the NoTA framework is not intended to provide services for a broad range of applications across different domains. Hence, the design of NoTA focuses on the provision of a minimal set of services that is required to facilitate the integration of applications provided by various parties.

Due to the similarities of both architectures and their non-contradicting architectural concepts, it seems possible to combine both concepts by realizing the NoTA interconnect as optional service on top of the GENESYS core services. This could beneficially influence both architectures: GENESYS by taking advance of a mature architecture from the consumer applications domain which may strengthen the position of GENESYS in this domain. NoTA by using a platform that is designed to provide fault-tolerance and resilience against transients [59] in order to improve the reliability of the products in the consumer domain. Given that a cost-efficient instantiation of the GENESYS architecture is available, the use of GENESYS as platform for the implementation of NoTA-based consumer applications could result in a substantial qualitative improvement of products of this domain.

8.2 Integrated Modular Avionics (IMA)

ARINC standard 651 [1] is known as IMA and addresses the design of architectures aimed at the separate implementation and integration of avionic applications. IMA represents an integrated system architecture that focuses on: (i) the use of shared resources for reducing unwanted resource duplication to a minimum for lowering the acquisition costs, weight, and volume of avionics equipment, (ii) the support of modular interchangeable hardware components that allow a high volume production, which will positively affect the production costs, and (iii) the introduction of improved diagnostic techniques to improve the scheduling of maintenance actions and reduce and eliminate the unconfirmed removal of Line Replaceable Units (LRUs) [66]. In the Boeing 787 Dreamliner, e.g., the use of the IMA approach enables a weight reduction of about 900 kg compared to previous aircrafts [67].

8.2.1 Avionics System Structure

In IMA the functionality of the avionics application is provided by multiple integrated cabinets which are interconnected by the global data bus. (cf. Figure 8.3). The functionality provided by one integrated cabinet is typically larger than the functionality of a single federated LRU, but smaller than the sum of all LRUs the cabinet replaces [27].

For example the Airplane Information Management System (AIMS) for the Boeing 777, which is one of the first systems that implements IMA concepts, replaces the conventional LRUs by two integrated cabinets [14]. The global data bus in the AIMS is realized by the ARINC 629 multi-transmitter communication bus [ARINC 1991b]. However, systems designed according to IMA are not restricted to particular communication networks. In the Airbus A380,

8.2. INTEGRATED MODULAR AVIONICS (IMA)

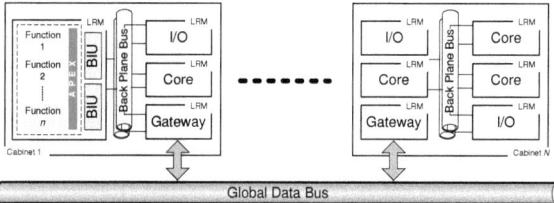

Figure 8.3: IMA Avionics Architecture

e.g., Avionics Full-Duplex Switched Ethernet (AFDX), an ARINC 664 standard network [5], is deployed for the interconnection of the integrated modules [11].

A cabinet is internally further structured into multiple Line Replaceable Modules (LRMs), which provide the necessary computational resources for performing the required application functionality. LRMs in an IMA platform can be classified into three categories [19] (cf. Figure 8.3):

Core module: Core modules are responsible for the execution of the applications. Typically, a single core module hosts multiple applications, which reside in dedicated encapsulated partitions ensuring that the individual applications do not interfere with each other.

I/O module: System components that are not part of the cabinet or not connected to the global data bus are usually connected by point-to-point communication protocols like ARINC 429 [4] to the I/O modules of the cabinet. These I/O modules provide the functionality to perform input/output operations with system components.

Gateway module: The gateway module is a specific LRM that handles the communication between the individual cabinets over the global data bus.

Considering the example presented above: for providing the functionality of Boeing 777's AIMS (e.g., flight management, display control, communication management, etc) each cabinet of the AIMS comprises 10 active LRMs and three spare LRMs for future functionality [55].

The interconnection of the LRMs within a single cabinet is established by a backplane bus - a fault-tolerant bus using a Time Division Multiple Access (TDMA) scheme for bus arbitration. The backplane bus is specified in the ARINC standard 659 [2]. A commercial implementation of this standard is Honeywell's SAFEbus [27], which is deployed, e.g., in the AIMS of the Boeing 777. The SAFEbus backplane bus is accessed by an LRM via a so-called Bus Interface Unit (BIU). All transmission or reception operations of the BIU are a priori scheduled and stored in a memory table within the LRM that is inaccessible by the functions of the cabinet. This way, a faulty function is prevented to effect the timing behavior of the backplane bus by changing the LRM's configuration [27].

CHAPTER 8. MIGRATION PATH AND RELATIONSHIP TO DOMAIN-SPECIFIC ARCHITECTURES

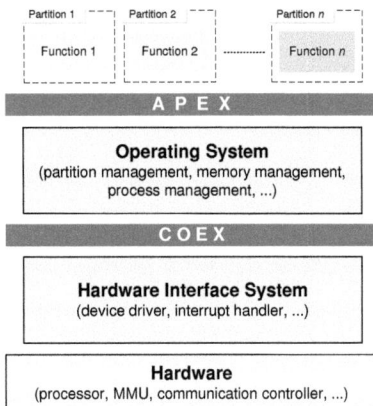

Figure 8.4: APEX Avionics Software Structure

8.2.2 Avionics Software Execution Environment

The Avionics Application Software Standard Interface specified in the ARINC 653 standard [6] defines the services of the avionics software environment, which serve as the basis for avionics function integration. This standard interface, which is known as APEX, provides services for partition management, process management, memory management, time management, inter-partition communication, intra-partition communication, and diagnosis:

Partition Management: For the integration of multiple avionic functions on a single LRM, partition management establishes spatial and temporal partitioning [70] for the individual functions. Therefore, each function is executed in a single partition. For temporal partitioning, the partition management performs a cyclic scheduling with fixed priorities. Each partition has assigned two constant parameters - period and duration - that specify the amount of time at which the partition has exclusive access to the LRM's resources (e.g., processing resources) [9]. In order to protect the memory of partitions and to avoid interference in the temporal domain (e.g., through a task overrunning its deadline or blocking a shared resource), APEX demands sufficient processing, I/O and memory resources from the used processor. Furthermore, APEX requires time resources, atomic operations, and mechanisms for transferring control to the operating system, if a partition attempts to perform an invalid operation.

Memory Management: For spatial partitioning, each partition has assigned a constant (defined at design time) memory area that can be exploited by its hosted function. Any memory access violating these boundaries is prohibited by a Memory Management Unit (MMU).

8.2. INTEGRATED MODULAR AVIONICS (IMA)

Process Management: Each partition comprises one or more processes that implement its avionic function. All processes share the resources of a single partition. With respect to other partitions, the processes are executed concurrently. Based on the attributes of a process (e.g., a given period for a periodic process, the process's deadline, and the priority of the process [9]), the process management is responsible for scheduling the processes within a partition. Tasks within partitions can employ also intra-partition communication mechanisms to avoid the runtime overhead of the inter-partition communication. Intra-partition communication mechanisms include buffers, blackboards, semaphores, and events.

Time Management: Time management in APEX provides system calls for the activation (release) of periodic and aperiodic processes. Aperiodic processes are characterized by the fact, that the future instants of activation are not known a priori (e.g., aperiodic processes could be triggered after the occurrence of a specific event like the reception of a message). For example, LynxOS-178 [53], a real-time operating system that establishes the APEX interface to its applications, provides the system calls TIMED_WAIT and PERIODIC_WAIT for time management.

Communication: APEX supports inter-partition and intra-partition communication services. Inter-partition communication is realized via message passing over physical channels and logical ports. Logical ports represent the communication endpoints within the partition. Multiple ports can be mapped onto a single physical channel. For inter-partition communication, two variants of message passing are defined in APEX: Using sampling ports, the arrival of a new message overwrites the previous contents of the port, i.e., the port is realized by a single message buffer. Queuing ports, on the other hand, provide a message queue where incoming messages are stored in First-In/First-Out (FIFO) order. In APEX back pressure flow control is used to handle full message queues. For intra-partition communication, standard inter-process communication mechanisms like shared memory and semaphores can be exploited.

Diagnosis: For the support of diagnosis, the ARINC standard 653 defines the concept of a health monitor, which is responsible for monitoring faults and failures of the hardware, the operating system, and the application. The purpose of the health monitor is to help on isolating faults and preventing the propagation of failures. The response to a fault, i.e., the measures triggered by the health monitor after fault detection, can range from logging of the occurrence of faults, over responses at partition level like the restart of a partition, to a response on the LRM level like reset or shutdown of an entire LRM [64].

In order to provide the above services for the application software, APEX employs the core software within an LRM. The core software consists of the O/S kernel and system-specific functions, while the application software comprises application partitions and system partitions:

- Application partitions execute software implementing application functionality. For error containment reasons, application partitions may only use ARINC 653 calls to interface the hardware and communication system.

- System partitions require interfaces outside of APEX services. System partitions are specific to the core software implementation.

- The O/S kernel provides the services defined by the APEX specification.

- System-specific functions implement device drivers, diagnostic, and maintenance functions.

As depicted in Figure 8.4, the APEX is located between application software and operating system. The operating system itself interfaces the underlying hardware via a standardized interface called COre EXecutive (COEX). Together with the hardware interface system (cf. Figure 8.4), it is the purpose of the COEX to provide a uniform interface for accessing different implementations of the LRM to the operating system. This facilitates the portability of the operating system. Operating systems that establish the APEX interface are, e.g., LynxOS 178 [53] or VxWorks 653 Edition [64].

8.2.3 Realization of IMA on top of a GENESYS Chip

We elaborate in this section how the structure of a typical avionic system based on IMA as depicted in Figure 8.3 can be mapped onto a system based on the GENESYS architecture. An outline of the realization of an IMA system on top of a GENESYS chip is shown in Figure 8.5.

The depicted mapping addresses all three integration levels of GENESYS: the chip level, device level, and the system level. At the chip level, each chip consists of a set of IP cores that are interconnected by a deterministic on-chip network. Similarly to the roles of LRMs within cabinets in IMA, we distinguish three different roles for IP cores within a chip: IP cores providing services that correspond to avionic functions executed in a single partition in the IMA system structure, IP cores establishing access to I/O modules via local interfaces, and IP cores realizing gateway functionality for connecting a chip to chip external networks, i.e., the backplane bus or the global data bus.

At the device level, several chips are integrated via a backplane bus (e.g., SAFEbus or TTP) to form a device. For this purpose, each chip requires a gateway IP core to the chip external network. The role of a single device in this system model can be compared to the role of a cabinet in IMA. Each of these devices provides a gateway to a device external network such as AFDX. This gateway is provided either as an IP core within one of the integrated chips (as depicted in Figure 8.5) or as a dedicated chip that serves solely for the exchange of data between the backplane bus and the global data bus.

Establishment of Partitions

One of the central services of every operating system that is deployed in avionic systems based on IMA is the provision and management of partitions that allow for the non-interfering execution of multiple avionic functions within a single LRM. Due to the inherent criticality of this service, thorough certification of partition management is required.

8.2. INTEGRATED MODULAR AVIONICS (IMA)

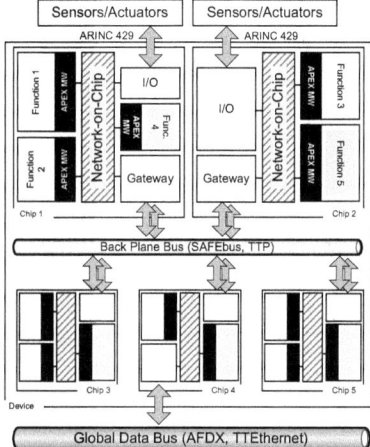

Figure 8.5: Mapping of IMA to GENESYS

When realizing IMA on top of GENESYS, the stringent requirement of a partition management support for the deployed operating systems is removed: The integration of avionic functions is not realized within a single shared CPU but on the basis of IP cores within a chip. Thus, each avionic function is assigned a dedicated IP core providing the resources required for the execution of the avionic function (e.g., computational resources such as soft-core CPU and on-chip memory). Similar to the structure of cabinets in IMA, the access to I/O modules is controlled by dedicated IP cores with local interfaces to the chip's environment.

The only way an avionic function hosted within an IP core can interact with other IP cores is via the exchange of messages over the deterministic NoC. This way, an avionic function can interfere with other avionic functions only by the dissemination of faulty messages. However, GENESYS provides hardware mechanisms to ensure spatial and temporal partitioning between IP cores. That is, even in the case of faulty software within an IP core, the integrity of information exchanged between any other two IP cores and the guaranteed availability of communication and computational resources (e.g., time of availability, duration or jitter of availability) to other IP cores cannot be affected. Thus, in GENESYS an IP core represents a Fault Containment Region (FCR) (due to the physical proximity of IP cores on a chip, the fault containment coverage with respect to hardware faults will be lower than the fault containment coverage with respect to design faults).

Since an IP core forms an FCR, errors can propagate to the outside of an IP core only by erroneous messages. Error propagation can be avoided, if erroneous messages are detected at the boundaries of an IP core by an independent FCR.

Realization of APEX Services

Besides partition management, APEX provides further services to enable the development and integration of multiple avionic functions within a single LRM. In order to facilitate the transition from classical IMA-based systems to systems having a GENESYS Multiprocessor System-on-a-Chip (MPSoC) as platform, the APEX interface for application development needs to be provided as an optional service within each IP core (cf. Figure 8.5). This middleware layer is in charge of providing memory management, process management, time management, communication services, and diagnosis services. The realization of many of those functionalities benefits from the architectural services provided by the GENESYS MPSoC:

Memory Management: Each IP core provides a certain amount of memory to its hosted avionic function. The protection of this memory from illegal access from other avionic functions is guaranteed by design: Avionic functions are solely empowered to interact via the exchange of messages via their LIFs. There are no software or hardware means to directly access the memory of other IP cores. Technological or economical reasons limit the amount of memory within an IP core. If the memory consumption of an avionic function exceeds the amount of memory provided by the hosting IP core, chip-external memory can be provided. The access to this memory region is controlled by a dedicated IP core, similar to the access to chip external I/O devices. This dedicated memory management IP core has to take care of access violations of memory regions allocated to an IP core.

Process Management: At the chip level, one of the major design drivers of GENESYS is to support the integration of independently developed IP cores on the basis of their LIF specifications. To simplify this composition from the point of view of the system integrator, the LIF specification abstracts from the internals of IP cores. Hence, the core services of GENESYS do not directly provide mechanisms for process management and inter-process communication. This functionality has to be provided by the APEX middleware within the IP core.

Time Management: With this service, APEX enables the timed activation (and release) of processes within partitions. The common time service of the GENESYS MPSoC provides a foundation for the implementation of this functionality within the APEX middleware: The common time service provides to each IP core a counter value that is globally synchronized (internally and externally). With this counter value, the temporal coordination of processes within a single avionic function but also the temporal coordination of avionic functions within and across chip boundaries is supported.

Communication: Using the GENESYS architecture as underlying platform for the realization of IMA, inter-partition communication is mapped to inter IP core communication using the deterministic NoC. APEX defines two types of inter-partition communication, both are natively supported by the communication modes of the NoC: The periodic message transport service is optimized for the transport of state information from one sender

8.2. INTEGRATED MODULAR AVIONICS (IMA)

port of an IP core to a set of receiver ports at destination IP cores. At each receiver port, the previous content of the message is replaced upon the reception of a new message. This communication paradigm corresponds to the use of sampling ports in APEX. The realization of APEX queuing ports is supported by the sporadic message transport service of GENESYS. Using this service, the sender places the message in an outgoing message queue. Under consideration of temporal constraints specified for the given communication channel (e.g., bandwidth, maximum latency) the message is transported to the receiving IP cores and placed in incoming message queues. As explained for process management, to define services for the internals of an IP core is not the focus of the GENESYS architecture; thus, the GENESYS architecture does not provide mechanisms that correspond to the intra-partition communication of APEX. This functionality has to be provided by an APEX middleware.

Diagnosis: The GENESYS supports a dedicated core service that supports the implementation of a health monitor service as specified in the ARINC standard 653. The network management and diagnosis service provides a coherent global view of the operational state of all IP cores. It provides a membership vector as feedback to the APEX middleware or the avionic functions, which performs a binary classification (correct or faulty) of the IP cores on the chip. In combination with the reconfiguration core service, the information about the operational state of IP cores can be exploited to trigger the restart of IP cores in order to recover from transient faults.

Connection to Chip-External Avionic Networks

A typical avionic system is connected to several networks: the backplane bus within cabinets, the global data bus between cabinets and peripheral buses to perform I/O operations. An attempt to establish a standardized gateway for data exchange among the different networks is the ARINC 655 [3] standard of the Remote Data Concentrator (RDC). Besides the standardization of physical properties and electrical signals (at least ARINC 629 and ARINC 429 interfaces, digital and analog inputs/outputs), an RDC shall support the following functionalities in order to support interoperability among different aircraft suppliers:

- partitioning among application / data of different criticality
- universality (not designed with respect to a dedicated application)
- reconfigurable (e.g. calibration of data inputs), monitoring of higher protocols
- protocol conversion
- inspection of correct software loaded on RDC
- built-in test

Among the most important characteristics of an RDC is the support for partitioning among applications, i.e. to protect disseminated data or memory regions of diverse application, in particular if they belong to different criticality levels. The component-oriented design of the GENESYS architectural style in combination with the message-based communication infrastructure facilitates the fulfillment of this requirement for avionic gateways: Firstly, different applications are hosted on different IP cores. As explained before, partitioning among applications is established per se. Secondly, communication is realized in GENESYS by passing a unidirectional message from one sender port to one or more receiver ports at the components. By ensuring at the gateway that each message receive port has assigned its distinct memory region (either a distinct queue for the reception of event messages or a buffer with update-in-place semantics for state messages), the data integrity can be preserved.

As listed above, an RDC shall be implemented independent of any avionics function and shall provide the means for being adapted to particular usage scenarios. For example an RDC shall transform a well-defined set of information chunks transmitted over the backplane bus (e.g., SAFEbus messages) to messages for the global data bus (e.g., ARINC 629 messages). This requires the selective reception of messages and property transformation. The concept of gateways in the GENESYS architecture fit very well to those requirements of an RDC: The gateway component is (at the chip level) an IP core that provides an interface to the on-chip network as well as an interface to an off-chip network (e.g., SAFEbus, AFDX, etc). The configurable communication infrastructure of GENESYS enables the selective reception of multicast messages at the gateway without the need to modify the sending component. Since, a gateway is a dedicated IP core and not add-on functionality of a particular application, once implemented gateway functionality can be reused on different chips and shared by multiple applications.

In order to guarantee the correctness of an RDC the ARINC standard 655 demands mechanisms to inspect the software loaded on the RDC as well as built-in test routines to check physical interfaces and memory regions. The reference architecture template of GENESYS describes optional services that help in the development of such mechanisms. Among the security services of GENESYS is the Secure Boot service, which verifies the integrity of an application that should be executed on an IP core. In addition, the robustness services of GENESYS include optional services for detection and correction of memory bit errors.

8.3 Automotive Open System Architecture (AUTOSAR)

AUTOSAR [25] is an attempt to exploit the benefits of integrated system architectures in the automotive domain. It is a joint initiative of several automotive, semiconductor, and software companies. According to [25], the motivations behind this standardization initiative in the automotive domain are:

- Management of E/E complexity associated with growth in functional scope
- Flexibility for product modification, upgrade and update
- Scalability of solutions within and across product lines

8.3. AUTOMOTIVE OPEN SYSTEM ARCHITECTURE (AUTOSAR)

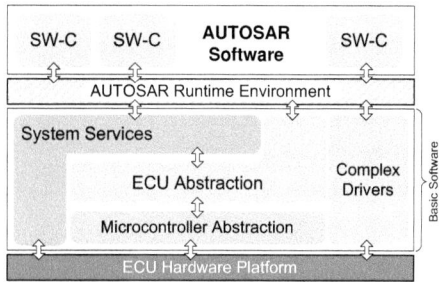

Figure 8.6: AUTOSAR Software Layers

- Improved quality and reliability of E/E systems in order to provide a higher level of abstraction

The main objective of AUTOSAR is to facilitate the reuse of AUTOSAR Software Components (SWCs). An AUTOSAR SW-C encapsulates an application which runs on the AUTOSAR infrastructure – between different vehicle platforms, Original Equipment Manufacturers (OEMs), and suppliers [72].

Furthermore, it is envisioned to improve software updates and upgrades over the entire vehicle lifetime [25]. For these purposes, AUTOSAR defines a standardized software architecture for each Electronic Control Unit (ECU) in an automotive system that provides a technology independent, i.e., independent from the ECU hardware and the underlying micro controller, infrastructure for SW-Cs. On one hand, this enables the decoupling between application development and development of the hardware platform of automotive systems. On the other hand, this will support the decoupling between the life-cycles of hardware and software [72].

8.3.1 AUTOSAR ECU Software Architecture

The structure of the AUTOSAR ECU architecture is schematically depicted in Figure 8.6. The software architecture of an ECU in AUTOSAR is vertically structured into Basic Software, the AUTOSAR Run Time Environment (RTE), and AUTOSAR software.

The Basic Software is a standardized software layer in each ECU that provides services to the SW-Cs, which are necessary to realize the actual functionality. Examples for those services are memory access, access to the communication system, operating system functionalities, etc. Basic Software itself does not provide any application specific services. It contains standardized, i.e., ECU-independent components, like System Services and Microcontroller Abstraction, as well as, ECU specific components like ECU Abstraction, and Complex Drivers [25].

Microcontroller Abstraction: The Microcontroller Abstraction decouples higher layers of the Basic Software from microcontroller internals. This layer contains microcontroller specific drivers like Input/Output (I/O) drivers, memory drivers, and Analog Digital Converter (ADC) drivers. It represents the lowest layer of the AUTOSAR Basic Software.

ECU Abstraction: The purpose of the ECU Abstraction layer is to hide the upper layers from the layout of the ECU, i.e., to provide an Application Programming Interface (API) to access the ECU's peripherals, regardless whether they are micro controller internal or external devices. Since it is built on top of the Microcontroller Abstraction, the implementation of the ECU Abstraction is microcontroller independent.

System Services: The System Services represent the highest layer of Basic Software and are used from the layers above the Basic Software to abstract from ECU and micro controller hardware. The System Services include operating system services, vehicle network communication services, memory management services, diagnostic services, and ECU state management. In addition, the System Services include basic library functions that can be exploited from ECU Abstraction, Microcontroller Abstraction, and Complex Drivers to implement their functionality (e.g., watchdog library).

Complex Drivers: The concept of Complex Drivers is introduced to handle complex sensors and actuators with strong real-time requirements or electromechanical hardware requirements, which cannot be directly mapped to a single layer of the AUTOSAR Basic Software. The implementation of a Complex Driver is highly dependent on the micro controller and the ECU hardware. However, to an upper layer – the AUTOSAR Run Time Environment (RTE) – Complex Drivers provide a standardized AUTOSAR interface.

Between the Basic Software and the application software resides the AUTOSAR RTE. The purpose of the RTE is to provide a uniform environment to all SWCs, i.e., to abstract from any implementation details of the Basic Software and from hardware aspects [24]. The RTE can be seen as the runtime representation of the Virtual Function Bus (VFB) on a specific ECU.

The VFB provides standardized communication services to the application software, which are defined independently whether the communication manifests after the integration of the system in inter-ECU or intra-ECU information exchange [25]. This way, the VFB decouples the application from the system infrastructure [72].

An application in AUTOSAR consists of interconnected AUTOSAR SW-Cs. SW-Cs are located in the ECU's application layer in the AUTOSAR stack. By introducing the VFB and standardized interfaces, the implementation of such a SW-C is independent from the ECU and the underlying micro controller. In addition, the VFB realizes location independence for the implementation of SW-C, i.e., the implementation of a SW-C has not to be aware of its physical location and the physical location of other SW-Cs.

An AUTOSAR SW-C is an atomic component, which means that each instantiation of a SW-C is allocated to exactly one ECU and cannot be distributed over several ECUs. In general, the implementation of an AUTOSAR SW-C is independent from the infrastructure in terms of the type of the micro

8.3. AUTOMOTIVE OPEN SYSTEM ARCHITECTURE (AUTOSAR)

controller and the ECU the SW-C is located on (due to the Microcontroller Abstraction layer and the ECU Abstraction layer of the Basic Software). In addition, it is in general also independent from the physical location of the SW-C, because of the abstraction provided by the VFB. However, in typical automotive applications there exist SW-Cs which are designed for a specific sensor or actuator (e.g., a car velocity sensor). By the use of a specialized class of SW-Cs – the Sensor/Actuator Software Components – such dependencies can be expressed within the AUTOSAR standard.

8.3.2 Compatibility of AUTOSAR Virtual Function Bus (VFB) and GENESYS

When designing an automotive application according to AUTOSAR, the VFB provides the means for interconnecting the individual components (software components) and enable their interaction – among each other and with the environment (i.e., via sensors and actuators). The VFB is a logical construct that defines the concepts for application modeling and design and abstracts from the implementation on the underlying hardware platform (e.g., the concrete distribution of SW-Cs on ECUs). In the following, we examine the compatibility of the concepts comprised in the VFB with the GENESYS architectural style.

Component-Orientation

The central concept in AUTOSAR applications is the software component (SW-C). The entire system is decomposed into smaller (reusable) units that provide a part of the required systems application functionality (application software component), some standardized ECU- or platform-related service (service component, ECU abstraction component, complex device driver component), or that interact with the environment (sensor-actuator component).

Similar to all types of components in AUTOSAR is their interaction via ports. AUTOSAR discriminates two types of ports: PPorts and RPort. PPorts are outgoing ports via which information is provided. RPorts are incoming ports that enable a component to receive information. The data elements exchanged via ports are defined in the specification of the port interface. AUTOSAR supports three types of interfaces: with client-server interfaces one or more clients are enabled to invoke operations provided by one server, sender-receiver interfaces are used to specify data exchange from one sender to multiple receivers, and calibration interfaces allow a component the access of static calibration parameters.

Those concepts fit very well to the GENESYS architectural style, which also follows a strict component orientation. However, in GENESYS the term component is defined as a self-contained hardware/software subsystem that can be independently developed and used as a building block in the design of a larger system. Thus, in contrast to AUTOSAR, a component in GENESYS is not a software component but always seen in relation to the concrete hardware platform that provides the foundation for component execution and interaction (e.g., the communication infrastructure).

Similar to AUTOSAR, components interact via ports in GENESYS. Those ports are specified via interface specifications. The Linking Interface (LIF) specification captures all information relevant for the integration of the component with other components (e.g., syntax and timing of the exchanged information); thus, it specifies the local application service of a component visible at its boundaries. The LIF matches the concept of sender-receiver and client-server interfaces of AUTOSAR, since it captures the services provided by a component and the data exchanged via a component's port. The concept of calibration interfaces is realized by the technology independent interface of a GENESYS component. This interface is used to configure a component, e.g. assign the proper names to a component and its input output ports, to reset, start and restart a component and to monitor and control the resource requirements (e.g., power) of a component during run time.

Data Exchange and Communication Semantics

The AUTOSAR specification defines two types of communication semantics for the data exchange between components via ports of sender-receiver interfaces:

Queued Communication: At the receiver side, the data element is put into an incoming data queue. At the sender side, each produced data element is stored in an outgoing data queue. For this communication paradigm *1:n* and *n:1* multiplicity is supported. *1:n* means that the data element produced by one sender is put into the incoming data queues of multiple receivers. The *n:1* multiplicity describes a topology where the data elements from multiple senders are placed into a single queue of one receiver.

Last-is-best Communication: At the receiver side the reception of a data element associated with a port with last-is-best semantics replaces the data element previously received via the respective port. Optionally, an instant of invalidation of the data element can be specified for this type of communication. The supported multiplicity for last-is-best communication is *1:n*, which means one sender and multiple receivers.

In order to efficiently support the above listed communication topologies, multicasting needs to be supported by the communication infrastructure. Furthermore, the communication infrastructure is responsible for the correct distribution of the data elements, i.e. the correct interconnection of sender and receiver ports. The sender of data elements in AUTOSAR is unaware of the number and name of the receivers of its data. Likewise, the receiver is unaware of the name (and in case of *n:1* queued communication of the number) of the sender of its received data elements.

The GENESYS architecture natively supports both types of communication semantics – the sporadic communication paradigm perfectly matches the queue communication. The periodic message transport service uses update-in-place of received messages and implements last-is-best communication. In addition, it is an architectural principle of GENESYS that multicasting has to be supported by the communication infrastructure. Thus, an efficient implementation of the communication topologies defined in AUTOSAR seems reasonable – except for the *n:1* communication topology for queued communication: Receiving data from different components at a single shared port opens up a source for error propagation in some rare scenarios. For instance a component exhibiting a babbling idiot failure would violate its bandwidth specifications and would be empowered to flood the incoming queue of the receiving component. Thus, messages of other (still correct) components could be delayed or even lost, leading to violations of the service of the components in temporal and/or value domain.

For client-server communication, AUTOSAR specifies a *n:1* multiplicity. That is multiple clients are empowered to invoke the service of a single server. For this purpose, a client provides a data value for each of the outgoing arguments (as specified in the port interface). As response, either the result of the operation or an error message is returned to the client.

Such client-server communication is not supported by GENESYS at the core service level. However, in order to account for the importance of client-server interaction as stated by several application domains, client-server interaction has been included as domain-independent optional service in the GENESYS reference architecture template. As the name implies, such an optional service is implemented on top of the core services as middleware within a component and can be included in a particular instantiation of the architecture if required.

Hardware Abstraction

The functionality of the VFB is realized by the RTE and the AUTOSAR Basic Software, which provide a standardized interface to AUTOSAR SW-Cs. This way, the RTE and Basic Software abstract from the concrete hardware of the underlying ECU enabling the reuse and relocation of (many) AUTOSAR SW-Cs to different ECUs. Of course, particular software components that are tightly coupled with sensors or actuators can only be deployed on ECUs with the respective hardware available. To achieve this abstraction, a layered software model is followed for the AUTOSAR Basic Software, which consists of a microcontroller abstraction layer, ECU abstraction layer, and a system services layer.

Of particular importance is the abstraction from ECU boundaries for software components. In order to enable the reuse of SW-Cs, a developer of a SW-C must not be required to be aware of the concrete location of the interacting SW-Cs. That is, from point of view of a SW-C, it should make no difference whether a SW-C is located on the same ECU or on a different ECU. For this purpose, the AUTOSAR COM module of the Basic Software provides mechanisms to route signals over ECU boundaries that are hidden to the sending as well as the receiving software component.

Abstraction from the underlying platform technology is also a primary design driver for the GENESYS architectural style in order to enable a seamless upgrade of the platform to upcoming technologies. This abstraction is realized in the GENESYS architecture by a Uniform Network Interface (UNI), which provides the functionality of the core services to the domain-independent and domain-specific middleware services as well as to the application services in a uniform way. Location transparency of SW-C as provided by the AUTOSAR RTE is also supported by GENESYS: Source and sink of all communication activities are ports. Sending components place their data elements in the component's outgoing ports, receiving components read data elements from the component's incoming port. The components themselves are not aware of the actual communication topology that interconnects the individual components. It is in the responsibility of the system integrator to configure the communication infrastructure accordingly to establish the required communication channels. In addition, by using dedicated gateway system components in GENESYS, the transparent (transparent to the application running in the IP cores of the MPSoC) data exchange across ECU boundaries (e.g. chip boundaries) can be achieved.

Basic Reconfiguration

AUTOSAR provides the applications (SW-Cs) and other Basic Software modules a mode management service, which enables to change the execution state of an ECU (e.g., to put an ECU into sleep state), supervise and take influence on the execution of application services (e.g., a watchdog that restarts an application missing the dissemination of a life sign), and change the configuration of the (physical) communication channels between ECUs. For this purpose, AUTOSAR needs to support the definition of modes, communication mechanisms that allow dissemination of mode changes as well as scheduling mechanisms for different modes.

As elaborated in Section 5.1.1, the GENESYS reference architecture template includes basic reconfiguration core services, which enable the implementation of the above mentioned mode management services of AUTOSAR. For instance the creation and modification of communication channels during runtime as well as mechanisms to control the execution state of cores is a functionality that has to be provided by every instance of the GENESYS architecture as core service. A watchdog service is not part of the GENESYS core services. However, the global time service in combination with the ability to restart cores simplifies the implementation of a watchdog as optional service on top of the core services.

8.3.3 Instantiation of AUTOSAR on top of GENESYS

Of course, the AUTOSAR Basic Software offers a plethora of services that are not covered by GENESYS core services or that are also not covered by optional services at that moment. For instance functions that are provided by AUTOSAR Basic Software are: access to non-volatile RAM, communication and diagnostic services, or ECU state and watchdog manager. The intention of GENESYS is to provide a platform that can be used across different domains and is further customized for the respective application domain – like the automotive domain in this case.

It is the purpose of this section to elaborate on a hypothetical customization of GENESYS for the automotive domain by outlining a possible instantiation of AUTOSAR on top of the GENESYS MPSoC platform. Figure 8.7 depicts a theoretical mapping of an AUTOSAR-based ECU to GENESYS components. Two types of components are distinguished: application cores and system components. Application cores implement the required automotive functionality. As shown in this Figure a radical one-to-one mapping of SW-Cs to application cores is proposed. The advantages of this approach are the reduced requirements on operating system functionality within a single application core as well as the inherent encapsulation of SW-Cs. A drawback is the increased overhead for SW-C to SW-C communication, since it always requires communication activities via the on-chip network.

8.3. AUTOMOTIVE OPEN SYSTEM ARCHITECTURE (AUTOSAR) 171

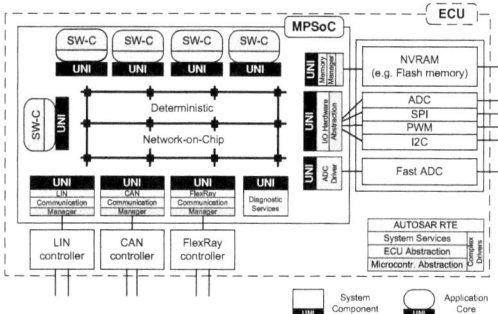

Figure 8.7: Mapping of AUTOSAR Basic Software to the GENESYS MPSoC

In order to provide an appropriate execution environment for SW-Cs, each application core requires a middleware layer that implements (at least parts of) the AUTOSAR RTE. This seems to be a reasonable level of abstraction, since it is the purpose of the RTE to decouple the SW-Cs from the underlying platform and from the mapping to a specific ECU by providing an interface to the SW-Cs that is completely independent from the ECU. SW-Cs are allowed to access via the RTE the following AUTOSAR services: system services, memory services (nvram manager), communication services (e.g., LIN, CAN, FlexRay), complex drivers, and I/O hardware abstraction.

The second type of components is system components. System components in GENESYS are components that implement application-independent optional services – either as software within a CPU or as dedicated hardware block. In the outline presented in Figure 8.7, the system components are deployed to implement parts of the AUTOSAR Basic Software.

Memory Manager: The functionality of non-volatile RAM management is sourced to a dedicated system component, which is connected for instance to a chip-external memory component (e.g., Flash memory) on the ECU. Compared to the layered software architecture of AUTOSAR, this component corresponds to the following parts of the Basic Software: It implements memory drivers from the microcontroller abstraction layer (e.g., driver for external Flash memory) in order to enable the low level access to the memory hardware. Furthermore, this system component needs to provide the functionality of the memory hardware abstraction of the ECU abstraction layer, which provides an abstraction from the type and location of the respective memory element. For instance Flash or EEPROM memory shall be accessible via the same interface. In addition, the system component has to provide the functionality of the system services layer. Since the system services layer in the presented setup does not directly interact with the RTE, but uses the UNI and the deterministic on-chip-network instead, the task of this layer changes with respect to the AUTOSAR specification. Instead of providing a standardized AU-

TOSAR interface, all tasks for non-volatile data management like saving, loading, checksum protection, etc. have to be built on the message-based UNI of the GENESYS architecture. This means, SW-Cs request data load/storage via AUTOSAR conformant operations to their local RTE middleware. The purpose of the RTE is than to translate these requests to operations on the message-based UNI, which are then forwarded to the memory manager system component.

Communication Manager (LIN, CAN, FlexRay): AUTOSAR provides the SW-Cs a uniform interface for vehicle network communication, which is independent from the actual targeted vehicle network (e.g., CAN, LIN, FlexRay). For this purpose, the AUTOSAR Basic Software provides communication drivers to different communication controller types, which are located in the microcontroller abstraction layer. On top of this, a communication hardware abstraction is built in the ECU abstraction layer. This layer is responsible for the abstraction from the number, type and location of the various communication controllers on a given ECU. This also establishes uniform access mechanisms to communication hardware, regardless whether it is on-chip or on-board. These mechanisms are exploited by communication managers in the system services layer of the AUTOSAR Basic Software to provide a uniform interface to vehicle networks (e.g., hide protocol and message properties from the application, uniform interface for network management).

As depicted in Figure 8.7, we propose to realize the functionality of a communication manager in distinct system components for each supported communication protocol instead of having a communication middleware replicated in each core of MPSoC. This would relax the resource requirements for the application cores, since most of the computational resources of the core are available for execution of the application software and not occupied by the execution of middleware services. In addition, the system components would be highly reusable in different ECUs based on the GENESYS MPSoC.

I/O Hardware Abstraction: A further functionality provided by the Basic Software that is proposed to be realized as a dedicated system component instead of a middleware layer is the uniform access to I/O devices. AUTOSAR has a two-layered model to provide a uniform access to I/O devices: At the microcontroller abstraction level, basic drivers for analog and digital I/O (e.g., ADC, PWM) and for peripherals like watchdog timers, general purpose timers etc. are provided. This first abstraction is exploited at the ECU abstraction layer to provide a signal-based interface that corresponds to the AUTOSAR interface standard.

As explained before, we argue for using a dedicated system component for this I/O hardware abstraction service, when instantiating AUTOSAR on top of the GENESYS MPSoC. The reason therefore is again twofold: simpler application IP cores, since they are tailored to the needs of the actual application only, and the potential for reuse for such system components in different designs.

Complex ADC Driver: The purpose of complex drivers in AUTOSAR is to interface complex sensors and actuators, which usually have strin-

8.3. AUTOMOTIVE OPEN SYSTEM ARCHITECTURE (AUTOSAR)

gent requirements on timing. Having a complex driver (e.g., for a fast ADC) as a system component has the advantage of a highly optimized implementation of the driver functionality. For instance even a hardware implementation is possible enabling an efficient interaction with the complex ECU peripheral. Furthermore, when implementing such complex drivers in middleware as part of larger software within a single general purpose CPU, stringent requirements on the deployed operating system arise. Thus, by outsourcing this functionality of the Basic Software to a dedicated (parallel) component, also the requirements for an operating system within an application IP core are relaxed.

Diagnostic Services: AUTOSAR provides a couple of diagnostic services that are capable of the detection of errors, dissemination and logging of errors, as well as of initiating fault treatment actions. These services could also be provided by a system component instead of middleware within application IP cores. Since all interaction between SW-Cs within one ECU as well as across ECU boundaries are performed via the NoC, they are potentially observable by a diagnostic system component to detect anomalies in the SW-C's behavior. In addition, basic functionality to (re)start and stop IP cores is part of the core services of the GENESYS MPSoC. Thus, such a diagnostic system component is empowered to change the execution state of individual SW-Cs (i.e., IP cores) via the core services.

8.3.4 Résumé

As elaborated in the previous sections, the core services of the GENESYS architecture as well as the system structuring at the chip level provide many means that facilitate the instantiation of AUTOSAR on top of GENESYS.

The most important part for enabling the reuse of existing AUTOSAR applications and the implementation of new AUTOSAR-conformant applications on top of the GENESYS architecture would be the provision of a domain-specific optional service realizing the AUTSAR RTE in each application core. In conventional AUTOSAR systems, the RTE provides the SW-Cs of a single ECU the access to the services of the Basic Software. In the approach presented in Figure 8.7 only a few services (e.g., timed or event-based activation of SW-Cs) are directly implemented within the RTE middleware in a core. The majority of services are provided by system components. Thus, instead of directly providing access to services that are running on the same processor, the RTE has to map service requests from SW-Cs to messages disseminated via the deterministic NoC. This presented approach of instantiating AUTOSAR on top of the GENESYS MPSoC and establishing a one-to-one mapping of SW-Cs to IP cores is kind of radical. However, it entails some interesting advantages:

Reduced complexity of operating systems within IP cores: Complex operating systems are not required in IP cores. There is no need for error-containment functionality, since only one SW-C is hosted in one IP core. Also temporal advantages can be achieved. For instance, AUTOSAR supports the event-based activation of SW-Cs. The response time, in particular the jitter of the response time of the activated SW-C depends on many preconditions in a traditional AUTOSAR system (e.g., utilization of the processor by other SW-Cs, used scheduling strategy). In the presented approach, a guaranteed response time can be achieved, since only a single SW-C is controlled by a less complex operating system.

Highly reusable system components: The proposed system components for realizing AUTOSAR services of the Basic Software have a high potential for reuse in different systems. In order to be GENESYS compatible the service of those system components needs to be captured by a precise LIF specification at the abstraction level of the UNI. This interface specification facilitates the reuse in different systems without the need to be aware of the internals of the system component.

Introduction of new "basic services" for automotive applications: Even reuse of non-AUTOSAR system components (e.g., for optimized memory controller or TTE controller) becomes possible in automotive applications. The important interface for component reuse is the UNI not the AUTOSAR interface. The RTE middleware is responsible for mapping AUTOSAR requests of SW-Cs to message of the UNI. This would enable an introduction of new communication protocols even transparent to the RTE.

Efficient implementation of drivers: For I/O hardware, sensors, actuators and in particular for realizing complex drivers an efficient implementation of drivers with system components would be possible. For instance, for dedicated peripherals that have stringent time constraints even a hardware implementation of a device driver would be possible. The choice whether a driver would be implemented in hardware or software is transparent to the RTE and the AUTOSAR applications.

Glossary

Application Service
The application service is the intended sequence of messages that is produced by a job via output ports at the LIF and the *controlled object* interface in response to the progression of time, inputs (via input ports at the LIF and the controlled object interface), and state.

Architectural Style
The architectural style consists of rules and guidelines for the partitioning of a system into subsystems and for the design of the interactions among subsystems. The subsystems must comply with the architectural style to avoid a property mismatch at the interfaces between subsystems.

Architecture Model
A set of descriptions that define an architecture or a configuration or a combination of an architecture and a compatible configuration (that obeys the rules defined by the architecture).

Architecture
A technical system architecture (or architecture for short) is a framework for the construction of a system for a chosen application domain. It provides generic platform services and imposes an architectural style for constraining an implementation in such a way that the ensuing system is understandable, maintainable, and extensible and can be built cost-effectively (see also federated architecture, integrated architecture).

Behavior
The behavior of a subsystem is the sequence of messages (i.e., intended and unintended) that is produced by the subsystem at its LIF.

Behavioral Model
A model that describes the dynamic internal evolution (operation) of the object of reference (system, subsystem, component) and its response to external stimuli.

Channel
A channel serves for the exchange of messages between ports. A channel is

associated with a communication topology, a data-direction (e.g., unidirectional or bidirectional), temporal properties and dependability properties.

Closed World System
In a closed-world system the number of clients is limited and known a priori. The clients can cooperate with each other or with a central scheduler in order to establish a coordinated schedule, such that the server is in the position to meet the requests of all clients within specified temporal bounds. Temporal guarantees can only be given in a closed world system (see also *Open World System*).

Cluster
A cluster is a physically distributed computer system that consists of a set of nodes interconnected by a physical network. If the cluster supports a single *DAS* only, we speak of a federated cluster. In this case, the DAS is physically separated from the clusters of other DASs. Since the *jobs* belong to the same DAS, they possess a common level of criticality. An integrated cluster, on the other hand, supports more than one DAS. Each of these DASs receives a share of the communication and component resources of the integrated cluster.

Component
A component is regarded as a self-contained subsystem that can be used as a building block in the design of a larger system. The component can have a complex internal structure that is neither visible, nor of concern, to the user of the component. A component is a self-contained composite hardware/software subsystem that can be used as a building block in the design of a larger system. In the context of embedded real-time systems, it is essential that the component behavior can be specified in the domains of value and time. Thus, a component is considered to be a self-contained computational element with its own hardware (processor, memory, communication interface, and interface to the controlled object) and software (application programs, operating system), which interacts with its environment by exchanging messages across *LIFs*.

Composability
Composability is a concept that relates to the ease of building systems out of subsystems. A system, i.e., a composition of subsystems, is considered composable with respect to a certain property (functional or non-functional) if this property, given that it has been established at the subsystem level, is not invalidated by the integration. Examples of such properties are timeliness or certification.
For example, some embedded systems closely interact with their environment and they have to produce intended results at intended points of time. Temporal composability is a prerequisite for the feasible construction of such temporally predictable systems of high complexity. In architectural styles that support temporal composability, determining the emergent temporal behavior of the resulting system is eased by the fact that the individual subsystems retain their temporal properties after integration.

Constrained Access
The access of the platform services through the application is temporally constrained in order to ensure consistency in read/write operations without explicit synchronization (e.g., semaphore). Constrained access depends on clock synchronization between application and platform for the temporal coordination of access operations. For example, the application temporally aligns the read operations to a memory that is written by the platform.

Controlled Object
The controlled object is the industrial plant, the process, or the device that is to be controlled by the computer system.

Core Platform Service
Core platform services (or core services for short) are mandatory in every instantiation of the *reference architecture template*. The core platform services provide the foundation for higher-level, *optional platform services*. For instance, a message transport service is a core service. At any given *integration level*, the core services form a waist that can be realized using a multitude of implementation choices. Also, they form the starting point for the domain-customization using optional services. Exemplary categories of core services are networking services, robustness services, and composability services.

Cross-Domain Architectural Style
The cross-domain architectural style consists of views, concepts, and design principles that have been consolidated from the different application domains. This includes the description of fundamental architectural principles, the identification of commonalities between application domains and the identification of different *integration levels* (e.g., ranging from the level of Electronic Control Units (ECUs) to car-to-car communication in the automotive domain) required in each application domain.
Examples for possible design principles are the ensuring of error containment or the partitioning of the system along precisely specified interfaces. In addition, the cross-domain architectural style provides an appropriate naming scheme that defines and interrelates the namespaces at the different integration levels.

Cross-Domain Development Methodology
The cross-domain methodology framework consists of a set of methods, techniques and tools for diverse development processes that are applicable across multiple application domains.

Declared State
The declared state is the state of a subsystem, which is considered as relevant by the system designer for future *behavior* of the subsystem (forward view).

Determinism
A model behaves deterministically if and only if, given a full set of initial conditions (the initial state) at time t_0, and a sequence of future timed inputs, the outputs at any future instant t are entailed.

Distributed Application Subsystem
A Distributed Application Subsystem (DAS) is a nearly independent distributed subsystem of a large distributed real-time system that provides a well-specified *application service*.

Examples of DASs in a present day automotive application are body electronics, the power-train system, and the multimedia system. Examples of DASs in a present day avionic application are the cabin pressurization system, the fly-by-wire system, and the in-flight entertainment system. DASs are often developed by different organizational entities (e.g., by different vendors) and maintained by different specialists.

Since DASs may be of different criticality (e.g., vehicle dynamics control vs. multimedia system), the probability of error propagation across DAS boundaries must be sufficiently low to meet the dependability requirements. A DAS is further decomposed into smaller units called *jobs*.

Error
An error is that part of the system state which is liable to lead to a subsequent *failure*. A failure occurs when the error reaches the service interface.

Error Containment
Although a *fault containment region* can demarcate the immediate impact of a fault, fault effects manifested as erroneous data can propagate across the boundaries of fault containment regions. For this reason the system must also provide error containment for avoiding error propagation by the flow of erroneous messages (see *Error Containment Region*).

Error Containment Region
The set of *fault containment regions* that performs error containment is denoted as an error containment region (ECR). An error containment region must consist of at least two independent fault containment regions. The error-detection mechanisms must be part of a different FCR than the message sender, otherwise the error detection service can be affected by the same fault that caused the message failure.

Event Message
An event message is a *message* that contains event observations. An event observation contains the difference between the "old state" (the last observed state) and the "new state". The time of the event observation denotes the point in time of the state change. In order to maintain state synchronization, the handling of event messages requires exactly-once semantics. The arrival of an event message usually gives rise to a control signal, which triggers subsequent computational and communication activities.

Fail-operational System
A fail-operational system is able to tolerate one or several *faults*. Fail-operational systems send correct messages despite the *failure* of their subsystems.

Fail-safe System
In a fail-safe system all *failures* are, to an acceptable extent, only minor ones.

Fail-silent System
A fail-silent system is able to fail cleanly by just stopping to send *messages*. Such a property is called Halt on Failure. Fail-silent systems send only correct messages. A system built out of $t+1$ fail-silent sub-systems executing the same task can tolerate t active faults.

Fail-stop (fail-halt) System
A fail-stop (fail-halt) system should satisfy the following properties: Halt on Failure - the system fails cleanly by just stopping to send messages.
Failure Status - the system failure is detectable from exterior.
Stable Storage - the state of the system is partitioned into stable storage and volatile storage. The contents of stable storage are unaffected by any failure and can always be read by any processor. The contents of volatile storage are not accessible to other systems and are lost as a result of a failure.
The last two properties are required for implementing systems whose correctness criteria involve generating outputs in a timely manner. A system made out of $t+1$ fail-stop sub-systems executing the same task can mask t active faults.

Fail-uncontrolled System
A system that does not possess any local error detection mechanisms and can thus produce quite random or even malicious behavior. t active faults can be masked by using $2t + 1$ fail-uncontrolled systems.

Failure
A failure occurs when the delivered service deviates from fulfilling its specification.

Fault
A fault is the adjudged or hypothesized cause of an error. Faults can be internal or external of a system.
Examples of types: An external fault (e.g. a malicious attack) causes an error, and possible a subsequent failure. An internal fault (i.e. vulnerability) allows an external fault to harm the system and has to pre-exist in the system.

Fault-Containment Region
A Fault Containment Region (FCR) is a collection of components that operates correctly regardless of any arbitrary logical or electrical fault outside the region.

Fault Hypothesis
The fault hypothesis is the specification of the *faults* that must be tolerated without any impact on the essential system services. The fault hypothesis states the assumptions about units of failure (see *Fault Containment Region*), failure modes, failure frequencies, failure detection, and state recovery.

Fault-Tolerant Unit
A fault-tolerant unit (FTU) is a unit consisting of a number of replica determinate components that provides the specified service even if some of its components fail.

Federated Architecture
In a federated architecture, each *DAS* is implemented on a dedicated distributed computer system, consisting of nodes dedicated to *jobs* (in the automotive industry called Electronic Control Units - ECUs) and a physical network (e.g., a CAN network) among the nodes. In a federated architecture, each DAS is physically separated from other DASs, which leads to clear boundaries for responsibility and error propagation.

Host
The host is the unit used to execute *jobs*.

Integrated Architecture
An integrated architecture is characterized by the integration of multiple *DASs* within a single distributed computer system. An integrated architecture possesses a single physical network that is shared among the DASs.

Integrated Resource Management
Integrated resource management is the simultaneous management of multiple resources (e.g., bandwidth, power, energy, memory) in order to globally optimize different resources.

Integration Level
The integration level denotes the layer in a system-of-systems at which it is composed out of its components. Different integration levels can be distinguished in embedded systems on between two extreme levels: the chip level and the open collaboration level. At the chip level IP (Intellectual Property) cores are integrated by a network-on-chip. This is a closed integration where a manufacturer provides a top down design of a chip. The open collaboration level, on the other hand, exhibits a bottom up ad-hoc integration of independently developed, autonomous components/services (e.g., ambient intelligence).

Interface State
The interface state contains the history of the component that is relevant for the future behavior of the component as seen from this interface. Interface *state* is defined between the intervals of activity on the *sparse time base*. Interface state is a subset of the state of the component and should be accessible from the interface.

Job
A job is a constituting element of a *DAS* and forms the basic unit of work. It interacts with other jobs through the exchange of *messages* in order to work towards a common goal and provide the *application services*.

Linking Interface
A *job* provides its real-time services, and accesses the real-time services of other jobs by the exchange of *messages* across its *Linking Interface (LIF)*. These messages have to be fully specified in a LIF specification which consists of an operational specification and a LIF service model specification.

Linking Interface Specification
The linking interface specification is the mediating middle between a service supplier and the service user. On the one hand, the *LIF* service specification should be complete in the sense that it contains all information required to understand and use the services of the component that are offered at the particular LIF. On the other hand, the LIF service specification should be minimal in the sense that it contains only information that is required by the user of the services.
The LIF service specification comprises a syntactic specification, a temporal specification, and a LIF service model specification. We subsume under the term operational specification of an interface the syntactic specification and the temporal specification. The syntactic specification forms out of the sequence of bits in a *message* larger (information) chunks (such as a number, a string, or a method call, a structure consisting of a combination thereof, or a complex data object, such as a picture) and assigns a name to each chunk.
The temporal specification of the messages defines their send and receive instants, e.g., at what instants the messages are sent and arrive, how the messages are ordered, and the rate of message arrival. This information can be formalized if an appropriate model of real-time is available. In non-safety critical applications the temporal specification can be expressed in probabilistic terms.
The LIF service model specification provides a conceptual interface model that relates the names of the chunks to the user's conceptual world and thus assigns a deeper meaning to the chunks generated by the syntactic specification. It follows that the LIF service model must be expressed in concepts that are familiar to the user of the interface services.

Message
A message is any data structure that is formed for the purpose of inter-job communication. This definition is very open. We also view a data exchange via common memory as a means of (state) message passing.
In order that errors in a message may be detected, an output guard and an input guard can be associated with a message. Such a guard is a predicate on values of the message, and relevant state variables that defines an application-specific acceptance criterion. Using such assertions, it is possible to classify messages as follows:

Attribute	Explanation	Antonym
valid	A message is valid if its checksum and contents are in agreement.	invalid
checked	A message is checked at source (or, in short, checked) if it passes the output assertion.	not checked
permitted	A message is permitted with respect to a receiver if it passes the input assertion of that receiver. The input assertion should verify, at least, that the message is valid.	not permitted
timely	A message is timely if it is in agreement with the temporal specification.	untimely
value-correct	A message is value-correct if it is in agreement with the value specification.	not value-correct
correct	A message is correct if it is both timely and value-correct.	incorrect
insidious	A message is insidious if it is permitted but incorrect.	not insidious

Meta Model
A meta-model defines the rules and constructs according to which a model is created in a predefined class of problems. A meta-model can be viewed from three perspectives; as a set of building blocks and rules used to build models, as a model of a domain of interest, and as an instance of another model

Ontology
Ontology is a shared knowledge standard or a knowledge model defining primitive concepts, relations, rules and their instances, which comprise the relevant knowledge of a topic. A formal ontology is a controlled vocabulary expressed in an ontology representation language. This language has a grammar for using vocabulary terms to express something meaningful within a specified domain of interest.

Open World System
We define an open-world system as a system where an (unknown) number of uncoordinated clients compete for the services of a server. The critical instant in an open world system occurs, when all clients request the services of the server simultaneously. Guaranteed real-time performance cannot be achieved in an open-world system. An example of an open-world system is the Internet. Another example of an open world system is standard Ethernet. It is thus impossible to establish temporal guarantees in standard Ethernet without restricting the access pattern that is characteristic for open world systems.

Optional Platform Services
The optional platform services which are built upon the *core platform services*

can be generic in the sense that they can be used in multiple application domains or specific for a focused domain. These services are optional in the sense that they are not required in every instantiation of the architecture. If needed, developers can pick them out of the GENESYS *reference architecture template*, which includes a set of existing, validated component libraries for the different levels of integration. For instance an encryption service could be a generic optional service.

Platform
A platform is the hardware/software foundation for the execution of applications. The platform comprises generic services for the development of applications, which are denoted as platform services (see *Core Platform Services* and *Optional Platform Services*).

Platform Services
Platform services facilitate the development of distributed applications and separate the application functionality from the underlying platform technology to reduce design complexity and to enable design reuse. We differentiate between two different types of platform services: Core Platform Services and Optional Platform Services.

Platform-Independent Model
A Platform Independent Model (PIM) is a model of a system that is independent of the specific technological platform used to implement it.

Platform-Specific Model
A Platform Specific Model (PSM) is a model of a system that is linked to a specific technological platform used in implementation.

Reference Architecture Template
The reference architecture template is a template for building concrete architectures. The reference architecture template provides specifications for a comprehensive set of *platform services*, including domain-independent services that can be used across application domains. In any specific application, a subset of these platform services can be selected and implemented. The selection and implementation of the platform services is part of the instantiation of the template used to arrive at a concrete architecture (e.g., a particular chip, a network platform running a distributed application).

Reliability
Reliability is the ability of a system or component to perform its required functions under stated conditions for a specified period of time.

Replica Determinism
Replica determinism is a desired property between replicated subsystems. A set of replicated subsystems is replica determinate if all subsystems in this set produce exactly the same output *messages* that are at most an interval of d time units apart, as seen by an omniscient outside observer. In a time-triggered system, the subsystems are considered to be replica-deterministic, if

they produce the same output messages at the same global ticks of their local clock.

Robustness
Robustness is the capability of a system to deliver an acceptable level of service despite the occurrence of transient and permanent hardware *faults*, design faults, imprecise specifications, and accidental operational faults. A system must be resilient with respect to unanticipated behavior from the environment of the system or of subsystems. In case such unanticipated behavior occurs, the system should still exhibit some sensible behavior, and not be completely unpredictable.

Service
The service delivered by a system (in its role as a provider) is its intended *behavior* as it is perceived by its users. The behavior is the sequence of observable outputs of a system.
In GENESYS, a service delivered by a *job* is part of the job's behavior as seen by the platform and the other jobs. Such a service is called an *application service*.
In GENESYS, a service delivered by the platform is part of the platform's behavior as seen by the platform and the other jobs. Such a service is called an *architectural service* or a platform service.

Sparse Time Base
If the time base of the global time in a distributed system is dense (i.e., the events are allowed to occur at any instant of the timeline), then it is in general not possible to generate a consistent temporal order of events on the basis of the time-stamps. Due to the impossibility of synchronizing clocks perfectly and the denseness property of real time, there is always the possibility that a single event is timestamped by two clocks with a difference of one tick.
By introducing the concept of a sparse time base this problem can be solved. In the sparse time model the continuum of time is partitioned into an infinite sequence of alternating durations of activity and silence. Thereby, the occurrence of significant events is restricted to the activity intervals of a globally synchronized action lattice. In this time model, the costly execution of agreement protocols can be avoided, since every action is delayed until the next lattice point of the action lattice.

State
The state enables the determination of a future output solely on the basis of the future input and the state the system is in. In other word, the state enables a "decoupling" of the past from the present and future. The state embodies all past history of the given system. Apparently, for this role to be meaningful, the notion of the past and future must be relevant for the system considered (see also *Declared State* and *Interface state*).

State Message
A state message is a periodic *message* that contains state observations. An observation is a state observation, if the value of the observation contains the

state of a real-time entity. The time of a state observation denotes the point in time when the real-time entity was sampled. The handling of state messages occurs through an update in place and non-consuming read.

State Recovery
State recovery is the action of (re-)establishing a valid state in a subsystem after a failure of that subsystem.

Subsystem
A subsystem is a part of a system that represents a closure with respect to a given property.

Unconstrained Access
Unconstrained access does not restrict the points in time of access operations performed by the application. In order to support consistency, asynchronous handshake protocols are employed that do not require clock synchronization between application and platform (e.g., handshake protocol for the producer/consumer problem based on read/write positions).

List of Project Partners

Name	Organisation
OBERMAISSER Roman	Vienna University of Technology
KOPETZ Hermann	
KUSTER Sibylle	
HUBER Bernhard	
EL SALLOUM Christian	
ZAFALON Roberto	STMicroelectronics
AUZANNEAU Fabrice	Commissariat à l'Énergie Atomique
GHERMAN Valentin	
KRONLOF Klaus	Nokia Oyj
WARIS Heikki	
CRISTAU Gérard	Thalesgroup
EDELIN Gilbert	
MILLET Philippe	
BORTH Michael	Embedded Systems Institute
COUVREUR Chantal	Interuniversitair Micro-Elektronica Centrum
SURI Neeraj	Technical University Darmstadt
BOKOR, Peter	
Dobre, Dan	
Serafini, Marco	
CAMPOS Sergio	European Software Institute
NOGUERO Adrián	
OVASKA Eila	Technical Research Centre of Finland
TIENSYRJÄ Kari	
GOEDECKE Michael	Infineon
HUFELD Knut	
GROPPO Riccardo	Centro Ricerche Fiat
SEBASTIAN Martina	TTTech Computertechnik AG
SCHLAGER Martin	

LIST OF PROJECT PARTNERS

Name	Organisation
BENINI Luca	University of Bologna
BENSALEM Saddek	Verimag
WICHERT Reiner	Fraunhofer IGD
TAZARI Saied	
BROY Manfred	TU München
FEILKAS Martin	
HUMMEL Benjamin	
HÖLZL Florian	
AVIZIENIS Algirdas	Vytautas Magnus University
GRIGONYTE Gintare	
PEREZ Antonio	Ikerlan
PEREZ Jon	
PATARICZA András	Budapest University of Technology and Economics
BALOGH András	
SANZ Ricardo	Universidad Politecnica de Madrid
VAN DER WOLF Pieter	NXP Semiconductors
HILLER Martin	Volvo Technology

Bibliography

[1] Aeronautical Radio, Inc., 2551 Riva Road, Annapolis, Maryland 21401. *ARINC Specification 651: Design Guide for Integrated Modular Avionics*, November 1991.

[2] Aeronautical Radio, Inc., 2551 Riva Road, Annapolis, Maryland 21401. *ARINC Specification 659: Backplane Data Bus*, December 1993.

[3] Aeronautical Radio, Inc., 2551 Riva Road, Annapolis, Maryland 21401. *Remote Data Concentrator (RDC) - Generic Description. ARINC Report 655*, April 1999.

[4] Aeronautical Radio, Inc., 2551 Riva Road, Annapolis, Maryland 21401. *ARINC Specification 429: Digital Information Transfer System*, November 2001.

[5] Aeronautical Radio, Inc., 2551 Riva Road, Annapolis, Maryland 21401. *ARINC Specification 664: Aircraft Data Network Part 1 – Systems Concepts and Overview*, January 2002.

[6] Aeronautical Radio, Inc., 2551 Riva Road, Annapolis, Maryland 21401. *ARINC Specification 653: Avionics Application Software Standard Interface, Part 1 - Required Services*, March 2006.

[7] T. Amnell, E. Fersman, L. Mokrushin, P. Pettersson, and W. Yi. TIMES: a tool for schedulability analysis and code generation of real-time systems. In *Proc. of FORMATS 03, number 2791 in LNCS*, pages 60–72. Springer-Verlag, 2003.

[8] ARTEMIS. *ARTEMIS Final Report on Reference Designs and Architectures – Constraints and Requirements*. ARTEMIS (Advanced Research & Technology for EMbedded Intelligence and Systems) Strategic Research Agenda, 2006. http://www.artemis-sra.eu.

[9] N. Audsley and A. Wellings. Analysing APEX applications. In *Proceedings of the 17th IEEE Real-Time Systems Symposium (RTSS '96)*, pages 39–44, Washington, DC, USA, 1996. IEEE Computer Society.

[10] A. Avizienis, J. Laprie, and B. Randell. Fundamental concepts of dependability. In *Proceedings of 34th Information survivability Workshop (ISW 2000)*, pages 7–12. IEEE, 2000.

[11] F. Brajou and P. Ricco. The Airbus A380 – an AFDX-based flight test computer concept. In *Proceedings of the IEEE Autotestcon*, pages 460–463, San Antonio, TX, September 2004.

[12] D.D. Clark. The design philosophy of the DARPA Internet Protocols. *Proceedings SIGCOMM 88, Computer Communication Review*, 18(4):106–114, August 1988.

[13] A.M. Davis. A comparison of techniques for the specification of external system behavior. *Communication of the ACM*, 31, 1988.

[14] K.R. Driscoll and K.P. Hoyme. The airplane information management system: an integrated real-time flight-deck control system. In *Proceedings of the Real-Time Systems Symposium*, volume 1, pages 267–270, December 1992.

[15] D. Dzung, M. Naedele, T. P. Vonhoff, and M. Crevatin. Security for industrial communication systems. *Proceedings of the IEEE*, 93, 2005.

[16] EUROPEAN AIRPORT MOVEMENT MANAGEMENT BY A-SMGCS (EMMA), Braunschweig. *D681 Recommendations Report*, 2006.

[17] A. Evesti, E. Niemelä, K. Henttonen, and M. Palviainen. A tool chain for quality-driven software architecting. In *Proceedings of 12th International Software Product Line Conference (SPLC '08)*, 2008.

[18] Message Passing Interface Forum. *MPI: A Message-Passing Interface Standard - Version 2.1*. High Performance Computing Center Stuttgart (HLRS), June 2008.

[19] C. Fraboul and F. Martin. Modeling and simulation of integrated modular avionics. In *Proceedings of the Sixth Euromicro Workshop on Parallel and Distributed Processing (PDB'98)*, pages 102–110, January 1998.

[20] M.-C. Gaudel, V. Issarny, C. Jones, H. Kopetz, E. Marsden, N. Moffat, M. Paulitsch, D. Powell, B. Randell, A. Romanovsky, R. Stroud, and F. Taiani. Final version of the DSoS conceptual model. *DSoS Project (IST-1999-11585) Deliverable CSDA1*, December 2002. Available as Research Report 54/2002 at http://www.vmars.tuwien.ac.at.

[21] S.S. Gokhale and M. Rung-Tsong Lyu. A simulation approach to structure-based software reliability analysis. *IEEE Transactions on Software Engineering*, 31(8):643–656, 2005.

[22] K. Goseva-Popstojanova and K.S. Trivedi. Architecture-based approach to reliability assessment of software systems. *Perform. Eval.*, 45(2-3):179–204, 2001.

[23] W. Hasselbring and R. Reussner. Toward trustworthy software systems. *Computer*, 39(4):91–92, 2006.

[24] H. Heinecke, J. Bielefeld, K.-P. Schnelle, N. Maldener, H. Fennel, O. Weis, T. Weber, J. Ruh, L. Lundh, T. Sandeén, P. Heitkämper, R. Rimkus, J. Leflour, A. Gilberg, U. Virnich, S. Voget, K. Nishikawa, K. Kajio,

T. Scharnhorst, and B. Kunkel. AUTOSAR – Current results and preparations for exploitation. *Proc. of the 7th EUROFORUM conference, Software in the vehicle*, 2006.

[25] H. Heinecke, K.-P. Schnelle, H. Fennel, J. Bortolazzi, L. Lundh, J. Leflour, J.-L. Maté, K. Nishikawa, and T. Scharnhorst. AUTomotive Open System ARchitecture – An Industry-Wide Initiative to Manage the Complexity of Emerging Automotive E/E Architectures. *Convergence 2004, Proceedings of the 2004 International Congress on Transportation Electronics, SAE/P-387*, pages 325–332, 2004. SAE-2004-21-0042.

[26] C. Hoefer. Causality and determinism: Tension, or outright conflict. *Revista de Filosofia*, 29(2):99–225, 2004.

[27] K. Hoyme and K. Driscoll. SAFEbus. *IEEE Aerospace and Electronic Systems Magazine*, 8:34–39, March 1993.

[28] IEEE Instrumentation and Measurement Society. IEEE Std. 1588 - 2002 IEEE Standard for a precision clock synchronization protocol for networked measurement and control systems. Technical report, IEEE, November 2002. ISBN: 0-7381-3369-8.

[29] A. Immonen. A method for predicting reliability and availability at the architectural level. In *Software Product-Lines – Research Issues in Engineering and Management*, pages 373–422, 2006.

[30] ITRS. International technology roadmap for semiconductors. Executive summary, ITRS, 2007. http://www.itrs.net/Links/2007ITRS/ExecSum2007.pdf.

[31] International Telecommunication Union (ITU). The Internet of things. executive summary. ITU Internet reports, ITU, November 2005.

[32] D. Jackson, M. Thomas, and L.I. Millett, editors. *Software for Dependable Systems: Sufficient Evidence?* The National Academies Press, 2007.

[33] R. Jain. *The Art of Computer Systems Performance Analysis: Techniques for Experimental Design, Measurement, Simulation and Modelling*. John Wiley & Sons, Inc., 1991.

[34] H. Kopetz. Sparse time versus dense time in distributed real-time systems. In *Proceedings of 12th International Conference on Distributed Computing Systems*, Japan, June 1992.

[35] H. Kopetz. *Real-Time Systems: Design Principles for Distributed Embedded Applications*. Kluwer Academic Publishers, Norwell, MA, USA, 1997.

[36] H. Kopetz. The complexity challenge in embedded system design. *IEEE International Symposium on Object-Oriented Real-Time Distributed Computing*, pages 3–12, 2008.

[37] H. Kopetz, A. Ademaj, P. Grillinger, and K. Steinhammer. The Time-Triggered Ethernet (TTE) design. In *Proc. of 8th IEEE Int. Symposium on Object-oriented Real-time distributed Computing (ISORC)*, May 2005.

[38] H. Kopetz and G. Bauer. The time-triggered architecture. *IEEE Special Issue on Modeling and Design of Embedded Software*, January 2003.

[39] H. Kopetz and G. Grünsteidl. TTP – a protocol for fault-tolerant real-time systems. *Computer*, 27(1):14–23, January 1994. Vienna University of Technology, Real-Time Systems Group.

[40] H. Kopetz, C. El Salloum, B. Huber, R. Obermaisser, and C. Paukovits. Composability in the Time-Triggered System-on-Chip architecture. *21st Annual IEEE International SoC Conference*, Sep. 2008.

[41] H. Kopetz and N. Suri. Compositional design of RT systems: A conceptual basis for specification of linking interfaces. In *Proceedings of the Sixth IEEE Int. Symposium on Object-Oriented Real-Time Distributed Computing*, pages 51–60. IEEE, May 2003.

[42] H. Kopetz and N. Suri. On the limits of the precise specification of component interfaces. *IEEE International Workshop on Object-Oriented Real-Time Dependable Systems*, 0:26, 2003.

[43] K. Kronlöf, S. Kontinen, I. Oliver, and T. Eriksson. A method for mobile terminal platform architecture development. *Advances in Design and Specification Languages for Embedded Systems*, pages 285–300, 2007.

[44] J.H. Lala and R.E. Harper. Architectural principles for safety-critical real-time applications. *Proceedings of the IEEE*, 82:25–40, January 1994.

[45] L. Lamport. Using time instead of timeout for fault-tolerant distributed systems. *ACM Trans. Program. Lang. Syst.*, 6(2):254–280, 1984.

[46] L. Lamport, R. Shostak, and M. Pease. The byzantine generals problem. *ACM Transactions on Progamming Languages and Systems*, 4(3):382–401, July 1982.

[47] A. Lappeteläinen. Extending NoTA for distributed products, 2008. Slides of the presentation at First International Network on Terminal Architecture Conference.

[48] A. Lappeteläinen, J.-M. Tuupola, A. Palin, and T. Eriksson. Networked systems, services and information. The ultimate digital convergence. *First International Network on Terminal Architecture Conference*, 2008.

[49] R. Lauwereins. Multi-core platforms are a reality, but where is the software support? In *6th International Forum on Embedded MPSoC and Multicore*, 2006.

[50] N.G. Leveson. Software safety in embedded computer systems. *Commun. ACM*, 34(2):34–46, 1991.

[51] N.G. Leveson. *Safeware: system safety and computers*. ACM, New York, NY, USA, 1995.

[52] J. Lilius, J. Lindqvist, I. Porres, D. Truscan, T. Eriksson, A. Latva-Aho, and J. Rakkola. Testable specifications of NoTA-based modular embedded systems. TUCS Techn. Report No 841, Turku Centre for Computer Science, Sept. 2007.

[53] LynuxWorks. *LynxOS 4.0 User's Guide*, 2006.

[54] D. Mills. Simple Network Time Protocol (SNTP) Version 4 for IPv4, IPv6 and OSI. Request for comments: 4330, University of Delaware, January 2006.

[55] M.J. Morgan. Integrated modular avionics for next generation commercial airplanes. *IEEE Aerospace and Electronic Systems Magazine*, 6:9–12, August 1991.

[56] R. Obermaisser. *Event-Triggered and Time-Triggered Control Paradigms - An Integrated Architecture*. Springer-Verlag, 2005. Real-Time Systems Series, Volume 22, 170 pages.

[57] R. Obermaisser, B. Froemel, C. El Salloum, and B. Huber. Integrating safety and multimedia subsystems on a time-triggered system-on-a-chip. In *Proceedings of the 6th IEEE International Conference on Industrial Informatics (INDIN 2008)*, pages 270–275, Daejeon, Korea, July 2008.

[58] R. Obermaisser, H. Kraut, and C. El Salloum. A Transient-Resilient System-on-a-Chip Architecture with Support for On-Chip and Off-Chip TMR. *Seventh European Dependable Computing Conference*, pages 123–134, 2008.

[59] R. Obermaisser, C. El Salloum, B. Huber, and H. Kopetz. Fundamental design principles for embedded systems: The architectural style of the cross-domain architecture GENESYS. In *Proc. of IEEE Int. Symposium on Object/Component/Service-Oriented Real-Time Distributed Computing*, March 2009.

[60] Object Management Group (OMG). *Smart Transducers Interface, Version 1.0*, January 2003.

[61] OMG. MDA Guide Version 1.0.1. Technical Report document number omg/2003-06-01, Object Management Group, June 2003. Available at: http://www.omg.org/docs/omg/03-06-01.pdf.

[62] OMG. MARTE (Modeling and Analysis of Real-time and Embedded systems). Technical report, Object Management Group, December 2008. Available at: http://www.omgmarte.org/.

[63] E. Ovaska, A. Balogh, S. Campos, A. Noguero, A. Pataricza, K. Tiensyrjä, and J. Vicedo. Model and quality driven embedded systems engineering. VTT Publication, VTT, Espoo, 2009.

[64] P. Parkinson and L. Kinnan. *Safety-Critical Software Development for Integrated Modular Avionics*. Wind River Systems Inc., Alameda, California, 2006.

[65] F. Pourbigharaz and M. Aleksic. NoTA imaging solution, 2008. Slides of the presentation at First International Network on Terminal Architecture Conference.

[66] P.J. Prisaznuk. Integrated modular avionics. In *Proceedings of the IEEE 1992 National Aerospace and Electronics Conference (NAECON'92)*, volume 1, pages 39–45, May 1992.

[67] J.W. Ramsey. Integrated Modular Avionics: Less is More. *Avionics Magazine*, January 2007. Available at http://www.aviationtoday.com/av/categories/commercial/8420.html.

[68] R.H. Reussner, H.W. Schmidt, and I.H. Poernomo. Reliability prediction for component-based software architectures. *J. Syst. Softw.*, 66(3):241–252, 2003.

[69] G. Rodrigues, D. Rosenblum, and S. Uchitel. Reliability prediction in model driven development. In *ACM/IEEE 8th International Conference on Model Driven Engineering Languages and Systems*, 2005.

[70] J. Rushby. Partitioning for avionics architectures: Requirements, mechanisms, and assurance. NASA Contractor Report CR-1999-209347, NASA Langley Research Center, June 1999. Also to be issued by the FAA.

[71] J.H. Saltzer and M.D. Schroeder. The protection of information in computer systems. *Proceedings of the IEEE*, 63(9):1278–1308, Sept. 1975.

[72] T. Scharnhorst, H. Heinecke, K.-P. Schnelle, H. Fennel, J. Bortolazzi, L. Lundh, P. Heitkämper, J. Leflour, J.L. Maté, and K. Nishikawa. AUTOSAR-Challenges and Achievements 2005. *VDI BERICHTE*, 1907:395, 2005.

[73] H.A. Simon. *The Sciences of the Artificial*. MIT Press, 1996.

[74] F. Singhoff, J. Legrand, L. Nana, and L. Marcé. Cheddar: a flexible real time scheduling framework. *Ada Lett.*, XXIV(4):1–8, 2004.

[75] R. Suoranta. New directions in mobile device architectures. *9th EUROMICRO Conf. on Digital System Design: Architectures, Methods and Tools*, pages 17–26, 2006.

[76] G.J. Whitrow. *The Natural Philosophy of Time*. Oxford Univeristy Press, 2nd edition edition, 1990.

Die VDM Verlagsservicegesellschaft sucht für wissenschaftliche Verlage abgeschlossene und herausragende

Dissertationen, Habilitationen, Diplomarbeiten, Master Theses, Magisterarbeiten usw.

für die kostenlose Publikation als Fachbuch.

Sie verfügen über eine Arbeit, die hohen inhaltlichen und formalen Ansprüchen genügt, und haben Interesse an einer honorarvergüteten Publikation?

Dann senden Sie bitte erste Informationen über sich und Ihre Arbeit per Email an *info@vdm-vsg.de*.

Sie erhalten kurzfristig unser Feedback!

VDM Verlagsservicegesellschaft mbH
Dudweiler Landstr. 99 Telefon +49 681 3720 174
D - 66123 Saarbrücken Fax +49 681 3720 1749
www.vdm-vsg.de

Die VDM Verlagsservicegesellschaft mbH vertritt

Printed by Books on Demand GmbH, Norderstedt / Germany